THE SOVIETS IN THE NHL

RED LINE

0 57812 69902 1

THE SOVIETS IN THE NHL

RED LINE

BY STAN AND SHIRLEY FISCHLER

Prentice-Hall Canada Inc., Scarborough, Ontario

Canadian Cataloguing in Publication Data

Fischler, Stan, 1932-
Red line: Soviet players in the NHL

ISBN 0-13-769902-6

1. National Hockey League. 2. Hockey players – Soviet Union.
3. Russians – Canada. I. Fischler, Shirley. II. Title.
GV847.8.N3F58 1990 796.96'2'0922 C90-094374-2

Prentice-Hall Inc., *Englewood Cliffs, New Jersey*
Prentice-Hall International, Inc., *London*
Prentice-Hall of Australia, Pty., *Sydney*
Prentice-Hall of India Pvt. Ltd., *New Delhi*
Prentice-Hall of Japan, Inc., *Tokyo*
Prentice-Hall of Southeast Asia (Pte.) Ltd., *Singapore*
Editora Prentice-Hall do Brasil Ltda., *Rio de Janeiro*
Prentice-Hall Hispanoamericana, S.A., *Mexico*

Editor: John Meyers
Design and Cover Illustration: Suzanne Boehler
Manufacturing Buyer: Lisa Kreuch
Composition: Heidy Lawrance Associates

ISBN: 0-13-769902-6

Printed and bound in the U.S.A.by R.R. Donnelley & Sons Co.

1 2 3 4 5 RRD 94 93 92 91 90

TABLE OF CONTENTS

ACKNOWLEDGEMENTS

It was not easy for the Russians to bring their act to the NHL. For Viacheslav Fetisov, it meant endless months of waiting and frustration before he got the green light to come to New Jersey. For Sergei Makarov, there was the anguish of being separated from his lifetime line mates Vladimir Krutov and Igor Larionov. For Alexander Mogilny, there was the challenge to conquer his fear of flying, not to mention the desire to prove that he did the right thing in defecting from the Soviet Union.

In each case, the Russian players needed help and each time they received considerable assistance from their respective teams. By the same token, quite a bit of help was required in putting this book together. Translations from Russian publications were necessary and innumerable interviews had to be conducted, not only with Soviet players but with officials and historians.

With that in mind, we would like to thank the following for their assistance in the research end of the project:

Nadia Moszkowicz, Jean Snyder, Teresa Faella, Tammi Marcotte, Damian Salvati, Charlie Higgins, Dan Sokolow, Brian Fishman, Rich Calder, Jeff Resnick, Greg Goldstein, Josh Sipkin, Sandra Carreon, Linda Lundgren, Kay Ohara, Andy Schneider, Dave Katz, Eli Polatoff, Joe Dionisio, Kathy Johnson, Arthur Staple, Dave Starman, Andy Cohen, Rich Deitsch, Kevin McKay, Chris Devine, Mike Mouat,

Jessica Gilsdorf, Alan Rozinsky, Joel Bergman, Kim Bozek, Dennis Glasgow, Michelle Dye, Jim McRae, Diane Gerace, Dave Zafris, Jeff Boudreau, Dave Ferry, Laurie Berger, Tim Haffey, Sandra McPherson, Mike Burton, Mary McCarthy and Toni Rumore.

In addition, a large measure of thanks is due NHL people for their aid, in particular Dave Freed and Mike Levine of the Devils Public Relations Dept., Barry Watkins and Ginger Killian from the Rangers Press Bureau, and Greg Bouris and Chris Botta of the Islanders.

Other NHL PR folks who provided major assistance include Heidi Holland, Boston Bruins; John Gurtler and Budd Bailey, Buffalo Sabres; Rick Skaggs, Calgary Flames; Jim DeMaria, Chicago Blackhawks; Bill Jamieson, Detroit Red Wings; Bill Tuele, Edmonton Oilers; Phil Langan, Hartford Whalers; Susan Carpenter, Los Angeles Kings; Joe Janasz, Minnesota North Stars; Michele Lapointe, Montreal Canadiens; John Halligan, New York Rangers; Rodger Gottlieb, Philadelphia Flyers; Cindy Himes, Pittsburgh Penguins; Nicole Bouchard and Jean Martineau, Quebec Nordiques; Susie Mathieu, St. Louis Blues; Bob Stellick, Toronto Maple Leafs; Darcy Rota, Vancouver Canucks; Lou Corletto, Washington Capitals; and Murray Harding and Mike O'Hearn, Winnipeg Jets.

Special help came from two special people, Lana Dixon, who came through with some excellent translations, and Devils strength coach Dmitri Lopuchin, the indefatigable interpreter.

But nobody was more important than our literary shepherds, Ed Brewer and Tanya Long of Prentice-Hall Canada, not to mention our agent, John Wright, who helped launch the project and guided it through to its fruition.

DEDICATION

To Ben and Simon,
our topliners before, during,
and after **RED LINE**. Our love
and gratitude for your
understanding while we
immersed ourselves in pucks,
sticks, and hockey players.

AUTHORS' INTRODUCTION

In order to chronicle completely the extraordinary integration of Soviet players into the National Hockey League we concluded that every angle should be covered.

To this end, we watched firsthand as many games as possible during the 1989-90 season involving the Russian players.

We also decided in advance that a special focus was necessary. With that in mind, we chose the New Jersey Devils experiment as our target.

After all, the Devils had caused the most commotion at the earliest day with their pursuit of Viacheslav Fetisov. The suspense built for more than a year, culminating with Slava's signing at Byrne Arena in the summer of 1989.

But that was just the start of the Devils melodrama. Fetisov brought a countryman, Sergei Starakov, with him and later would (much to his dismay) find still another Soviet, Aleksei Kasatonov, at his side.

We zeroed in on the Fetisov–Starikov–Kasatonov story just a bit more than the others because there were so many interesting points and counterpoints, including Starikov's failure, Fetisov's feud with his comrade Kasatonov, the gooning of Slava by Toronto Maple Leaf Wendel Clark and the major role Fetisov and Kasatonov were given in the Devils desperate race for a playoff berth in the homestretch. Nevertheless, we did not overlook the contributions of Sergei Makarov, Igor Larionov, and the other Soviets.

What they did was a truly courageous and remarkable thing. Although they didn't become instant superstars, they did have an impact that no doubt will be felt for years to come and likely into the next century.

It was gratifying as both fans and historians to chronicle this unique epoch in NHL history.

The sum total, we believe, is as comprehensive a look as possible at what has been a truly exciting adventure in hockey annals–the year of the Soviets.

Shirley Fischler
Stan Fischler

FOREWORD

When Stan and Shirley asked me to do a foreword to their book on Soviet NHL players, I quickly agreed to do so. I have known Stan and Shirley since I became involved in NHL player representation in the early sixties and our friendship has endured for nearly thirty years. In 1966, Hockey Canada was formed with an ambition to create a competition between Canada's best hockey players and any other country's best hockey players. It took six years to reach this goal. In September 1972, Hockey Canada organized games between Canada and three other countries, Sweden, Czechoslovakia and the USSR. Two games were scheduled between Canada and Sweden in Stockholm; Canada won one and tied the other. One game was scheduled between Canada and Czechoslovakia in Prague; Canada tied the game with two seconds left on the clock.

The series between Canada and the USSR consisted of eight games. The first four were played in Canada. Canada lost the first game in Montreal, won the second in Toronto, tied the third in Winnipeg and lost the fourth in Vancouver. The last four games were played in Moscow. Canada lost the fifth game, and had to win the last three games if it was to win the series.

Canada won the sixth and seventh games and the series was tied. On September 28, 1972, with eighty-five percent of Canada's population tuned in, and with Canada coming to an almost complete halt to watch or listen to the game, the most important goal in the history of Canadian hockey was scored. Canada started the third period with the score USSR 5, Canada 3. Led by the outstanding performances of Phil Esposito, Pete Mahovlich and Yvan Cournoyer, Canada tied the game at 5–5. Suddenly, with 26 seconds left to play, Espo stole a puck in the Soviet end, and shot it towards the Soviet goal. Paul Henderson picked up the rebound and on his second shot, put the puck behind the brilliant Soviet goalie Vladislav Tretiak.

Three thousand Canadians in Moscow's Sports Palace went wild with excitement. Across Canada, twenty-five million Canadians celebrated Henderson's goal.

The games involving Canada, Sweden, Czechoslovakia and the Soviet Union proved beyond any doubt that there were some great hockey players in Europe. It was only a matter of time before they came to the NHL. Borje Salming and Inge Hammerstrom joined the Toronto Maple Leafs from Sweden in 1973. They were followed by Ulf Nilsson and Anders Hedberg and many other Swedish players. The Czechoslovakians were led by the Stastny brothers, Peter, Marian, and Anton, who defected to Canada and the Quebec Nordiques. They were followed by several of their colleagues. Some came with permission of their hockey federation, others defected from the CSSR to Canada or the US. Players from Finland were quick to follow, and outstanding contributions have been made to the NHL by players such as Jari Kurri of the Edmonton Oilers. Uwe Krupp from Germany joined the Buffalo Sabres.

The only gap was the lack of a quality hockey player from the USSR. In 1979, attempts were made by Hockey Canada to arrange an exchange of players for at least one year. I met with the Canadian ambassador to the USSR, with the Soviet ambassador to Canada, and with the sports ministers of both countries. It would be the most unusual trade in the history of hockey. Ken Dryden would spend a year in Moscow and play with Moscow Red Army, and Vladislav Tretiak would join the Montreal Canadiens for the 1979-80 season. At the last moment the Soviets said the exchange was impossible because Tretiak was an army captain and had to complete his army service.

In 1981, two Soviet players told me that they wanted to play in the NHL, but were not interested in defecting. They asked me to intercede with their hockey federation. I had preliminary discussions with federation representatives and was told in no uncertain terms that the players were not available.

The possibility of Soviet players coming to the NHL was discussed on several occasions during the late eighties. In the summer of 1987, I learned that the Soviets might consider permitting some of their older players to join NHL clubs. At the Olympics in Calgary in 1988, the Soviet Hockey Federation told me that such players as Fetisov, Kasatonov, Makarov, Larionov and Krutov — the Soviet "Big Five" — would be released in 1988 or 1989. When I disclosed this to a national television audience on ABC with Al Michaels, all hell broke loose. The Detroit Red Wings had a team meeting and told the National Hockey League Players Association that they didn't want the Russians taking NHL jobs. An agent who had acted for some Czechoslovakian players (who *took* NHL jobs) stated that I should be fired as executive director of the NHLPA for bringing the Soviet players to the NHL.

The NHLPA position on foreign players is clear and simple. We welcome the best players and we don't put up barriers against them. If we tried to stop Soviet players from playing in the US we could expect complaints from US Immigration about Canadian players playing for US teams. I expect to see more Soviet players join players like Fetisov and Makarov. I don't know how long any of them will stay. While they are here, if they contribute to our game, I welcome them all.

Stan and Shirley Fischler have reported thoroughly on the important events that led up to the Soviet invasion of the NHL. (Some invasion — nine players out of 540 in the NHL). The 1972 Canada—Russia series, the 1979 Challenge Cup, the 1980 Lake Placid gold medal win for the USA, and the Canada Cup tournaments from 1976 through 1987 are all part of North American and Soviet competition. International hockey is a major part of NHL success. Stan and Shirley have given us an interesting outline of the events that created the opportunity for nine Soviet players to come to play in the NHL during the 1989—90 season.

—*R. Alan Eagleson*

PART 1

C H A P T E R 1

IN THE BEGINNING

"A coalition army is the easiest to beat."
—*Napoleon*

Once upon a time the thinking in National Hockey League circles had it that Canadians — and *only* Canadians — were capable of producing Stanley Cup-winning teams. Napoleon's dictum for winning battles was essentially worshipped by NHL general managers until 1960, when an upstart American Olympic team led by a brash coach named Jack Riley and a virtually impenetrable goaltender, Jack McCartan, annexed a gold medal at Squaw Valley, California.

Within hours of the victory celebration, New York Rangers general manager Murray (Muzz) Patrick grabbed a telephone and invited McCartan to Manhattan. The St. Paul native, who had never in his wildest dreams imagined that he would become a big-leaguer, accepted the invitation, and before he could say Lord Stanley of Preston, McCartan found himself starting in goal against the immortal Gordie Howe and the Detroit Red Wings.

There were two significant aspects to McCartan's debut at Madison Square Garden in March 1960. Very early in the game the husky goaltender faced Howe on a clean breakaway and stopped the league's foremost shooter with consummate ease; it signalled a breakthrough for Americans in the NHL and that, in turn, would eventually result in the influx of Swedes, Finns, Czechs and, finally, Soviets.

In 1960 the suggestion that Soviets might someday be skating side by side with players from Flin Flon, Manitoba, Trois Rivieres, Quebec and Nelson, British

Columbia, simply was dismissed out of hand. When a Russian team visited Madison Square Garden that year, the redshirted squad was regarded with a curiosity one might have exhibited had they been deposited at Eighth Avenue and 49th Street by a spaceship from Mars.

"Everything about them was different," said Tom Lockhart, who had been business manager of the Rangers and president of the Amateur Hockey Association of the United States. "Our guys were out there for practice taking the usual shots from the blueline. The Russkies did things we never saw before. They were gathered in groups, each one doing some special kind of routine: some passing, some shooting, others stickhandling. It was pretty obvious that they were treating hockey in a scientific way."

The Soviet invasion was a curio and not one that anyone considered significant in terms of the NHL. "They came and left," said Lockhart, "but those of us involved in international hockey had a suspicion that, sooner or later, they'd be back again. It was just that we didn't know when it would happen."

Certainly, Lou Lamoriello had no idea. A native of Providence, Rhode Island, Lamoriello played hockey for Providence College and later coached its hockey team before becoming the university's athletic director. "In the sixties," Lamoriello recalls, "the NHL was the dominant force in terms of hockey interest. The six-team league reached its peak in the mid-sixties, and then came expansion. As far as the Russians were concerned, we thought about them only in an international context."

That changed in 1972 when Toronto lawyer Alan Eagleson orchestrated an eight-game tournament involving skaters from his NHL Players Association, of which he was executive director, and a select squad of Soviet stars. Although Team Canada annexed the series with a dramatic comeback in Moscow, the Russians were so unexpectedly dazzling — not to mention competitive — that major North American hockey executives realized that at least a dozen of the comrades were proficient enough to star in the NHL.

"Much as I disliked them," said Phil Esposito, one of Team Canada's prime heroes, "I had to admit that they had talent. That goalie in particular showed me a lot."

Vladislav Tretiak displayed the kind of goaltending proficiency seen only in such NHL immortals as Glenn Hall, Terry Sawchuk and Frankie Brimsek. He was one of several arresting Soviets, including Boris Mikhailov, Aleksander Yakushev and a young defenseman named Viacheslav Fetisov who, in time, would be inextricably linked with Lamoriello.

"At the time," said John Ferguson, who was Team Canada's assistant manager, "nobody figured the Russians had a place in the NHL simply because their top players meant too much to the success of Soviet hockey. And on top of that, the Communist state being what it was at the time, who could imagine that they'd ever allow any meaningful athlete to just leave and play in a capitalist country?"

One man could imagine such a breakthrough, although nobody believed him at the time. John J. McMullen, a onetime commander in the United States Navy who became a millionaire naval architect and marine engineering mogul, bought the Colorado Rockies NHL franchise in 1982 and moved the club to New Jersey, renaming them the Devils. "I had had many dealings with the Russians through my businesses," said McMullen, "and I could see the day when we would be able to deal more freely with them on the athletic front."

McMullen's foresight was evident at the annual NHL draft in June 1983. At a time when the Minnesota North Stars made Brian Lawton the first pick overall, the Winnipeg Jets selected Bobby Dollas as their top choice and Montreal Canadiens went for Alfie Turcotte, the Devils unobtrusively waited for the eighth and twelfth rounds for their extraordinary moves.

"My feeling was that if there were Soviet players with NHL ability, we should grab a couple," said McMullen. "They could be further down the list and that way we'd have nothing to lose. Then, maybe a few years down the line the political climate would change and we'd be lucky enough to get 'em."

With that in mind, the Devils picked Viacheslav Fetisov in the eighth round. The Russian defenseman thus became the 150th pick overall. In the twelfth round — which normally draws nothing but yawns from the audience — New Jersey opted for another Soviet backliner, this time Aleksei Kasatonov. He was number 213 on the list.

"We didn't think much of it at the time," said Jimmy Devellano, vice-president of the Detroit Red Wings. "Usually, the focus is on the top two or three guns. I drafted Steve Yzerman that year and I remember the Devils' top pick was John MacLean. Then they went after Shawn Evans, a defenseman, and Chris Terreri, the goalie. But when you get down to the one hundred group or two-thirteen, like Kasatonov, there's not a lot of interest. And even if there was, who would think the Devils would be able to sign them? Nobody."

Of course the Devils didn't sign them. Fetisov and Kasatonov continued to star in the Soviet Union although their careers began dramatically separating like two sets of railroad tracks splitting off from a switch.

Kasatonov emerged as the darling of Soviet national coach Viktor Tikhonov. Aleksei was known as a player who took orders well and was easily led. By contrast, Fetisov, a hero of many a Soviet international victory, became disenchanted with Tikhonov — he was not alone in this regard — and was not bashful about stating his case.

In a sense it was much easier for Fetisov, nicknamed Slava, to go public with his anti-coach position. In his upper twenties, Slava was considered Marx's gift to hockey, a player none other than Wayne Gretzky described as "one of the greatest players in the sport." As Russians go, Fetisov was among the upper crust. He drove a Mercedes-Benz, wore high-top sneakers unavailable to the average comrade, and was revered as the ace of Central Red Army by everyone but Tikhonov.

The coach had good reason for his displeasure. By Soviet standards, Slava had done the unthinkable: he publicly criticized Tikhonov for poorly managing the army team. The punishment was not exile to Siberia, but harsh by an athlete's standards: Fetisov was benched, Tikhonov demanded an apology.

Slava was adamant in his refusal. "The coach pretends to take care for his athletes, but he cares only for himself," he snapped.

This was early in 1989, a time when the Devils could almost see Slava in a New Jersey red, white and green uniform. The iron curtain had not quite fallen apart but glasnost was the order of the day, and ever since the 1988 Olympic Games in Calgary it appeared that Fetisov's emigration to East Rutherford, New Jersey, would only be a matter of time. Who could doubt it after Al Eagleson, hockey's supreme power broker, had gone on record that the Russians would ease their restrictions.

"It may have seemed easy to a lot of people," chuckled Lamoriello, "but the difference between talking about getting a player here and actually *getting* him here is very, very big."

Lamoriello spoke first-hand; since the '88 Olympics, the Devils president had been laying the groundwork for Fetisov's arrival in America. In the summer of 1988 he visited the Soviet Union to speak with Fetisov, confident he would return with a new defenseman. It didn't help that the media had seized the Russian story and turned it into a fait accompli.

"What the press didn't understand but we in the NHL knew was the red tape involved in such a procedure," an NHL official revealed. "It was unrealistic for the media to think — poof! — it would happen just like that."

Lamoriello's first obstacle was the Soviet Army's refusal to allow Fetisov to resign his commission as a major. There had been no precedent for such a move and the Russians were baffled about untangling the red tape.

"Lamoriello had sought to head off potential problems by talking to everyone who could affect negotiations," noted John Dellapina of the *Bergen* (New Jersey) *Record*. "He also tried to set a stage that would make it not only attractive but imperative for the Soviet authorities to grant Fetisov permission to come."

If there was any move that would help, Lamoriello made it. When the Devils played an exhibition game against Fetisov's Central Red Army team at Byrne Arena, Lamoriello saw to it that Soviet Ambassador to the United States Yuri Dubinin was invited to drop the ceremonial first puck, along with owner McMullen and US Deputy Secretary of State John Whitehead.

When Dubinin and Fetisov huddled, the Soviet diplomat quietly inquired about Slava's true desire to play for the Devils. When Fetisov assured him that he did, Dubinin replied that he would send a message to Moscow urging that the move be allowed.

Ah, but who would move Tikhonov? The coach and his captain were barely co-existing, although Viktor insisted that he would not blockade Fetisov's attempted move to New Jersey. Few believed him. When Tikhonov's name was announced over the public address system at Byrne Arena the Devils fans lustily booed.

"The truth cannot be hidden from the people," Fetisov said.

Devils fans had reason to yearn for Slava. In 1988, when Fetisov was being courted in Calgary, the New Jersey sextet launched a major offensive that resulted in the club's first entrance to the Stanley Cup playoff round. Under coach Jim Schoenfeld, the Devils reeled off stunning upsets over the New York Islanders and Washington Capitals, and extended the Boston Bruins to a seven-game series before being eliminated at Boston Garden. "All in all," said Schoenfeld, "it was a satisfying finish."

But 1988-89 was a consummate disappointment for Schoenfeld and his troops. The darlings of spring 1988 had become the ugly ducklings of autumn. Clearly, the club needed help on defense, and that made Fetisov so conspicuous by his absence. But never did McMullen, Lamoriello or Slava himself give up hope.

After his exhibition game in New Jersey, Fetisov was overwhelmed by the warmth displayed to him by Devils players. He held a press briefing in an interview room and then walked out into the corridor, where Devils captain Kirk Muller called to him down the hall, "Slava!"

Fetisov wheeled around, walked toward the home team dressing room and embraced Muller; Kirk said, "I hope I see you in one of these uniforms soon." Slava grinned his toothy smile, patted Muller and walked away.

Unfortunately for the Devils, Tikhonov remained in the way. The Devils continued their desultory play, missing the playoffs, and making it even more compelling for Lamoriello to force the Soviets' hand. While he was waiting for the green light, the Calgary Flames announced that Sergei Priakin had received permission from Soviet authorities to sign with the Smythe Division leaders.

Lamoriello didn't know it but Priakin's arrival would have considerable significance for his club. For one thing it demonstrated that, yes, Russian players could be lured to North America, and for another, the Priakin experience would demonstrate that players don't just come to the NHL to be welcomed with open arms. There are problems — *big* problems.

In Priakin's case it was a matter of disrupting a team that was hellbent for its first Stanley Cup. This was a concern of coach Terry Crisp; when the Russian arrived, Crisp explained to the curious media his general plans for the Soviet rookie. "He isn't here to take anyone's job. He's no different than Joe Nieuwendyk, Brett Hull or Jiri Hrdina. We brought all of those guys in late in the season."

The media didn't buy that line. They believed that if Priakin played he would significantly disrupt the Flames' chemistry (unless he was the second coming of Wayne Gretzky), or that he was being used as a lever to pry open the Russian gate, behind which loomed a bigger prize, namely, Sergei Makarov. The perceptive Vancouver *Province* columnist Tony Gallagher was right when he noted, "Getting Priakin helps the Flames toward their ultimate goal of landing speedy winger Makarov in the fall."

To intercept any problems, the Flames held a team meeting; players were told that Priakin wouldn't be disruptive. Other Smythe Division coaches hoped and prayed that he would be at least an annoyance to other Calgary players. "I hope they do use him," said Vancouver Canucks coach Bob McCammon. "But unless he does something great, I don't think we'll be seeing much of him."

How prophetic. Priakin was a dud. He played in a total of two regular season games and was a non-factor for the Flames in their march to the Stanley Cup. His major importance, ironically, was in not getting on his teammates' nerves enough to cause overwhelming dissension.

Then again, how could the wealthy Flames become upset with a rookie, Soviet or otherwise, who was allowed to keep just $1,200 a month of his salary? Priakin's contract was for $500,000 spread over two years, but only $1,200 went to the player; the rest went to the currency-desperate Russians. "That was the best way for Priakin to fit in with his teammates," observed Gallagher. "They felt so pitifully sorry for him they went out of their way to make him feel good. Anyone crazy enough to play in the NHL for that pittance deserved everyone's loving care."

While Priakin was riding the pines at the end of the Flames bench or, more often, sitting in the press box wondering whether he'd ever get into a playoff game, Lamoriello was putting into place his final plans to win the release of Fetisov.

CHAPTER 2

THE SLAVA-SERGEI SHOW

"It's easier to play hockey than deal with bureaucracy. But with the changes in the Soviet Union it's time for people to take a stand. When it comes down to it, you have to fight for what you want."
— *Viacheslav Fetisov, New Jersey Devils*

The Devils' 1988–89 season ended on Sunday, April 3, 1989, at the Byrne Arena in East Rutherford, New Jersey. They played the Washington Capitals, a team they had humbled a year earlier during their outrageous playoff run. This time coach Jim Schoenfeld's crew defeated the Caps 7–4, but no one was impressed, least of all the boss, Lou Lamoriello. His club finished with 27 wins, 41 losses and 12 ties for a total of 66 points. That left them a big 14 points away from fourth-place Philadelphia and the coveted playoff berth.

"Considering what we had done the year before," said defenseman Craig Wolanin, "and what had been expected of us, the ending was disappointing, if not embarrassing."

Wolanin didn't know it but his future would be inextricably linked with that embarrassment and the mission to Moscow his employer, Lamoriello, had embarked on when the Devils' season ended. Following the annual NHL draft meetings in Bloomington, Minnesota, Lamoriello jetted across the Atlantic for his decisive meeting with the Soviet authorities. The top-secret negotiations were completed on Monday, June 26, 1989, and sealed with a communiqué Lamoriello personally dispatched from Moscow:

"Laying to rest long-standing rumor and speculation, we have signed Soviet defensemen Viacheslav Fetisov and Sergei Starikov. We are delighted with the fact that both these players have been signed and we look forward to them joining our team."

Lamoriello had ensured that each had been granted their visitor's visas and that permanent visas would be arriving shortly. "We anticipate no further problems in this regard."

But Lamoriello's problems had just begun, and they would remain with him from that day forward. In fact they began the moment the first reporter phoned Devils defenseman Randy Velischek to get his reaction to the new acquisitions.

A hero of the Devils' 1988 playoff uprising, Velischek lost no time wasting his new teammates. "I believe their place is to play in Russia," said the multilingual defenseman. "It's fine, we have the Swedes and Finns but we're at the point, once you open the door, it's going to be a flood. They are taking jobs, taking money out of our pockets. And they're not going to stay. These fellows will be over here a few years, earning a lot of money and heading back home after a couple of years. I don't think it's appropriate."

Yet Velischek, who can be interviewed in English, French or German, allowed that he was of two minds on the Soviet import subject. Randy, the subjective survivor, wanted to protect his position with his NHL team. Randy, the objective purist, understood that Fetisov was a world class player who could lift the Devils into a playoff berth. "Randy Velischek the defenseman would like to see Fetisov in our lineup, too," he went on. "I know that may seem hard for people to understand, but I have a lot of different feelings about this, and I think that goes for a lot of our players."

By the end of June the arrival of Fetisov was being anticipated by local hockey writers the way pop music reviewers would have awaited a reunion of The Beatles at Giants Stadium. Each morning Devils public relations official Dave Freed listened to his phone ring off the hook with "When are they coming?" queries. Fetisov and Lamoriello would be accompanied by a little-known

Russian defenseman named Sergei Starikov, whose acquisition merely added spice to the already appetizing menu.

Finally, on the morning of July 7, a bulletin was dispatched to all New York sports media: "Devils Press Conference — Winners Club, Byrne Arena, Noon."

Long before noon the elaborate Winners Club dining room was packed to capacity. This in itself was highly unusual for a hockey press conference; normally, only beat writers turn out for such affairs, but the arrival of the Russians had been heralded for so long by so many different reporters that even non-hockey types were seen at the New Jersey fete.

One of the earliest to arrive was Devils owner John McMullen. Dapper in a blue suit, the white-maned leader of the New Jersey club had been regarded as a maverick ever since he bought the Colorado Rockies franchise. McMullen, who also owned the Houston Astros baseball club, had many dealings with the Soviets through his assorted business connections. McMullen's wide grin betrayed his feelings about the new acquisitions from Moscow. "I sensed a long time ago that there's going to be a thaw in our relationship with the Soviets," he revealed. "Naturally, we would like to have had Slava and Sergei sooner, but we're happy to have them now."

When they were finally escorted to the dais, Fetisov and Starikov were a study in contrasts. Slava was accompanied by his tall, stunning, blond wife, Lada. Neither spoke English, but the Devils had provided an interpreter, Dmitri Lopuchin, who had been the team's conditioning coach for several years. The shorter and stockier Starikov was arm in arm with his wife, Irene, who was fluent in English, although her husband had to rely on Lopuchin.

Shepherding the quartet was Soviet Ambassador Yuri V. Dubinin, who squelched all suggestions that some unknown obstacle would somehow still prevent Slava and Sergei from moving into the NHL. "There is no danger of them not playing here," the ambassador said. "If they weren't going to play for the Devils, they wouldn't be here today. This opens a new avenue and follows the example of Gorbachev and Bush trying to improve the relationship between the two nations. This is a new element in our relations with the United States."

No stone was left unturned; at least not by the Soviets. In order for Fetisov and Starikov to obtain clearance from their army duty, the players had to make contributions from their Devils salary to the Soviet Children's Fund. "Ultimately, they got what they wanted," said the 31-year-old Fetisov. "A piece of the action."

The players endured the press extravaganza calmly. First came the formal introduction by McMullen and Lamoriello. Added attractions were coach Jim Schoenfeld and team captain Kirk Muller. Schoenfeld, whose job was on the line following the dismal performance in 1988–89, was asked how he would communicate with players who could not speak English. "They know 'pass' and 'shoot'," grinned the red-haired coach.

Introductions were followed by two segments featuring the newcomers. Fetisov and Starikov first met with the print media people, and then went head-to-head with the television and radio interviewers. A constant source of questioning dealt with Fetisov's frosty relationship with Soviet coach Viktor Tikhonov. Fetisov had long ago strained relations with Russian hockey authorities by blasting Tikhonov and his country's political stranglehold on athletes. "It's easier to play hockey than deal with bureaucracy," said Fetisov, softly, but with firmness. "But with the changes in the Soviet Union it's time for people to take a stand. When it comes down to it you have to fight for what you want."

Fetisov remained at centre stage, while Starikov captured some attention as a good secondary act. The bulky 30-year-old was built up as a potential defensive sleeper by the Devils corps of experts. "He reminds me of Bill Juzda, who played on the Maple Leafs' Stanley Cup-winners in the late 1940s," said Devils vice president Max McNab. "He's built like a fireplug and, from what I gather, he can throw a pretty good bodycheck."

Starikov was as low-key as Fetisov; he allowed that he had been offered playing jobs with European teams but opted for the United States. "When this offer came," he chuckled, "I took it in fifteen minutes."

The media marvelled at their patience and humor. Fetisov, whom many already were calling Slava, told a story about his first visit to Manhattan's fashionable Fifth Avenue shopping strip. "We were walking about Saks department store and my wife and I got separated in the crowd," he remembered. "When I found her she was in tears."

Nobody seemed too concerned about the missive from the Soviet Ice Hockey Federation, a letter for NHL President John Ziegler sent earlier in the week requesting that the two defensemen not be permitted to play in the league. The Soviet contention was that their negotiations were not conducted through Sovintersport, the official Soviet sports agency that customarily handles such matters. The presence of Ambassador Dubinin underlined the fact that Lamoriello had scored a coup.

"The last week in the Soviet Union everything was finalized," Lamoriello assured interviewers. "It was a long process, especially because of the media exposure. I never tried to put doubt in my mind because I approach things positively, but there were certainly highs and lows."

For the Devils, at that time, there was nothing but a collective high. Not only had Lamoriello landed one world class defenseman, and another who had the makings of a solid defensive player, but he had been vigorously wheeling and dealing in other areas. The New Jersey general manager had dealt hard-checking Pat Verbeek to Hartford for Sylvain Turgeon. Although Verbeek had been a fan favorite in earlier years, his play had dramatically tailed off during the 1988–89 season, coincidentally (perhaps not coincidentally) following a substantial raise in salary. Turgeon, who had been no less disappointing in a Whalers uniform, was a gamble. He once had been a high scorer, but suffered injuries and fell into disfavor with the Hartford management. Lamoriello expected him to find himself in East Rutherford.

The same held for Walt Poddubny, once a hero across the Hudson River when he skated for the New York Rangers. Lamoriello dispatched disappointing defenseman Joe Cirella and feisty Claude Loiselle to Quebec for

Poddubny, who arrived at Byrne Arena as enthusiastic as the Soviets. Obviously, Poddubny had not enjoyed playing in Quebec for truculent coach Michel Bergeron. As an added fillip the Devils signed fleet Finnish defenseman Reijo Ruotsalainen, who had been playing in Switzerland, but previously had worked for the Oilers where he helped win a Stanley Cup. The mobile Ruotsalainen was targeted as the point man on the Devils' power play, which had been deficient in the past.

"We want to win the Stanley Cup," proclaimed McMullen, and many listened. The New York *Post* was so excited about the club's prospects it ran a banner headline: GREAT EXPECTATIONS.

Certainly, the demeanor of Fetisov and Starikov would not indicate otherwise. The pair handled the press conference with aplomb and spoke with cautious optimism about their NHL futures.

Time and again, Fetisov was pressed about the culture shock of coming to the NHL, especially the prospect of big-league goon hockey, the intimidation and possible absence of artistry. He stickhandled through the queries without missing a step. "Hockey is hockey," Slava insisted. "You play and you react to situations accordingly. There's no point in complaining or mixing words."

Standing off to the side, handsome, red-headed coach Jim Schoenfeld grinned through the proceedings. Some in the press gallery wondered about Schoenfeld. He had been the hero who bailed out the club late in 1987–88, after the Devils had floundered under the previous coach, Doug Carpenter. Emotional and articulate, Schoenfeld was hailed for his efforts during the Devils' amazing playoff run in the spring of 1988. Likewise, he was castigated — albeit with less vigor than he had been praised — for the disappointing 1988–89 campaign. A few critics actually believed that Lamoriello would fire him before the 1989–90 season began and replace him with assistant coach John Cunniff, who had been signed right after the 1988–89 season had ended.

Schoenfeld's reprieve merely added to the drama. The coach had problems with some players in his first full season in Jersey, especially Verbeek, and there were questions about his ability to meld the Soviets into the lineup and give them proper direction.

"Fetisov will be a key part of our team," said Schoenfeld. "He has great leadership qualities, although it may take a while for him to be a leader in the dressing room, where he is going to stand up the way Kirk Muller does. But he'll lead by example on the ice. He was a great leader for the Soviets and we expect the same thing here. Leading by example. Great defensive skills, great offensive skills, power play, penalty killing; the works. He is a big guy to the success of the team, for sure."

It was mentioned immediately to Schoenfeld that NHL players already were voicing disappointment over the potential influx of Soviet players. Point-blank, the coach was asked about Fetisov's ability to withstand NHL intimidation tactics. Schoenfeld grinned again. "He's played in the highest level of competition against our best players from the NHL in the Canada Cup," Schoenfeld pointed out. "He is big, strong, tough. That's what our players perceived of him when he came to Jersey last season [in an exhibition game]. This guy is a tough son-of-a-gun. He's a North American-type player."

In mid-summer, predictions about the fall have a utopian ring. Nobody could blame Schoenfeld for his glowing optimism but, in the crunch of regular season play that fall of 1989, he would be proven dead wrong about Fetisov being "a North American-type player." At times, Schoenfeld seemed aware that he was being too much the Pollyanna. "Sure, Slava will be challenged," he went on. "That's the difference between making it or not making it in the NHL. Other European players have come over here and found that the NHL brand just wasn't their style of hockey."

The more he was pressed on the subject, the more Schoenfeld drifted from the public relations line over to the realm of NHL reality. "Any time a club has a key player, the opponent is going to give more attention to the guy because that guy can hurt you. He's the one who can beat your team. We expect that with Fetisov, just as we have come to expect it with Kirk Muller, John MacLean and Patrik Sundstrom. They're key players. As far as having someone out on the ice to protect Slava, I don't think it will be necessary."

One of the reporters covering the event was Frank Brown of the New York *Daily News*. Himself a goaltender who had occasionally practiced with the New York Rangers, Brown was one of the most knowledgeable journalists on the scene, and one who had a special feel for the game. Brown observed that the most important personality on the Devils in 1989–90 would be captain Kirk Muller. "He's the one who's going to have to bring all the divergent personalities — and nationalities — together," said Brown. "If he does, everything with the team will be hunky-dory. If not..." He never completed the sentence.

Muller also took questions at the press conference. Obviously, the Devils wanted this to be as official an occasion as possible and the captain had emerged as the most visible — and in many ways most likeable — member of the team. Kirk also was as Canadian as one could get. A native of Kingston, Ontario, the ebullient forward played junior hockey for Guelph and Kingston as well as the Canadian Olympic team, before moving to New Jersey in 1984 as the Devils' number-one draft choice.

Muller was aware of teammate Randy Velischek's hostile remarks about the arrival of Fetisov and Starikov. He didn't have to be briefed about the questions that would come, particularly the one about the Soviets' effect on the Devils' team chemistry.

"As a member of the Devils," Muller began, as diplomatically as possible, "it's going to be a unique situation. They're such great hockey players that they're certainly going to help us and change our style a little bit. They're offensive-type players. I think this will allow us to open it up a little more. I know there's going to be a lot of different views about them joining the team, whether we're allowing too many imports in our game right now. It's something you can't hide. It's the way a lot of people are going to feel, but I don't think there are going to be any problems with our club. I think once our players get into training camp and see that they can help our club that much more, then they'll be excited to welcome them to the team."

Well said. The cameras clicked, the video cameras floated around the room shooting the Soviets, Lamoriello, Schoenfeld, the ambassador, Muller and McMullen. Even the more cynical among the New York media agreed that, as press conferences go, it was a signal triumph for the Devils. But it was also acknowledged that the debut of the Russians raised many questions. Now that they were here, what would happen to the hockey team and how would they be greeted by the league?

"There are a lot of players in the league who are big, strong players and aren't that keen on the Russians," said Devils goalie Sean Burke. "They're going to get their share of abuse and will have to prove themselves night after night. These guys aren't going to have to earn a spot in camp, so they are going to be taking jobs away from two of our players, and we have some pretty close ties on this team. But if they come in and play the way they're capable of, they'll be accepted very quickly."

Certainly, Fetisov's emigration was accepted in the Soviet Union by just about everyone but Tikhonov and the Soviet Ice Hockey Federation. Fetisov had never forgiven the coach for what, he was convinced, was an unnecessary pigeonholing of his release after the 1988 Olympics, and then caused a stir by leaving the Central Red Army team. Tikhonov counterpunched by dropping Fetisov from the national team for the world championships in Stockholm. Tikhonov eventually took Fetisov back after teammates Igor Larionov, Vladimir Krutov and Sergei Makarov announced on Soviet television that they would boycott the tournament.

Fetisov was named outstanding defenseman in the world championships; afterward he was granted his release from the military, but he never forgave Tikhonov for his meddling. "I wanted to assert myself so that Soviet athletes would have some rights," said Fetisov. "The sports committee could always do whatever it wanted. What I did was a very difficult process. But there was a powerful group of athletes who stood behind me."

Lamoriello: "You have to see the respect Slava is held in over there to understand how he was able to accomplish that. It helped that our desire to get him had become a conversation piece in the Soviet Union."

As a conversation piece, Fetisov and Starikov became less significant once the fallout of the press conference became dissipated in the heat of a baseball season and the National Football League training camp openings. That, however, did not lessen the pressure on coach Schoenfeld, who had to devise a formula for working his new acquisitions into the lineup, maintaining team morale and, at the same time, saving his job.

"A lot of the changes I made," said Lamoriello, "were made with the Russians in mind. One of our liabilities is speed and puck movement and I think Fetisov will help us improve that."

For Schoenfeld, the puzzlement began with a look at his incoming defensemen. Tommy Albelin, Ken Daneyko, Bruce Driver, Tom Kurvers, Randy Velischek and Craig Wolanin all had played capably at one time or another for the Devils. All but Albelin had been on the 1988 miracle playoff crew. Then there was gifted Eric Weinrich, a prospect who was doomed to stay with Utica in the American League because of the defense glut. Add to that the impending arrival of Ruotsalainen, and Schoenfeld was a coach with a defensive roster at overflow level.

But that wasn't Fetisov's fault, nor his concern at the moment. The defenseman and his wife settled into a suburban New Jersey home and began seeing the sights of the Greater New York area. Culture shock set in almost immediately. "On one street corner in New York you can have a multimillion-dollar townhouse and have people lying there sleeping on the street," said Fetisov. "The contrast amazes me. The pace of life here is much faster."

How much faster it would be on the ice Fetisov could not possibly imagine, but he would soon find out with the start of training camp. In the interim, he acclimatized himself to the new world and watched with glee as his comrades set up households in Vancouver, Quebec, Buffalo and Calgary.

CHAPTER 3

SOVIETS IN VANCOUVER, CALGARY, QUEBEC, BUFFALO

"You can't hate the person. You do not like the politics of his country, but the human being is warm and modest, and he will help this team."

— Peter Stastny, New Jersey Devils

Igor Larionov was a 28-year-old centre who had dazzled European audiences with his creative passes for wingers Vladimir Krutov, 29, and Sergei Makarov, 31, on the Central Red Army and Soviet national teams. In a fairy-tale world the Larionov-Krutov-Makarov trio would have been reunited in the NHL on the same club. But the NHL is not utopia, and the Calgary Flames had laid claim to Makarov while the Vancouver Canucks embraced the remaining linemates.

News that British Columbia hockey fans would have the opportunity to view even two Soviet aces over a 40-game home schedule in 1989–90 was hailed as a major event from Victoria to Nanaimo. A portion of the enthusiasm was rooted in the not-too-distant past. After a dismal run during the early and mid-eighties, the Canucks underwent a managerial metamorphosis. Pat Quinn, a former NHL player who had become an attorney, was hired as president and general manager and he imported Brian Burke, a former New England sports agent, as his aide. Combined with coach Bob McCammon, they were one of the more intelligent front office teams in the NHL, and one that finally gave victory-starved Vancouver hockey fans some cause for optimism.

The enthusiasm multiplied during the 1988–89 season. Quinn had acquired swift young Greg Adams, a forward, and goalie Kirk McLean from the New Jersey Devils a season earlier, and then added rookie Trevor Linden after the 1988 draft. Not only did the Canucks make the playoffs, they gave the Calgary Flames an awful fright in the opening playoff round. Heavily favored, the first-place Flames found themselves extended to overtime in the seventh game at the Saddledome. "It looked like they had us beaten twice," recalled Flames coach Terry Crisp, "but [goalie] Mike Vernon came up with a few big saves and then we got the winner."

Heart-wrenching as the defeat was for Vancouver fans, it merely whetted their appetites for the next season, and when the word flashed that Larionov and Krutov had won their release from the Soviet Hockey Federation less than a week after Fetisov had obtained his visa, cheers could be heard in the offices of Pacific Coliseum. Something to smile about, crowed a headline in the Vancouver Sun. Everything's Coming up Roses as Canucks Head Into Promising 1989–90 season.

The bottom line for any NHL team is spelled profit, and the addition of the Soviets was immediately reflected in a projected revenue increase. Long before the new season had started, Canucks marketing director Glen Ringdal reported that season ticket sales had cleared the 10,000 mark and were climbing. "We're selling hope," Ringdal explained, and the fans reflected the party line.

"I wouldn't rule out first place in the Smythe Division," said Royston Francis, a transplanted Englishman who had become a Canucks devotee. "We have as good a chance as anybody."

The reason it seemed so hopeful then was simple. Take a team that had extended the Stanley Cup-champion Flames to seven games and then add two world class players like Larionov and Krutov, and the result had to be an even better Vancouver club.

Of the two, Larionov created the most interest. The

fascination over him began in June at the NHL's annual meeting in Bloomington, Minnesota. It was then that Canucks officials revealed that Igor might choose the Finnish hockey league rather than the NHL. "There have been so many curves in this road," said Pat Quinn, "you almost hate to respond to the everyday twists."

Eventually, Larionov abandoned the idea of playing in Finland and opted for Vancouver. His arrival during the summer of 1989 was perfect timing. Like Fetisov and Starikov, Igor would have time to acclimatize himself to the new surroundings and even meet some of his future teammates. Like many NHL players, some of the Canucks spent parts of the summer working out at local rinks. In Vancouver, Harold Snepsts, Jim Sandlak, Garth Butcher, Larry Melnyk, Steve Weeks, Jim Benning and Steve Tambellini rented ice at the Moody Park Arena in New Westminster. Late in August, another Canuck was added to the Moody Park roster, Igor Larionov.

Brian Burke met Larionov at the airport and the Russian's first question to the Canucks executive was, "Can I skate tomorrow?" Burke obliged by setting him up with Snepsts-Sandlak & Co., and the newcomer fit in easily. Of course it helped that he had a solid command of English, something that many of his compatriots did not. "Igor doesn't get nervous much," said Burke. "Figure it out; it took a lot of nerve for him to get out of the Soviet Union, so why should he get shaken up over here."

At his first skate with his teammates-to-be, Larionov was the very soul of aplomb. Rather slight physically, he glided around the rink with the ease of a Paul Coffey. If there was any tension among the Canucks it was dissipated when Larionov skimmed a pass to Doug Lidster, who was camped near the enemy goal. Lidster accepted the pass and then fired the puck past the yawning goal. The Canucks on the bench razzed Lidster something awful. "Hey," yelled Barry Pederson, "Makarov doesn't miss those ones!" Larionov got the message and a broad smile creased his face.

Larionov's every exquisite move was carefully studied and analyzed by the enraptured audience. "The hand-eye coordination that makes him one of the best centres in the world became immediately apparent after he skated through a crowd, split the defense and beat Weeks in close with a little shovelled backhand shot," noted Pete McMartin of the Vancouver *Sun*.

Nobody was more impressed than Burke and the Canucks. "Some of those guys out there better shake their heads," said the club executive. "He can play. Eight of the forwards have already asked me if they could play with him."

Burke's propaganda line was to be taken only semi-seriously. Both Burke and his boss, Pat Quinn, were acutely aware of the potential problems that would develop once Larionov and, later, Krutov, settled in. While admiring Igor's skill, a couple of Canucks already had expressed displeasure at the Larionov-Krutov axis, much in the manner of Randy Velischek and the Soviet Devils. "From a personal viewpoint," said Butcher, "I'd rather see Canadians playing in the NHL than Russians."

Another concern, at least on Quinn's part, was motivating the Soviets. Nobody disputed their talent, but there already had been indications that at least some of the Russians tended to be lazy and were as much interested in partying as playing hockey. "We know the reputation," said Quinn. "Mr. Gorbachev has expressed concern about the [drinking] problem in his country, and we will watch it closely. It was discussed and I don't think there will be a problem."

Many players were torn between their feelings of Canadian chauvinism and the desire to see their team improved with high-quality talent. "Igor can help us all put some points on the board," added Sandlak. "And the fact that he's a Russian doesn't bother me. We've had Swedes, Czechs and Finns coming over here for years. And they should play in the NHL, but I think it might get to the point down the road someday where they have to put some kind of quota on how many European players they allow in the NHL."

Some of the Canucks masked their displeasure behind a facade of teamsmanship. Others simply tossed out a welcome mat as if Igor was a rookie, the way Trevor Linden had been the previous year. Team captain Stan Smyl, who once had been one of the team's more dominating players, but who had slipped markedly, helped Igor find a house while Pederson, whose job with the Canucks was jeopardized by Larionov's arrival, drove Igor to and from practice. "I'm very pleased with the hospitality," Larionov acknowledged. "I feel welcome. The guys on the team have been nice and I have not seen any of the resentment that some people have mentioned. It's good for Soviet players like me to play in the NHL. We'll help world hockey step up."

Bernie Nicholls, then with the Los Angeles Kings, wasn't so sure about that. The moment Larionov set foot in Vancouver, Nicholls blasted the newcomer in the newspapers, suggesting that he, like the other Russians, would get a tough time because the Soviets carry their sticks too high. This amused a number of NHL critics, who recalled that Nicholls frequently used his hockey stick like a machete.

The Vancouver media seemed anxious to lean over backward to welcome Larionov. Unlike the New York newspapers' handling of Fetisov and Starikov, where there was a big splash one day and no followup stories for weeks thereafter, British Columbia journalists kept an Argus eye on Igor, encouraging him at almost every turn.

"Let us agree right now to do Igor Larionov a tremendous favor," said Vancouver *Province* columnist Jim Taylor. "Let us not assume he is faster than a speeding bullet, more powerful than a locomotive, and can leap tall buildings in a single bound. That was CCCP on his jersey all those years, not S. Amid the hysteria to come, it would be wise to remember that.

"What the Vancouver Canucks have purchased is an extraordinarily gifted 29-year-old centre, on the smallish side for the bump and grind of the NHL, who'll be adapting to a new style in a strange league in a strange land on ice surfaces that will look like postage stamps compared to the icy prairies of the international game in which he's thrived."

The average fan, however, was not inclined to be so patient or understanding. Having been tempted by the success of 1988–89, the Canucks supporter couldn't help but be impressed by the headlines surrounding Larionov. And just when they began to abate, along came his longtime pal, Vladimir Krutov, alias The Tank.

Unlike Igor, who seemed eager to move to North America and did so long before Vladimir arrived, Krutov arrived in the midst of training camp under almost clandestine conditions. Canucks management attempted to sneak their second Soviet into the city, but enough of the media learned of his arrival to dispatch a squad of photographers and reporters to Vancouver International Airport as the new addition arrived after a 19-hour journey from Moscow.

Among the greeters were collegians Walter Sheloff and Julie Wierenga, each of whom spoke Russian and wore T-shirts inscribed with words in the Cyrillic alphabet that read, "No More War!" Sheloff said he was inspired to greet Krutov to make him feel more comfortable. "There's been so much hype about the hockey aspect," said Sheloff. "I gave him my home phone number and told him to call. I want him to feel more comfortable."

It was a thoughtful gesture, but one that would not immediately work. While Larionov behaved like a Canadian, Krutov would be conspicuous in his failure to adapt to his new land. Larionov already had displayed a sense of humor and, because of his knowledge of English, felt right at home, particularly with coach Bob McCammon, a witty sort invariably given to the droll riposte.

One day at the Canucks' Parksville training camp, Larionov indicated to McCammon that he was not feeling well. "In Russia, we have small apartment, small car, no food, but we're healthy all the time," said Igor. "In Canada we have big house, big car, lots of food and we're sick all the time."

Visitors to Parksville were impressed with Larionov's photographic memory. For example, he recalled playing against Canucks defenseman Paul Reinhart in the 1982 World Championships in Finland. "I remember that game," Igor told Reinhart. "You played centre. You scored one goal against me." Then, a pause and a smile. "I remember. That was the game I scored four goals!"

Any time a member of the Canucks high command wanted to outquip Larionov, they merely had to mention his nemesis, Soviet coach Viktor Tikhonov, the very same instructor who had earned the enmity of Slava Fetisov. McCammon wouldn't let this bit of information slip by and, after a scrimmage, the coach picked up the phone in the training room while Larionov was having his temperature taken. "Igor, it's for you," McCammon winked. "It's Viktor!" Onlookers reported that Larionov almost fainted.

Canucks players almost fainted at the dexterity of Larionov's play during training camp. "Igor is incredible," said Jim Sandlak, who was one of several players who hoped to play alongside Larionov. "I keep my stick on the ice and he hits the tape. I don't know where the puck is coming from sometimes, but all of a sudden, it's there."

With every rave about Larionov, members of the Vancouver media grew more bullish about the club's prospects. Quinn tended to be conservative. "The expectations may be a little unfair," the president admitted. "After that great playoff we had, people were bubbly, saying we almost made it to the Stanley Cup. But that's bullshit. We had a good playoff, that's all. We would have had three more teams to beat after that."

The signing of Krutov merely added to the optimism. At 29, Krutov was hardly in Larionov's class physically. Vladimir had the look of Sergei Starikov, built more like a fire hydrant. After he signed a three-year contract, an enterprising Vancouver distributor began marketing T-shirts with the inscription, "The Russians are coming." However, the words "are coming" were crossed out and replaced with "have come!"

Some Vancouver dreamers nurtured the hope that the Canucks could swing a deal with the Cup-champion Flames, who a year earlier had dealt Paul Reinhart to the BC sextet. The idea would be for Quinn to somehow wangle Sergei Makarov from Calgary and thereby reunite him on what once was Central Army's famous KLM line.

"Everybody would like to do that," acknowledged McCammon, "But Calgary is not going to give Vancouver any more help. I'm sure [Flames president] Cliff Fletcher is not going to throw any more crumbs our way."

McCammon was right. He knew that he had to somehow integrate Larionov and Krutov with a third forward, who could not possibly match Makarov in skill but, hopefully, would keep pace with the Soviets.

Integration into Canadian society, meanwhile, was progressing at a healthy pace, although there were some arresting moments. Captain Smyl was in a better position to observe than most because of his interest in helping his teammates adjust to Canadian life.

"One night," Smyl recalled, "I was driving Igor, his wife Lena, and three-year-old daughter Alena back to the hotel when we stopped for some milk. This grocery store is not a big one but I wish we could have had cameras to capture the expression on their faces. They stopped for a toothbrush and wanted to keep going down the aisles. The next day my wife, Jennifer, went back with Lena; when Lena saw the meat department, she tried to grab it all in one day. She wanted to take it home and freeze it right away. It was all Jennifer could do to convince her it would all be there again tomorrow.

"Lena had been a national junior figure skating champion in Russia, but she never coached after her career was over because of standing in line all day. She simply didn't have that much time. If you want good milk, you have to get in line early. Igor has been telling me that we must realize how much we have here in Canada and how lucky we are. After listening to him, I believe it. The tough part is, I don't think he quite realizes how much money he could be earning, how much of this he could have, if he was here under normal circumstances."

If the Soviet rookies realized anything, it was that they were living in an NHL fishbowl. Their every move seemed to be watched and usually chronicled and, not surprisingly, Larionov and Krutov were invariably compared both as players and personalities. The tendency, because they had played together so long, was to assume they were like brothers, but those who managed to get a closer look at them discovered otherwise. "These guys are twins," chuckled Tony Gallagher, "like Arnold Schwarzenegger and Danny DeVito were twins in the movie.

"Larionov is the classy, almost aristocratic thinker who rebelled against the Communist way of hockey at the very least. Krutov, on the other hand, is the stereotypical, raw-boned, rural rustic who says hockey is the same anywhere. He greets every question from the interpreter with a shrug first, saying he 'doesn't mind meeting with the media, but not often.' While Larionov has dreamt of the NHL, Krutov comes because a European release for less money would have been tough and his friend talked him into it, rather than spending the year Viktor Tikhonov wanted from him."

Right from the start, Larionov exuded optimism and a joy about being in Canada. He seemed genuinely interested in helping the Canucks to a winning season. By contrast, Krutov, consciously or otherwise, delivered negative vibrations. More often than not, Vladimir would leave one wondering just why he bothered travelling so far if he cared so little about playing hockey in Canada.

"Igor influenced my decision to come here," Krutov explained, "and he did it in a phone call. It wasn't an easy decision between playing in Vancouver and playing in Europe. He helped me make up my mind."

Krutov's image hardly was enhanced by his potbelly. The Canucks listed his playing weight at 195 pounds but his bulging midsection suggested a 210 minimum. Long before he had arrived, Vladimir had developed a transcontinental reputation as a connoisseur of vodka. In fact coach McCammon once quipped that he would drink with Krutov if it meant persuading him to play in the NHL. McCammon was also acutely aware of Krutov's endless passion for frankfurters. "I swear," said McCammon, "one of these days he's going to miss a flight chasing a hot dog."

During his first workouts with the Canucks, Krutov looked as out of place as a Gordie Howe coming out of retirement for another NHL fling. The Tank looked more like a whale, and the coach was worried. "Vladimir is going to have a lot tougher time," McCammon mused. "We're going to have to be patient. We're not talking about fringe guys. At least he'll be worth waiting for."

The muffled enthusiasm over Krutov's long-range prospects was based on his past performance in the Soviet Union. If Larionov was the brain of the KLM line and Makarov the artist, Krutov was the muscleman who could work the corners as well as a John Tonelli and park himself in front of the net, remaining as immovable as the Washington Monument. "Krutov is a tough son-of-a-gun," said Team Canada coach and general manager Dave King. "He's the kind of guy you love to have on your team, but hate playing against."

Krutov had been named the outstanding player in Europe in 1986–87 and was runner-up to Makarov in the 1988–89 Soviet League scoring race. Despite his bulk, Vladimir was admired for his exceptional acceleration and goal-scoring ability. Unfortunately, none of this was apparent after his first scrimmage in Vancouver.

After a few sprints, Krutov appeared to be skating in pain. He had what one observer described as "an agonized look on his puffy face" after a brisk 45-minute workout. It would be a portent of things to come, although nobody in the Canucks high command would dare admit it. "I didn't skate for the last two weeks," Krutov later admitted. "I'll get back into shape in a couple of weeks."

While Larionov was able to converse one-on-one with reporters, Krutov required the assistance of an interpreter. "My main goal," he said, "is to play hard and be involved. I'm ready for the first game."

McCammon wasn't so sure. The coach noted that he would have to make a major adjustment to the Canadian lifestyle, but he remained hopeful that Krutov would synchronize easily with his club. "Of all the Soviet players," added McCammon, "Krutov is best suited for the NHL with his style of play. He'll be all right, hockey-wise. Patience is going to be the key for both of them, understanding the way we play and making the adjustment with their teammates."

As training camp unfolded and the exhibition season began, Krutov remained a disappointment. Already there were signs that he regretted his decision to leave the Soviet Union, and discouraging words were heard up and down the hockey grapevine. "Of the Soviets' big three forwards," Dave King pointed out, "Krutov has always been the one who gets most easily discouraged. He doesn't respond well to tight checking. It'll be interesting to see if he can overcome that."

There were few precedents on which to make judgements about who would or wouldn't be able to handle the grind. Whenever historians looked back at Soviets in the NHL, they inevitably turned to the case of Victor Nechaev.

A native of Kuibshevka Vostochnaya, Siberia, Nechaev was the first Soviet-trained player ever to skate in the NHL. Nechaev preceded Sergei Priakin of the Calgary Flames by nearly seven years.

Signed by the Los Angeles Kings, Nechaev made his NHL debut against the New York Islanders on October 16, 1982. Shortly thereafter, he scored his first NHL goal, taking a pass from Daryl Evans and beating New York Rangers goalie Steve Weeks with a wrist shot from the blueline. "I was tired like the devil," Nechaev recalled. "It was my third game in three nights. I played in New Haven [of the American League] and then they picked me up for two games in New York and I felt dead."

Nechaev clearly was a cut or two below NHL calibre and was soon relegated to the minors. He was a pioneer, but only because his wife, Cheryl Haigler — whom he married in Moscow in 1980 — was an American, and therefore he was allowed to leave the Soviet Union in 1982. (The couple divorced in 1985.) "When I played in the NHL," added Nechaev, "I may have been a pioneer, but I was like a blind puppy. I tell them in Los Angeles, 'I don't want to play here,' and they put me on bench and they make a reputation about me. The next year, some teams were interested, but again they expected me to try out. I just gave up. I felt I was too old for that."

When Krutov and Larionov had settled into Vancouver, Nechaev was a 34-year-old part-owner of

Russian-American Television in Los Angeles. He followed their progress carefully and was cautiously optimistic about their NHL chances. "They can dominate as soon as they adapt," Nechaev predicted. "Krutov needs to learn English because monkey communication is very difficult. Here, he'll have to learn to take care of himself. It should be tough, especially for someone who has been with the national team ten or twelve years."

Interestingly, Nechaev had no idea that he was not the first Russian-born player to skate in the NHL. That was Johnny Gottselig, who was born in 1904 near Odessa in the Ukraine and emigrated to Regina, Saskatchewan, with his family a year later. In every other way, Gottselig was a Canadian-bred hockey player. He played 16 years under the nickname "The Mad Russian" and scored 177 goals with 195 assists in 589 career games in 1928–29 and 1944–45. Gottselig won the Stanley Cup with the Blackhawks in 1933–34 and 1937–38. He also coached the Hawks for four years and was the team publicity director from 1948 to 1963.

If Gottselig was unknown to the Soviet NHL pioneers of 1989, the same, in a different sense, could be said of the least-trumpeted of the Russian émigrés, goalie Sergei Mylnikov, who had been signed by the Quebec Nordiques.

A native of Chelyabinsk, Mylnikov, 31, had national team experience although he certainly wasn't in the goaltending class of the legendary Vladislav Tretiak. But like Tretiak, who never had the opportunity to play in the NHL, Mylnikov was thrilled by the challenge. "Playing in the NHL," the goalie allowed, "is the last thing left for me to try."

Mylnikov reported to Quebec and was suitably greeted by the local French-Canadian media, but his arrival went virtually unnoticed around the rest of the NHL. In a sense the goalie was fortunate; the Nordiques' captain Peter Stastny hailed from Eastern Europe (the eastern province of Slovakia in Czechoslovakia), and spoke Russian fluently.

But Stastny was not fond of Russians — and for

good reason. Peter was an 11-year-old when Soviet tanks invaded Czechoslovakia in August 1968. Without jogging his memory, he could explicitly detail how he heard radio broadcasts that resistance by the Slovaks would be foolish. He remembered that road signs between his grandparents' village of Pruzina and the city of Bratislava had been reversed, to confuse the invading Russians. Peter watched the Soviet tanks clank their way through the Bratislava streets on the banks of the Danube. "I hated them," Stastny recalled. "We could only defeat them in one arena and that was on a hockey rink. We had plenty of good hockey players and our games with the Russians were as intense as anything you could imagine. When we beat them — which did happen occasionally — it was like David beating Goliath."

In a sense, Mylnikov was the David to Stastny's Goliath when they sat together in the Nordiques' dressing room at Le Colisée in Quebec. Peter was the most distinguished performer in Nordiques history, the idol of the ancient city's French-speaking crowds. Mylnikov was an NHL babe in the woods, listening to Stastny as he explained the blueprints of Quebec coach Michel Bergeron. A decade earlier, it would have been impossible to visualize a scene where the Russian-hating Stastny would be playing uncle to a Soviet hockey player.

"You can't hate the person," Stastny explained to a curious reporter. "You do not like the politics of his country, but the human being is warm and modest, and he will help this team."

But would he? Nobody could be certain just who would do well and who would flop, although there were predictions galore. The consensus was that Sergei Makarov of the Flames would have the easiest time: there already was a Soviet player in Calgary, Sergei Priakin; the Flames, as Stanley Cup champions, could carry Makarov until he adjusted; and pound for pound, he was the most talented of the Russian players.

"Makarov will be the best of all," said Starikov of the Devils.

"Makarov is a great one-on-one player, one of the best in the world," noted Dave King. "He will have to learn to be more direct with his plays. He tries to get too cute sometimes, but he's likely to adjust."

A minority bloc chose Alexander Mogilny as the Soviet Most Likely to Succeed. In many ways, Mogilny deserved to be favored. He was younger than any of his compatriots and, in the estimation of some critics, was the bravest of them all, since Mogilny escaped from Russia the hard way — through the trap door.

CHAPTER 4

THE MOGILNY "MEGILLAH"

"I understand everything, everything. My decision can show other people how to think. Nobody there would ever believe I would do this."
—Alexander Mogilny, Buffalo Sabres

It was not unprecedented for players to defect from behind the iron curtain to the NHL. The Stastny brothers, Peter and Anton, escaped from their native Czechoslovakia by way of Austria and eventually wound up in Quebec City, where they signed on with the Nordiques. Older brother Marian followed a year later. But unshackling oneself from the Soviet hockey bureaucracy and making one's way to Buffalo and a contract with the Sabres was a melodrama of another sort.

Alexander Mogilny, a 20-year-old winger whose hockey gifts had become the toast of Europe, was the chief protagonist in a tale that would have been evaluated at Twentieth Century Fox as worthy of a grade-B Hollywood script.

The saga began early in 1988. Mogilny, whose speed matched the fastest NHL skaters, caught the eyes of Sabres scouts. They recommended that the club draft him at the annual meetings that June. Sure enough, when the fifth round arrived the Buffalo contingent announced their intention of drafting Mogilny, and his name was placed on the list as the 89th overall pick. At the time, Mogilny was relaxing in Moscow, having no idea what his hockey future would be outside the Soviet Union.

But in December 1988, Alexander was a member of the Soviet team participating in the junior world championships at Anchorage, Alaska. Scouting the young players was a tall, curly-haired ex-forward with the Buffalo Sabres named Don Luce. Luce was now employed by the Sabres club as its director of amateur evaluation and development. During a break in the games, Luce cornered Mogilny and told him that the Sabres were interested in him, that they were very excited about having him on the potential players roster. "If we can ever be of service," said Luce, subduing his enthusiasm while strongly underlining his point, "don't hesitate to call."

Luce's message registered firmly in Mogilny's mind. The young Russian had to consider some big decisions: Did he have the courage to defect? If he did, when would he do it; how would he make the move; who would help him?

After considerable thought, Mogilny concluded that the most propitious time to take the big leap would be in the spring of 1989. That was when the Soviet national team was scheduled to be in Sweden for the annual World Championships at Stockholm. When he left home late in April, Alexander took nothing but the minimum essentials for a road trip. Although the temptation was great to take some personal belongings with him, he decided against it, knowing that Soviet authorities might get suspicious and thwart his getaway.

On May 2, 1989, the phone rang in Luce's office. The Sabres' aide couldn't believe his ears. "Alexander Mogilny is prepared to defect, if you are interested," Luce informed his boss, Sabres general manager Gerry Meehan, a former NHL player who had become an attorney and now a hockey executive. Before making another move, Meehan wanted to be certain he wasn't being duped by a ruse. He checked, double-checked and triple-checked, until he was persuaded beyond a doubt that the call was authentic.

That done, Meehan and Luce booked seats on the next jet to Stockholm. They had a lot to talk about and much of the discussion centred on the character of the young man they were pursuing. Was he worth the trip? That puzzled them, particularly since Mogilny's immediate past was not all that lily-white, at least not by Soviet standards.

Conservatively speaking, Alexander was a rebel. Playing in a system that is rigid and demands teamwork over individual aspirations, Mogilny rocked the boat. During the junior world championships in Anchorage, a high-ranking Soviet accused Mogilny of putting his own interests above the game's. "He even predicted that 'Sasha' would be out of the game within two years," said *Inside Hockey* magazine editor Steve Dryden, "a victim of his own selfishness."

Like comrades Slava Fetisov, Igor Larionov and Sergei Makarov, Mogilny had no use for national and Central Red Army coach Viktor Tikhonov. "The difference," Dryden explained, "was Mogilny's willingness to go outside the system to achieve his goals. Alex had no encumbrances — nothing to hold him back, save devotion to his mother, father, brother and girlfriend. He did not have to steal away in the dead of night with a wife, child and full trunk in tow."

The other major difference was age. Compared to the others, Mogilny was a mere youth, a junior lieutenant in the army, who supposedly would be a key to the Soviet national hockey teams for years. But Mogilny was looking in another direction.

"I didn't want to become an officer," Mogilny explained, "because I was thinking about my future. I saw a lot of my teammates — like Fetisov. They were officers and they had to play until they were 30 years old before they could go abroad and play. If he hadn't become an officer, maybe they would have let him go abroad to play when he was 25 or 26.

A native of Khabarovsk in the eastern USSR — an eight-hour flight from Moscow — Mogilny left home at age 15 to play with the Red Army club. While others regarded the experience as a privilege and honour to play for so distinguished an organization, the iconoclastic Mogilny found skating under the autocratic Tikhonov more onerous than fun.

"During the five years it was terrible because they did everything for me," Mogilny asserted. "I wasn't thinking for myself and didn't have my own life. I didn't make any decisions. They made all those decisions for me. Also, I didn't have any free time to see my friends or have a social life. They were treating me in such a bad way. And I'm so young. The coaches were older and did not know how to relate to younger people."

If Meehan and Luce have one virtue it is an ability to deal with young people, and so it was hardly surprising that Mogilny took a liking to them when the rendezvous finally was arranged in Stockholm. Having met with the Sabres officials, Mogilny was convinced that he was making the right move. He phoned his parents from Stockholm and advised them that he planned to defect — immediately.

Nadezhda Mogilny, his mother, was traumatized by the news, as any mother would be. She grasped the consequences of her son's decision and pleaded with him to change his mind and return home, but his choice was irrevocable. Before he could elaborate, there was a click on the telephone, and Alexander realized that the call had been cut off, likely from the Russian end. (Without having any proof, Mogilny theorizes that the conversation had been monitored by the KGB.)

Meehan was no less concerned than Nadezhda Mogilny. He wanted to be certain that his potential sharpshooter knew what he had in store for him, and the two had a heart-to-heart. "I talked to him about how he felt about North America, and whether he realized the gravity of what he was doing," Meehan remembered. "He convinced me that he understood."

The Buffalo representatives wanted Mogilny to know that NHL opponents would not lay out a red carpet for him. Alexander convinced Meehan that he was ready for anything. "I know that always the first year somebody comes from Europe to play in the NHL," he said, "it takes like maybe one season to get really used to the team, the audience and the style of play. I know that maybe a lot of players are going to try to hit me because I am a Russian and because I am in my first year."

Meehan left their meeting assured that Mogilny was as prepared for the defection and ensuing complications as he ever would be. Arrangements were made for Mogilny, Luce and Meehan to leave for North America the next day. There were no major hitches and, sure enough, Alexander walked without obstruction through the security maze at Stockholm Airport and lounged with his new friends in the passengers-only section. He turned to Meehan and smiled. "I am free now."

When he uttered the words, Alexander was thinking of Tikhonov, who had become his *bête noire,* just as the coach had for Fetisov and Larionov. When Mogilny discussed Tikhonov his words dripped with contempt. "Only his wife and dog like him," Alexander clucked, "and I do not understand how they do."

At first, the Soviets did not understand how Mogilny could have jumped the team. The embarrassment was keenly felt from Leningrad to Vladivostok. Even *The New York Times* took due note of the event with a bylined story on page one of the news section: SOVIET HOCKEY STAR IN BUFFALO AFTER DEFECTING TO U.S. TEAM.

No sooner had Mogilny landed at Kennedy Airport in New York City, enroute to Buffalo, than Soviet officials were denouncing the defection. The Russians accused the Sabres of "piracy" and depicted Mogilny as a money-hungry ingrate, who earlier had been singled out as a malcontent by Soviet hockey authorities.

"The player showed by his action that it's not happenstance that he didn't have friends among his contemporaries on the team and that he was a person of secret intentions," said Tikhonov.

As the number of Mogilny headlines multiplied, so did the number of denunciations and reports of his questionable character in his homeland. Tikhonov reported that before leaving for the world championships, Mogilny had asked the authorities for a better apartment because he planned to marry. There also were reports that he had been fined a month's salary, stripped of his Master of Sports decoration and suspended for ten games for fighting, an unusual offense in Soviet hockey.

No less concerned were NHL officials. Just days before Mogilny's defection, league president John Ziegler had been crowing about how glasnost had spread to NHL-Soviet relations. Now Tikhonov was warning that the blossoming relationship between the NHL and Russian hockey authorities could be "seriously damaged" by the defection.

A spokesman for the Immigration and Naturalization Service in Washington explained that Mogilny had been allowed to enter the United States under a procedure in which aliens are sometimes given permission to enter pending a later determination of their status. Despite the rhetoric, everyone in the Sabres organization was convinced that American red tape would be quickly cut, and Mogilny would take up life in Buffalo just as he had hoped.

"I understand everything," said Mogilny, "everything. My decision can show other people how to think. Nobody there would ever believe I would do this. They are all such a part of the system that they could never even think about something like that."

Somebody asked Mogilny if he felt like a traitor. He wasted no time replying, "No way!"

Whether he would become an adequate professional hockey player and justify the Sabres' cloak-and-dagger move was another story, to be answered later in the year. Now there was a summer of rest, rehabilitation and new residency to enjoy before training camp began. In addition there would be an endless demand for interviews. The Sabres' public relations office handled requests, as did Mogilny's North American agent, Toronto lawyer Don Meehan.

Everyone attempted to cushion the change for Alexander. He was temporarily housed with the couple who shepherded him from Stockholm to Buffalo: Lena Nilsson, a Swede, and her husband, Sergei Fomitjov, a Soviet émigré, occupied a townhouse in a Buffalo suburb called Amherst.

If there was any doubt that Mogilny was making the adjustment quickly, it was dispelled whenever he went shopping. At the local Chevrolet dealer he bought a black Corvette. During a stop in Manhattan, he picked out a $400 shirt. It was enough to suggest that the young man would be travelling in the too-fast lane, but agent Meehan seemed unconcerned.

Others were not so sure. *Inside Hockey*'s Steve Dryden pointed out that Mogilny could well fall into the same traps as Petr Klima, "another young player with sudden wealth, from a Communist country." Klima's indiscretions while playing for the Detroit Red Wings had been so well-documented that even Mogilny was aware of them. "The problems Petr had with alcohol," Alexander insisted, "I would never have those problems." He added that he had never heard the word cocaine "until I came here."

His love life also became a subject of debate. While he talked about a girlfriend — or fiancée, depending on the occasion — in the Soviet Union, he also was linked with an Alaskan, Tera Harrington. Pressed about his romances, Mogilny snapped, "This is none of your business."

As for his hockey business, the word almost instantly was optimistic from the Buffalo camp. The Sabres' crack defenseman Phil Housley scrimmaged with him at a local rink and rhapsodized over the young Russian's skills. "He has great lateral movement and good takeaway speed," Housley reported. "He can skate and stickhandle. That's difficult to do. His hands and his feet are quick. I would say he's going to be an impact player. Maybe not right away, but he'll make a difference in some games.

Meanwhile, other NHL teams were kicking themselves for not beating Buffalo to the punch and signing Mogilny themselves. The Edmonton Oilers, in particular, were upset. The Oilers' chief scout Barry Fraser allowed that he knew in the spring of 1988 that Mogilny planned on fleeing Mother Russia, but the Sabres had surprised him by drafting the youngster.

"I had heard stories that he wanted out of the Soviet Union," Fraser admitted, "but you can't believe them all. I was more wary when it was a Russian they were talking about defecting than a Czech. Still, we got the information about Alexander from a very reliable source. We thought the defection would be at the junior world championship at Anchorage. We had planned to select him in the same round. I don't know how Buffalo found out...maybe the same guy who tipped us told them.

"Mogilny put up a smokescreen in Alaska and made like everything was fine. I guess he wanted to play in the world championship in Sweden."

Many observers were surprised that the Soviets were caught flatfooted by Mogilny's move. Shouldn't they have been more vigilant with a player who already had been notorious as a malcontent? Weren't the Russians expecting his attempted leap to freedom?

"Does a guy tell his wife he's going to rob a bank?" Fraser countered. The Oilers aide pointed out that it was relatively simple for Mogilny to bolt the Soviet national team while in Stockholm. "What were they going to do, shoot him? He can spit in a KGB guy's face and walk away if he wants."

Some Russians, such as Mogilny, obviously would dare stare down a KGB agent. Others were more hesitant. That was the case with Mogilny's last Soviet roommate, Sergei Federov, who was with him in Stockholm before he made his move. Just minutes before he packed his bags and departed the hotel room, Mogilny tried to persuade Federov to accompany him to North America. "Oh no!" Federov protested. "I couldn't. My father. My mother. My family. What about them? No, you go, Alex. 'Vsevo Khoroshevo.' Best of luck to you in your new life."

Federov and Mogilny had been two-thirds of a line that, with right-wing Pavel Bure, was heir apparent to the famed KLM (Krutov-Larionov-Makarov) unit. The Red Wings had chosen Federov in the 1989 draft, whereas Bure had been selected by the Canucks. Both Bure and Federov were committed to remain in Russia.

Mogilny soon was well ensconced in Buffalo, and now the Sabres were trying to figure out how to fit him into their retooled team. For 1989–90 the Buffalo club had a new coach in Rick Dudley — who had no NHL coaching experience — and a brilliant prospect in Pierre Turgeon, who led the team in scoring, with 88 points during his second full NHL season.

The idea of uniting the French-Canadian ace with the Russian gunner was positively intriguing to the Sabres general staff, not to mention Turgeon himself. "This is exciting," said Pierre, when asked about his teammate. "He's a Russian guy, he's come over here. It's a big thing for him and for us. It's going to be fun."

Dudley, new to his position but wise in the ways of public relations, realized that it was important not to create a buildup-to-a-letdown around Mogilny. On the other hand he didn't want to dismiss his sharpshooter out of hand. "Alex is a skilled, skilled hockey player," said Dudley. "He's fun to watch and the fans are going to love him. He's exciting and he obviously revels in the crowd.

"Style-wise, he's superb. People on the defense have to move with him. When he goes wide on people they have to try and play him. When he goes wide like that you see a little bit of [former Sabres great] Gilbert Perreault in him."

Buffalo's media hardly was subdued about Mogilny. "He seems destined to carve more notches in a stick than Billy the Kid ever cut with a gun," predicted Jim Kelley of the *Buffalo News*. "He's a bona fide rookie of the year candidate even before he steps on the ice."

In early practices it became evident that Mogilny's trump card was his speed. During his first exhibition game he dazzled onlookers with a play he made standing still. Unguarded, off to the side of the Hartford Whalers' net, Mogilny accepted a quick pass on his backhand. The lateral was unexpected, the type that normally would baffle the average skater. Alexander not only tamed the puck but flipped the backhand shot through an opening just a millimeter larger than the puck itself. "One shot," noted Kelley. "No wasted motion. Deadly accurate. Instantly, a legend was born."

Coaches and managers went out of their way to study Mogilny's moves and, for the most part, were singularly impressed. "You can see he's not just a product of the Soviet system," said the Chicago Blackhawks' erudite coach Mike Keenan. "He does have the skills you would expect from a player out of their system, but you can see that some of his talents are innate. Some of the things he can do are things you simply can't teach."

Mike Smith, the equally thoughtful Winnipeg Jets general manager, likened Mogilny to "an artist with his stick. The puck is there and then it's gone, and he knows exactly where it's going."

Reporter Kelley marvelled at Mogilny's ability to create offense during an exhibition game against the Blackhawks. "Once he drew three Blackhawks to him at centre ice just inside the blueline. They were big Hawks and very much interested in making a big hit. Just when it appeared they had taken away any chance for Mogilny to make a play, he snapped a wrist shot at goalie Alain Chevrier. It didn't go in, but it was so quick, hard and unexpected, the goalie couldn't handle it and Ray Sheppard stroked home the rebound.

"Later in the game Mogilny slipped over the blueline and wristed another shot at Chevrier from about 40 feet. It was high and wide, but it moved so fast that Chevrier was still raising his glove hand when the puck exploded off the glass behind him. It happened so fast, Chevrier appeared to look behind him in a futile search for the cause of the sound. Hard and fast with a quickness not seen in these parts for a long, long time. You've got to like this cowboy."

Sabres fans were ready to like the Russian skater. What remained to be seen was how much Mogilny would like Buffalo. Before the season even started there were hints that his reaction would be negative. In interviews Mogilny said he missed Moscow's teeming throngs, there weren't enough people in Buffalo, and California suited him better.

"A premature (and realistic) assessment," noted Steve Dryden of *Inside Hockey,* "but it does raise the most pertinent question of all: Why would anyone defect to Buffalo?"

It was a question Alexander Mogilny would be asking himself throughout the 1989–90 season.

CHAPTER 5

THE NHL VISITS MOSCOW

"The players will be together in a different environment and if there ever was a chance for togetherness early, this should be it."

— Bryan Murray,
then Washington Capitals coach

The arrival of Viacheslav Fetisov and comrades was a sensational event, to be sure, and the defection of Alexander Mogilny was an NHL version of a Tom Clancy thriller. But these all were office affairs and not genuine confrontations of Soviet and North American players between the two goals.

"We all were looking forward to the new season because of the Russians," recalled Craig Wolanin, a former New Jersey Devil, since traded to the Quebec Nordiques, "but there were so many things happening with them beforehand that it was almost as exciting as the upcoming games themselves. And one aspect we all were wondering about was the exhibition tour of the Flames and Capitals."

If ever there was proof that glasnost was alive and in high gear, it was the landmark agreement between the NHL and Soviet hockey authorities for a Friendship Tour (as John Ziegler called it) of Washington and Calgary teams to Russia before the start of the 1989–90 season.

According to the plan hammered out by Ziegler and his Soviet counterparts, it would be unlike any training camp ever held by an NHL team before. Not only would the Capitals and Flames practice and play in Moscow, but Calgary would make a side trip to Czechoslovakia, while the Capitals would do the same to Sweden.

In many ways each team was an ideal choice. The Flames had won their first Stanley Cup championship in May 1989, and Calgary management, headed by general manager Cliff Fletcher, was respected in hockey circles for its progressive approach to the game. What better choice than the NHL's foremost team?

Washington was an equally admirable selection. Under GM David Poile, the Capitals featured some of the game's classiest performers including Rod Langway, Scott Stevens, Mike Ridley and Kelly Miller. It didn't hurt that they represented the capital of the United States.

While the tour appeared to be a diplomatic coup for the NHL, the coaches, Terry Crisp of Calgary and Bryan Murray of Washington, were not so sure how the transatlantic journey would affect their players immediately and over the course of an 80-game season.

"It will be full of surprises," warned Boston Bruins general manager Harry Sinden. "There's an awful lot of travel involved and there will be harassment. Who knows what impact it will have on the teams."

Sinden had been to Moscow as coach of Team Canada in 1972, when an NHL squad played an eight-game series — four in Canada and four in Moscow — against a select Soviet squad. At that time hostility between the Soviets and Canadians was more intense than in 1989. Still, nobody was quite sure what to expect.

"This will be totally different," said Crisp. "I've been through so many years of training camps and they're all the same. Go to the rink, skate, have lunch, take a nap, go back to the rink, skate some more, play a few exhibition games. Now we're going to play six games in countries where most of us have never been."

The majority of players involved were either interested or ambivalent about the trip. Few were openly opposed. Capitals defenseman Grant Ledyard had been to the Soviet Union before, to play for Canada in the 1986 World Championships. "It was a great experience," Ledyard said of his 1986 visit. "They treated us first class and we had team meals at different restaurants throughout Moscow. We did everything — a Kremlin tour, Lenin's Tomb. It was fantastic.

"The hockey was great, too. We played on the big rinks and the games were very competitive. The only downer was that Chernobyl occurred with four days left to our trip and they never told us about it. They checked us back home as we got off the plane, but we all checked out okay."

Ledyard warned his teammates that they would have some trouble getting accustomed to the Russian cuisine. "I remembered having potatoes at every meal and that there was no milk, so we drank a lot of pop."

The teams took some precautions for proper diet. "We're more concerned about the water than the food," said Crisp, "and the possibility of getting a virus. We're taking distilled water and we've made arrangements to have our own water over there."

When the Capitals learned that there was no pasta in Russia, they made their own arrangements to supply the high-carbohydrate food. Thousands of pounds of pasta and hundreds of jars of sauce were ordered by the team's vice president of marketing.

Although the NHL attempted to play down the competitive aspects of the exhibition tour, the eight games figured to be well-contested, particularly since the Stanley Cup champions would be involved. "It's very important to the Soviets to win," said Poile. "Their goal is to win all eight games from Washington and Calgary. Our mentality in regard to pre-season is different. We would like to be competitive, but we're more concerned with deciding individual situations rather than results."

The Capitals itinerary would begin in Karlstad, Sweden, where coach Bryan Murray would put his club through intensive drills. The Capitals would play two exhibition games in Sweden before leaving for Russia. Unlike the Flames, who had reached the pinnacle just a few months earlier, the Capitals looked upon the European trip as a means of escaping an annoying trend that they had established.

Entering their sixteenth year, the Washington sextet invariably got off to a shaky start in just about every campaign and always failed to do well in their quest for the

Stanley Cup. Not once had they escaped the Patrick Division playoffs. "We've tried everything else," said Poile, "so why not this? It will be the first time since I've been manager that we've faced a competitive training camp. We're hoping it makes us sharp for the start of the season. Obviously there are difficulties."

There would be several disadvantages, not least the difference between international and NHL ice surfaces. Teams like the Flames and Capitals are accustomed to playing on a rink that measures 85 by 200 feet. The international surface is about 15 feet wider than in the NHL. Apart from the disadvantage presented by the larger ice, the teams would be playing at a high level after only a few days of training. Meanwhile, the Swedes and Soviets had been training since early July. "It's one of those inequities that occur whenever you're trying to do something new and different," Poile added. "Both sides were all for the exchange, and we hope the benefits to the NHL overbalance the competitive disadvantages."

The trip would have particular significance for Bryan Murray. Having coached the Capitals for nine years, Murray had established himself as one of the more competent leaders during the regular season. But the Capitals' playoff record under Murray was so dismal that there were credible murmurs that his job would be on the line in 1989–90. So it was imperative for him to get off on the right foot in Russia. Murray, himself, was optimistic about the prospects. He believed that the trip would boost club morale and conditioning for the regular season.

"The players will be together in a different environment," he said, "and if there ever was a chance for togetherness early, this should be it. I see it as a chance for a lot of players to compete at a high level without a lot of physical play. From a conditioning point of view, that should be good."

For the Flames there were several motives; one was an opportunity to view first-hand their prized 1989 draft pick, Robert Reichel, an 18-year-old star with the Czech national team. On their arrival in Prague, several Flames officials journeyed to nearby Pribram to watch Reichel work out with the Czech club.

"He's a good technical player," said Jiri Hrdina, the Czech-born Flames forward, "but he's small — like Theo Fleury."

Following the practice, Reichel chatted with the Canadian media accompanying the Flames. "I knew I'd been drafted by Calgary," the teenager acknowledged, "and I was very, very pleased when the Flames sent me a sweater and souvenirs. I would like to come there as soon as possible. Everybody realizes the NHL is our goal. It is the best league in the world. Everyone hopes to play there. To me, the money is secondary."

His coach, Pavel Wohl, had been preparing for the exhibition game with Calgary for weeks. Armed with a trusty VCR, he had been running tapes of the Flames-Canadiens Stanley Cup final. "I welcome the opportunity to play Calgary," said Wohl. "The Flames are what I call a world team, with players from Europe as well as Canada and the United States. We realize how strong Calgary is."

All 14,000 seats at the Prague ice rink had been sold for each of the two games, but Czech hockey officials estimated that at least 120,000 tickets could have been sold because of the overwhelming interest in the matches.

The Czechs had been training two months, the Flames less than a week. "They're going to be geared for us," warned Calgary's Smythe Trophy-winning defenseman Al MacInnis. "On the other hand, we did play until the end of May. It's been a short summer so we shouldn't need as long to get rid of the rust."

But the rust was apparent in the opening game. The Czechs conceded a two-goal lead to the visitors early in the first period and then tied the score 2–2 before the period had ended. Tomas Jelinek scored the winning goal early in the second period before 14,500 at the Sports Hall. The hosts added the clinching goal early in the third period.

"They didn't lose their discipline," commented an admiring Crisp, "even when they were down two goals. They skated so well, and on the bigger ice surface it simply was that they played their positions better than we did and we were chasing them."

When the Flames weren't chasing the Czechs they were cursing them. "All the camouflage and irritating nastiness of European hockey pricked the nerve centre of the Flames," said George Johnson of the Calgary *Sun,* who accompanied the team on the tour.

"All the crap that went on frustrated us," beefed Calgary centre Joe Nieuwendyk. "They stick you, then don't say anything. I guess that's the worst part. You can't even have the satisfaction of mouthing off at them. They just turn away."

Teammate Doug Gilmour added, "People always think the North Americans are the instigators, the bad guys. Well, it's just not so."

Or Jamie Macoun: "I've been here before, so I expected it. Those guys never go into a corner first. They wait until you're there and then come in. They hook, hold, spear you as you're going to the bench. That's the way it's played."

The second game was not much different except that the visitors were even more peevish. They lost 4–1 and were infuriated by Czech defenseman Leo (The Lip) Gudas, who hit any Flame within his reach and was attacked by several Calgary players, who took four penalties against him in one period alone. After taking one particularly jolting bodycheck, Gudas lashed his right skate up and tried to jab Jonas Bergqvist with it. Another time he blew kisses at the Flames as he passed their bench. "He wouldn't get away with that in the NHL," barked Nieuwendyk.

"It was a friendship tour for the first two shifts on the ice," said Flames left wing Gary Roberts.

If the Flames were upset with the Czechs' playing style, the Capitals were even more disturbed by diarrhea, which afflicted them in Karlstad. On the other hand, Sweden was a delight for the Washington players, who seemed more unified than during the regular season. "We had all our meals together, which is the way they ran training camp in the old days before my time," said Poile. "I really thought that symbolized what a team should be doing this time of year. We were in a small city so you really sense the togetherness. When we're training in Washington, a town of three million people, and the veteran players live at home and commute to the practice rink, you don't get that type of situation."

As for the games, Washington fared better than Calgary did in Czechoslovakia. The Capitals won both their games, defeating Farjestads 7–4 at Karlstad, and Brynas 3–1 at Gävle.

If there was one major distinction between the Flames' focus and that of the Capitals it was the assimilation of Sergei Makarov to the Calgary team. Crisp already had done basic training with 25-year-old Sergei Priakin, who had emigrated to Calgary in March. "All you need," the coach insisted, "is a blackboard, some chalk, some X's and O's and away we go. No problem at all communicating."

Priakin was not overly publicized and certainly did little to create attention during his springtime stint with the Flames. Very few critics expected him to be a star and his performance indicated that they were on target. Makarov, billed as the most skilled of the Soviets, was another story and, judging by media accounts, a much bigger one. Before he even pulled on a Flames jersey, Makarov was being analyzed.

"The key," said Flames veteran Jim Peplinski (who would retire before the season was half over), "is personality. From what I've seen of the Eastern bloc, the people there are a little less vocal, and are more introverted. The difference with a guy like Makarov is whether he'll be willing to take the risk of mispronouncing a word. If he can make mistakes, laugh at them and learn from them, it'll be much easier."

It wasn't easy for Makarov, at least not in the beginning. At best, his performances against the Czechs were mediocre. He made his debut on a line with an American, Paul Ranheim, and a Czech, Jiri Hrdina. On the plus side was a natural talent that had him graded the most complete Soviet forward of the 1980s; on the minus side was his unfamiliarity with the Flames' system.

"The principles of the game are different," said Makarov. "We're much more used to improvising. I didn't feel too well out there."

Ranheim: "I found myself all over the place — left wing, centre, right wing. I'm trying to read off him, and it's hard with Makarov because I'm trying to play the game wondering where the other guys are."

Nobody was terribly concerned after a couple of exhibition games, but there were enormous expectations once Makarov had flown with his teammates to Leningrad, where the Flames would open their Russian tour against Khimik, a team from a small city near Moscow.

Before the games, members of the Calgary entourage were taken on a sightseeing tour of Leningrad. One of the sites was the Hermitage museum. Carrying a tiny Canadian flag, the guide directed the group to Rembrandt's "The Return Of The Prodigal Son." The guide pointed to the canvas and then looked over at the Flames. "That is like when Mr. Makarov comes back here to play."

It was a good line, and the visitors beamed, including Makarov, who was preparing for his first performance against a Soviet club.

"All my life I've been with the Soviet national team and Red Army," said Makarov. "I've played against and with a lot of these players. How would you feel?"

While the NHL maintained that the tournaments were a "Friendship Tour," the Soviets trumpeted the games as "Super Series 89." This did not go unnoticed among the Flames. "What can you expect," said Theoren Fleury. "People say the NHL is the greatest league in the world so we're just expected to win all the time. It's not fair, but what can you do?"

What the NHL representatives did was play a winning brand of hockey. In their opener at Moscow, the Capitals outscored Spartak 8–7 on a sudden-death overtime goal by defensive forward Doug Wickenheiser, once the best junior in Canada. After Washington goalie Olaf Kolzig made a big save on Alexander Fatkullin two minutes into the extra period, Wickenheiser worked himself in close for a shot that sailed wide and bounced out toward the left point. Bob Gould retrieved the puck and flipped it goalward, where Wickenheiser deflected it past Spartak goalie Sergei Goloshumov.

"That wasn't the Washington Capitals' normal way of playing," explained coach Bryan Murray. "It's usually

2–1, not 8–7." But the crowd of 10,350 didn't seem to mind and, according to western viewers, they displayed more emotion than the usual Soviet hockey gathering. Many observers regarded the atmosphere as Olympian in nature. "The Capitals players," noted Robert Fachet of the Washington Post, "were besieged by youngsters seeking autographs and enthusiastically trading pins."

The Capitals had less trouble adjusting themselves to the Luzhniki Sports Palace than they did to the 1,777-room Cosmos Hotel where they were staying. They had no problem figuring that guests on odd-numbered floors took elevators at the far left of the huge lobby and those on even floors took one at the far right. What confused them was the key lady stationed on every floor. As soon as a player arrived at his floor the key lady greeted him, took his temporary hotel card — issued when the hotel takes the player's passport — and gave him the key to his room. The player was advised that when he left, he could reclaim his card.

One such key lady stunned goalie Bob Mason after she knocked on his door and tried to sell him a large jar of caviar. Another key lady had an interesting episode with Capitals' strength and conditioning coach Frank Costello. He was trying to find centre Mike Ridley, who was staying on an even-numbered floor. Trouble was, Costello was on an odd-numbered floor.

"I wanted to find a way of avoiding an elevator ride to the lobby," Costello explained, "and another ride up."

The key lady tried to assist and guided him on so curious a path of corridors that Costello became confused and the key lady, unable to speak English, turned forceful, at one point virtually hurling him down a corridor.

"I saw her shoving Frank," said defenseman Kevin Hatcher, "and I thought he'd done something wrong. If she was just giving directions, I'd hate to see her mad at somebody."

The Capitals found other aspects of the hotel fascinating, if not confusing. The lobby was dotted with slot machines and several bars. For a US dollar a player received four tokens to play the machines. At the bar, rubles were not accepted, only foreign currency.

Meanwhile, the Flames had landed in Leningrad. Goalie Mike Vernon had visited in 1982 as a member of Canada's junior team, along with Mario Lemieux, Sylvain Turgeon and other youngsters who soon would be playing in the NHL. Vernon was 19 years old at the time and remembered the train ride from Helsinki to Leningrad.

"I recall the train rolling past barracks with barbed wire all around them and high guard towers," he said. "It looked like Stalag 13 on *Hogan's Heroes*. They used to stop the train to switch you from one track to the other. One time, I stuck my head out the window to see what was happening and this soldier pointed a gun right in my face. He said: 'No. Go back!'

"What I remember about Leningrad was the food lineups three blocks long, even in the winter. Everybody wore the same color — black. But the poverty is what I remember most. It must have been like Canada was in the Great Depression."

While many of the players accepted the trip as a gesture of glasnost and assumed that it was a necessary part of the warmer feeling between the NHL and the Soviet hockey federation, others were publicly critical and more than a bit confused. "Why are we here?" asked Vernon. "I ask myself that question. I saw [NHL executive vice president] Brian O'Neill and wanted to ask him that. This trip is not benefitting the NHL in any way. Sergei Makarov and Sergei Priakin coming over will improve relations between the two countries, but the bottom line is that their federations are hurting for money. With the Olympics, don't tell me that they won't be coming back. It's automatic."

Nobody believed it would be automatic for the Flames to beat the Khimik club coached by Vladimir Vasilyev. Having gone 0–2 on their Czechoslovakian trip, the Flames then underwent a conditioning drought that disturbed Crisp. Once his club had settled down in Leningrad, the Calgary coach put his skaters through rigorous drills. "Every time it's Russia versus Canada," said Crisp, "you're talking a monumental game. Whether it's pee wee, midget, you name it. It's like Calgary–Edmonton."

His counterpart, Vasilyev, was succinct in his appraisal of the opposition. "We're aware we're dealing with the best NHL team. This is enough recommendation for me."

More than 12,000 fans paying ten rubles a ticket poured into the Leningrad Sports Palace and soon learned why Calgary were Stanley Cup champions. Just 31 seconds into the game, Gary Roberts accepted a dump pass from Joe Nieuwendyk and beat Khimik goalie Alexei Chervjakov. Not long afterward, Khimik received consecutive penalties. With a two-man advantage, Al MacInnis drilled in a wrist shot at 4:02. The result was sealed at 14:59, when Paul Ranheim lifted a wrist shot over Chervjakov's shoulder.

The final score was 4–2 for Calgary in a game that ended with the visitors receiving an abundance of trophies. MacInnis got a prize for best defenseman, while Makarov took a souvenir for being best offensive forward. Even Fleury was rewarded — as youngest player. "Geez," laughed goalie Rick Wamsley as the awards were being distributed, "if you can't win a trophy in this game, you might as well just forget it."

Vasilyev suggested to Crisp that he forget about the result. The Soviet coach insisted that his young players were too nervous at the sight of the champs and that opposition would be more formidable in the games ahead. "It will be very difficult for Calgary when they meet our other teams," warned Vasilyev. "We had not much experience in these sorts of games."

Crisp would not dispute his opposite. Having finally won his first game in Europe, the Calgary leader merely grinned broadly and advised all within earshot, "The beer is sure gonna taste good tonight, the best it has for 11 days!"

Although Makarov received an award, his play was disappointing to many of the onlookers, including Vasilyev. "Makarov is a historic player in Soviet hockey, but neither he nor Priakin was in very good form. They can play better."

Their next test would be provided by Sokol team in its home city of Kiev. Even more of a test would be the flu bug that had afflicted the Flames: Jamie Macoun, Joe

Nieuwendyk, Paul Ranheim, Joel Otto and Jonas Bergqvist all were contaminated.

But the game at Kiev Sports Palace indicated that the Flames were 100 percent healthy. They spanked Kiev Sokol 5–2 in a game that had some historic importance; Sergei Priakin became the first Soviet to score for a National Hockey League team when he netted a breakaway goal in the first period.

Sokol's amiable coach Anatoli Bogdanov echoed Vasilyev, noting that his players were nervous and confused by the sight of the Stanley Cup champions. "I agree with the general observation that if a team like Calgary comes here more and more times," said Bogdanov, "it will help our preparation and development of ice hockey."

If the Flames had any complaint it had to do with the condition of the ice at Kiev Sports Palace. "It was hard," said defenseman Dana Murzyn, "like skating on cobblestones."

What interested Crisp and his boss, Cliff Fletcher, more than anything was the ability of Makarov to fit into the lineup. Nobody disputed Sergei's innate talent, but some critics wondered whether he would be correctly assimilated into the Calgary game plan. Former Flames coach Bob Johnson, who had become executive director of USA Hockey, was one who expressed doubts.

"Makarov is not easy to play with," Johnson explained. "He's the exact opposite of Lanny McDonald, who was an up-and-down winger. Lanny would try to go between the defenseman and the boards or tuck it between the goalie's legs behind the net. You could predict what Lanny was going to do. With Makarov, when the puck is going forward, he is going back the other way. He's not going to be an up-and-down winger. He's not going to play a slow game.

"I told [Vancouver Canucks GM] Pat Quinn: 'You've got to give your best player to Calgary for Makarov and put the KLM line together again, because I don't know many players on Calgary who can play with Makarov.' Mind you, Sergei is a great player, but not as good as he once was. Theoren Fleury might be the best for him."

Anatoli Bogdanov: "Makarov is not an extraordinary player on the Flames. He is just on the level of the others, but if I had a chance to take one player from Calgary, it would be Sergei."

Having run up a three-to-none lead over the Soviets, the NHL squads had visions of a clean sweep as the Capitals prepared for their second match against Moscow Dynamo. Sponsored by the KGB, the Soviet secret police, Dynamo was not a team to take lightly, especially as coach Vladimir Jurzinov had been training his team for the meeting with Washington.

For the first time since the tour began, Russian audiences caught a glimpse of NHL hockey at its ugliest. As any North American fan understands, it is not unusual for a team losing by a wide margin to switch to vengeful, goon hockey in the latter stages of a game. Such nastiness prevailed in Moscow, as Dynamo sped to an easy 2–0 lead in the first period and mauled the Capitals 7–2.

"Whenever we get frustrated," said Washington captain Rod Langway, "we want to hurt them. And in this one we were embarrassing ourselves."

In the second period, belligerent Washington defenseman Scott Stevens slugged it out with Dynamo's Oleg Miculchik. The second period lasted 48 minutes — half as long as the games in Sweden — and the game itself disgusted coach Bryan Murray. "We weren't a good team," he said. "We looked tired, playing against a team that moved the puck very, very well, played a physical game from the outset and played a very good checking game from the early part of the game."

Unbeaten in Russia, the Flames next played Soviet Wings at Luzhniki Arena before a crowd of 7,000. Crisp had planned to start young goaltender Steve Guenette, but he was bedded down with the flu, so Mike Vernon got the assignment and played a superb game through 60 minutes. The score was tied 2–2 after regulation time but in the sudden-death Priakin fed Doug Gilmour, who swatted the rolling puck into the net.

After four days in Moscow, the Capitals moved on to Riga, the capital of Latvia, and a match against

Dynamo Riga, the undefeated (6–0–1) leader of the Soviet Elite League. The Capitals received a royal welcome in the Baltic metropolis. The team was greeted at the airport by top civic and sports officials, and youngsters waving American and Latvian flags as well as the Dynamo Riga banner. Teenaged girls presented roses to the wives of players and management.

Interest in the game was immense. Riga's arena seats only 4,000, but 200,000 fans had hoped to see the game. The solution: a lottery was held to apportion the tickets. Those who did get seats were treated to another close hockey game. The teams were tied 1–1 after regulation time. In the sudden-death period, Tim Bergland deflected a Wickenheiser shot at 2:56, giving the NHL a commanding 4–1 lead in games.

The Capitals weren't doing as well in the food department. The next morning team marketing director Lew Strudler wanted coffee for the club. Instead: "Every time I didn't specify something in detail, I ran the risk of not getting it. And I forgot to write down coffee for the group. So what did we get — tea. When we asked for coffee they said, sorry, it hadn't been ordered."

Caviar had been ordered when Sergei Makarov dined with a western friend and the Canadian neglected to touch the appetizer. "Is good," said Makarov. "You try. Red caviar. Is good. Is best!" It *was* exquisite.

The Capitals had brought considerable food with them from the United States, but were still having their communication problems. Lew Strudler was in charge of the Capitals' pasta department and at the hotel advised the chef to cook the spaghetti. "Unfortunately," said Strudler, "I forgot to tell them to cook the sauce as well. They served hot spaghetti and ice cold sauce."

The Flames' final match with Central Red Army was first-rate, as Calgary completed its tour in Moscow. Central Red Army was the perennial Soviet Elite League-winner. In the eyes of many this was tantamount to a world championship match, yet others insisted that it would be foolish to overdramatize its significance.

"Is this really red caviar they're serving up," asked George Johnson of the Calgary *Sun,* "or just a pile of fish eggs? If the Flames lose today, will anybody remember when the screws tighten in May? If the club slumps in December, could anyone be expected to recall a stirring victory on September 20? Of course not. In truth, the players are beat from the travel, time change and sightseeing. Most have colds. They're counting the hours till Friday's flight home from London. The Soviets' courageous efforts must be commended, but the food is still not what we're accustomed to."

To which defenseman Gary Suter added, "I ate more when I had my jaw wired shut!"

The Flames would later eat crow on ice when they collided with Central Red Army at Moscow's Luzhniki Sports Palace. Terry Crisp and his skaters were well aware that the finale was being billed as a pseudo-championship match by the Soviets, and Calgary was expected to respond with a first-class effort. When the game was concluded, the Flames insisted that they were satisfied with their effort, but the final score was Red Army 2, Calgary 1.

"They're a better team right now than we are," said Joe Nieuwendyk after a second period goal by defenseman Aleksei Kasatonov and a third period score by centre Igor Chibirev put the game out of the Canadians' reach. Rookie Paul Ranheim tallied for the Flames late in the third period, but they could not beat goalie Maxim Mikhailovsky again, although they pressed hard in the final minutes.

Soviet coach Viktor Tikhonov proved himself an able strategist and the Flames themselves admitted that Red Army's defense was as good as they had seen in a long time. "They plug up the middle," said Brad McCrimmon. "Once you get to the outside, it's not the same as the NHL. You're way outside. There's a big difference. That was their strategy and they executed it well."

Clearly the most disappointing player on either team was Makarov, who had been a longtime Central Red Army hero. Makarov was not a major factor in the contest. The loss also was a downer for the Flames although their record in the Soviet Union was 3–1 at the end. No less unsettling was the need for the Calgary players to resort to alibi and rationalization for their defeat.

"A lot of people said we were in a no-win situation, and we were," said Jamie Macoun. "We've been on the road for three weeks, living in hotels, eating their food — you can't exactly run down to the corner and get yourself a grilled sandwich here if you're hungry. The Russians were fresh and ready to go.

"They would have a lot of difficulty on an NHL rink. I'm convinced we'd beat them at home because their style wouldn't work on our ice surface. It just wouldn't."

The Capitals' side of the tour concluded with a 5–4 Washington victory over SKA, leaving both teams with identical 3–1–0 records in the Soviet part of the Friendship tourney. Despite the "hardships," many among the NHL troupe found the visit rewarding.

"It was very educational, seeing how the Russians live," said Capitals assistant coach Doug MacLean. "It was gratifying. We all realize how lucky we are now and the things we take for granted. You walk down the streets of Moscow and a kid comes up to grab your sweatsuit to feel the material. Driving down the streets and seeing people in 1950s and 1960s cars. It was like going back in time.

"We gave the guy who interpreted for us a US $50 bill and he almost started crying. On the black market he could get 500 rubles for that. He said that would pay his apartment rent for two years. About the food; a lot of guys complained about it but what I did was cover it with ketchup and it tasted fine."

The majority of the players favored Leningrad and Riga over Moscow, although Alan May of the Capitals was fearful about drinking the Leningrad water. "I put tape over my mouth when I had a shower," said May. "I didn't want to get sick."

Everyone seemed to have his own pet peeves. May complained about the Soviet airline Aeroflot. "They had no flight attendants and no rules. You don't have to do your seat belt up. There were no announcements. Nothing."

There was an abiding respect for the Soviet players who work for considerably less than their North American counterparts. "In Riga," said MacLean, "the average player makes 200 rubles a month, but they were offered 700 rubles each if they beat us. It was really competitive."

Makarov's return, while eagerly anticipated by Soviet hockey fans, was not thoroughly enjoyed by Tikhonov. The dean of Russian coaches still was bristling over the summer-long criticism directed at him by Viacheslav Fetisov and Igor Larionov, who had been released to play in the NHL. Before the Flames and Capitals departed, Tikhonov defended his methods and lashed out at the expatriates.

"You can be criticized by your wife," said the Soviet coach, "but criticism levelled by former players who I've brought from greenhorn to hockey stars — this does hurt. And I will remember this the rest of my life. We will see who is right in the future."

Fetisov and Larionov had criticized Tikhonov for, among other things, keeping players separated from their families for extended periods at a national training centre. "Sport differs from every other important activity because it has an index — a result. The governing bodies of sport do not want a coach who will lose."

In one sense Tikhonov was right. His club and national teams a year earlier had won every important championship — the Soviet league, Izvestia, World; everything except the Stanley Cup. "In hockey, no one can build a border separating the totalitarian regime from a democracy," Tikhonov asserted. "There should be a nice combination."

Not surprisingly, Tikhonov was less than enthusiastic over Makarov's performance. "This was not the Makarov I had known," the coach explained. "We were used to seeing him on the offensive. Here, he is secondary, helping others. Maybe he has a new task for this team. His best games are yet to come."

Having completed their obligations, the NHL teams packed their gear and prepared to return to their own hockey world. As the Flames and Capitals jetted home, the questions most often asked were, was the trip worth it, and would the teams want to return to train in the Soviet Union again?

Most of those questioned tried very hard to be diplomatic for the sake of the NHL and not to insult the Soviet hosts who had gone out of their way to be hospitable. When Bryan Murray was asked by a Soviet journalist if he would like to return in 1990, he half-ducked the question. "Maybe some time in the future," said Murray, "but not next year." When he was far enough away from the questioner to whisper to a friend, Murray added, "Some time, way off in the future."

Murray confided that he did, in fact, believe that the trip would be beneficial to his club in terms of the regular NHL season. His aide-de-camp Lew Strudler began preparing a report on the tour for future NHL visitors to the Soviet Union. "Many of the problems the Capitals faced could have been overcome had there been a greater understanding of the Soviet mind. It is not enough to accept the Soviets' assurances of 'ne problema.' One must dig deeper and ensure attention is paid to details," added Robert Fachet of the *Washington Post.*

Of course there would be more visiting NHL teams. That was part of the Soviet deal with Ziegler and it would not be broken. To get a feel for the trip, Ziegler had invited Munson Campbell to accompany the two NHL teams. Campbell, a longtime hockey enthusiast and former president of the California Seals when Oakland was represented in the league, enjoyed travelling through Russia, but marvelled at the paradoxes of Soviet living. "In Moscow they have chandeliers in the subway but you can't find a bar of soap. In Leningrad they have the world's largest collection of Rembrandts and you can't drink the water."

What they did have was lots of hockey players and a major organization confident enough in its development to lure two of the best teams in the world to their rinks. If nothing else, this development of glasnost-on-ice underlined a very vital point; that hockey from Siberia to Smolensk had come a long, long way in a very short time.

CHAPTER 6

AFTER WORLD WAR II

"They're way ahead of us. The Russians are picking up momentum and pretty soon you'll see them challenging Canada for the top spot."
— Jack Riley, Coach,
US Olympic Team, 1960

The story of the arrival of Soviet hockey players in the NHL begins immediately after World War II. The simple fact is that, until 1946, there was no hockey played in the Soviet Union — no hockey, that is, played by international or NHL rules.

What was played was a form of "bandy," or field hockey, called Russky hokkei, played on ice with shorter, rounded field hockey-type sticks on a rink of any dimensions, usually about the size of a soccer pitch.

However, the Soviet Union made a major policy decision on international sports, and the intention was clear: to dominate as many sports as possible in international play. The USSR now had annexed several formerly independent nations, and one of the "imports" from satellite nations was sports. Specifically, the Soviet Union turned to Czechoslovakia in order to create the sport of hockey, Russian-style.

In the late 1940s the USSR invited the Czech national hockey team to Moscow for a tournament, and afterward the Czechs left behind both their equipment and a style of play called, significantly, Canatsky hokkei, which had never been seen in the Soviet Union before. This signalled the birth of Soviet hockey. By the 1960s, it would be called hokkei shibah, or hockey-with-a-puck, as opposed to field hockey, which was hokkei myatchom, or hockey-with-a-ball. But where and how had the Czechs learned Canatsky hokkei?

The Czech version of Canadian ice hockey came about in the decade before World War II, largely because a young forward, Mike Buckna, from the Trail (BC) Smoke-Eaters happened to accompany a friend to Czechoslovakia in 1935. While the Czech-born friend was shopping for a bride in Prague, Buckna decided to watch a couple of hockey games.

Buckna was struck by one thing: he was sure he could play as well as anyone he saw on the ice. Eventually the young Czech-Canadian approached the rink manager, who also managed the local hockey club, and asked him for a tryout. The rink manager was so impressed with Buckna's skating and puckhandling that he immediately offered the 21-year-old a slot on the team.

As Buckna played with the Czech team in 1935, he found that the object of their brand of hockey was simply to prevent goals being scored. There was almost no offensive strategy: defensemen never touched the puck nor moved from in front of their net, and the concept of forechecking was never dreamed of by the forwards. Whenever a team lost the puck, all five players would drop back to defend their goal.

"They either had old hockey players," Buckna reminisced many years later, "who taught the same things over and over, or coaches who'd never played hockey at all, but soccer or tennis. The problem was definitely the coaching."

With his background in Canadian hockey, which was then a passing, puckhandling game with plenty of forechecking, Mike was invited to lead coaching clinics his first season. The following year he was invited enthusiastically to return, this time to oversee the whole Czech national hockey program. Until the Canadian government insisted that he come home in 1939, just before Canada's entry into World War II, Buckna coached and played on the Czech national team.

As soon as hostilities had ended, Buckna rushed back to Czechoslovakia, to find that nine of his former juniors were now competent seniors. It only took a year for him to get the Czech national team back together, and in 1947 they won the world championship. Buckna's team then won the silver medal in the 1948 Olympics at St. Moritz, when they tied Canada in a grueling 0–0 match. Mike left Czechoslovakia and returned to Canada after that, but the team he had coached won the world title again in 1949. It was *that* team that travelled to the Soviet Union and left such an indelible impression on the minds of Russian sports czars.

While Europe, and specifically Russia, learned to play a Mike Buckna-devised brand of hockey, something else was happening to "Canadian" or NHL-type hockey. The NHL had condensed into a six-team league by World War II, and it would be these same six teams — the Montreal Canadiens, the Toronto Maple Leafs, the Boston Bruins, the Detroit Red Wings, the New York Rangers and the Chicago Blackhawks — who spent each season playing no one but each other. Furthermore, the style of play had set into what many called "the alley style."

"The NHL style was all up and down the alley," said Czech-born George Gross, executive sports editor of *The Toronto Sun* and chronicler of hockey for decades. "It was dump the puck at the blueline, chase it in and slam guys in the corners."

Introduction of the red centre line to NHL hockey in the 1943–44 season changed the North American game, seemingly forever.

"When the red centre line was introduced to the NHL," said Emile Francis, president of the Hartford Whalers, "puck control was sacrificed for pure scoring."

But that was not the brand of hockey that would be adopted in Europe, and expanded in the Soviet Union. Instead, Europeans took to the flowing game of passing, puckhandling and forechecking that Mike Buckna had imported from pre-War, pre-red centre line Canada.

Canada's first inkling that its lock on world domination of hockey might be coming to an end came in 1954. It was the Soviet Union that dealt the blow, only five seasons after the Czech team had left Moscow. The world championships took place in Stockholm, Sweden, in that fateful year and the heavy favorite to win it all was an industry-sponsored Canadian Senior B team, the East York Lyndhursts.

Somehow, incredibly, when the Lyndhursts reached the final and decisive match for the world title, it was the lowly Russian team that had survived to challenge the Canadians. Furthermore, the hockey world was astounded when the Soviets proceeded to romp over the stunned Canadians, 7–2.

A story from *The New York Times* described the upset, as well as a Russian team that performed feats on the ice that could have shown the Canadian hockey world what was to come:

"A fast-skating, hard-checking Russian team won the world ice hockey championship today by routing a heavily-favored but highly nervous Canadian team, 7–2, before 17,000 fans at the Olympic Stadium in Stockholm.

"The Russians, playing in their first tournament, skated the Canadians off their feet. They opened with a four-goal onslaught in the first period, added three more in the second session and then coasted the rest of the way.

"The Russians took a leaf from Canada's book by body-checking fiercely and by racing to meet the Canadians before they had time to start plays. As a result, the Canadian attacks were limited to stray sorties and the Russians' brilliant rear guards took care of everything that came their way."

Prophetically, the leader of the Russian team, Boris Mjakinkov, said after the upset, "Even though we beat the Canadians fairly easily today, we still intend to press for a tour of Russia by a Canadian team."

The fact that Canada's Penticton V's went over for the world championships in 1955 and walloped everything in sight, including the Russians, supplied only a short-lived sense of revenge to Canada. Domination of the international hockey scene by the nation that had spawned the game was coming to an end, and since 1961 Canada has not won a world hockey championship.

What had the Soviet Union done in five short years to become a power in the international hockey domain? One man who played on the 1954 Soviet team was Anatoli Vladimirovich Tarasov, also a physical culture expert. Tarasov was asked after retirement as a player to construct the Soviet national hockey program. Tarasov would be a primary architect of Soviet hockey, and he delineated the basic Russian philosophy toward the game, as well as their training techniques, in his book, *The Road to Olympus,* published in English in 1978.

"The most difficult thing in mastering this game was the tactics," said Tarasov. "In many respects, we had to start from scratch: I am sure that if we tried to copy the Canadians, we would be doomed to play second fiddle forever."

So, while it was an early form of Canadian hockey that was introduced to the Russians, they immediately began to develop a hockey program that was unique in many aspects. One thing the Russians would not be was a copycat of the Canadians. And it was true that nearly every major team in Europe had Canadians helping to mold their development as coaches or at least as consultants. While the European countries developed their hockey as a variation of the North American brand, the USSR went its own way, virtually in isolation behind the iron curtain, until they felt they were able to compete in international play.

Many of the more experienced Soviet players who went to Stockholm in 1954 originally had been bandy players, from the old school of Russky hokkei. Tarasov claimed in his book that the speed Russian players displayed from their entry to international play was derived from bandy, as well as the Soviet concept of teamwork. For instance, Boris A. Mayorov, head of the Soviet Ice Hockey Federation in 1981, accompanied the Soviet national team to North America when they defeated Team Canada that year. Mayorov had begun as a Russian bandy player in 1938, switched to hockey in 1956, and was the man who set up the winning goal against Canada in the1967 World Championships in Vienna.

Most North American hockey enthusiasts look to 1972 as the year the Russians "arrived" in North America, but that was merely the year they finally confronted the National Hockey League. Russian teams had been coming to the United States and Canada to play amateur teams for 16 years before they finally met the NHL in 1972!

The hockey world championships were held in Moscow in 1957 and the Canadian entry was conspicuously absent. Soviet troops had squelched the Hungarian revolt in 1956, and the West decided to protest by withdrawing. Ironically, it was that same year, 1957, that a Soviet team was brought to North America for the first time.

It was good old hard cash that brought about a rapid thaw in Soviet–Western relations, at least in sports. The Soviets needed the hard western currency a tour in North America would bring. Furthermore, the Canadian Amateur Hockey Association (CAHA) and the International Ice Hockey Federation (IIHF), along with NHL owners who also operated rinks (like Stafford Smythe of Toronto's Maple Leaf Gardens), finally realized that a Soviet team tour could bring in big profits for everyone involved. But because the Soviets did not want to lose their status as amateurs, the possibility of playing a professional team in Canada was never even broached. The eight-game series would be played by international rules against Canadian junior and senior teams. Anatoli Tarasov was the coach of the team, known as the Moscow Selects.

The Soviet team, culled from the best of the Moscow hockey clubs — Central Army, Spartak, Dynamo, Locomotif and Wings *(Krylia)* — first played the Whitby Dunlops of the OHA Senior A circuit, who were heavily favored to win the title at the upcoming world championships in Oslo, Norway. The Dunlops indeed walloped the Soviets, 7–2, and the Canadian hockey world expected the rest of the tourney to pass in similar fashion. Much to North America's shock and dismay, the Soviet team — after losing two games and tying one — proceeded to win its last five games, smashing the junior Canadiens 10–1 in the last contest.

"They have won friends for themselves and for European-style hockey with some of the best skating and passing seen on this side of the ocean in any kind of league in the past 20 years," wrote Len Taylor, sports editor of the *Kitchener-Waterloo Record.*

Jack Kinsella of the *Ottawa Citizen* reiterated the shocked reaction of Canadian hockey pundits to the Soviet style of play: "The net result is a much faster, free-wheeling type of game, with the accent on skating, passing, shooting and other allied skills which in recent years have tended to be neglected [in North America] in favour of refined mayhem."

The Moscow Selects arrived in Canada stating that they had to come to learn, and learn they did. Al Nickelson, writing in *Hockey Pictorial,* said, "In the first game, it was the Dunlops' forechecking which helped defeat the Russians. In the second game [two days later, against the Windsor Bulldogs], it was the Russians who forechecked, and they tied the Bulldogs, 5–5."

Nickelson also noted that the Russian goaltending, flawed when the team arrived, improved rapidly with each game.

"At first," said Nickelson, "they jumped and leaped about with rare abandon. Their bodies did most of the work. It was colorful, but the netminder usually wound up on his pants, fair game for a rebound.

"Halfway through the tour, the Russian goaltenders were using their hands and arms to ward off shots. One even purchased a Canadian goaltender's mitt [like a first baseman's mitt]."

More than a decade before the conditioning and fitness craze would occupy North American sports, Canadian writers who looked behind the on-ice scene noticed that the Russians had developed a unique conditioning program.

"They played soccer for more than an hour," marveled Nickelson, "in pre-breakfast workouts, even on the day of a game. Pre-game dressing room calisthenics included hopping and leaping around in full equipment."

Nickelson's non-technical terms — "hopping and leaping" — and his amazement at hard work on the day of a game make it clear that the Russian conditioning and fitness program looked very strange to North America in 1957! In a nutshell, Nickelson admitted that the Russians were "25 per cent better when they left than when they came."

The Soviets were upset in the 1960 Olympics by an upstart, heavily-underdog US entry. Coached by Jack Riley, the team included an unknown goaltender named Jack McCartan who stood off the favored Russians, but later wouldn't last in the National Hockey League.

Then, in the 1961 World Championships in Geneva, Switzerland, the USSR finished third behind Canada (actually the Trail, BC, Smoke-Eaters, Mike Buckna's former team!) and Czechoslovakia. Canadian experts began to think that the rampaging Russian bear had been a mere fluke in international hockey. But the Russians put on a five-game tour of American cities not long after their defeat, and Connie Pleban, coach of the '61 American team, tried to warn the rest of North America: "I was amazed at their progress. They've learned to bodycheck. Our players would go into the corner with them and *they'd* come out with the puck. They'd wear our guys out, just by leaning on them."

On the eve of the 1962 hockey world championships in Colorado Springs, Colorado, Jack Riley cautioned: "They're way ahead of us. The Russians are picking up momentum and pretty soon you'll see them challenging Canada for the top spot."

Commenting on the fact that the US team would be beefing up its roster with players from the International and Eastern leagues, a Canadian scribe uttered fateful words regarding Canada's chances at the world tournament: "For Canada, victory is even more important. It doesn't want its reputation as the world's leading hockey power to vanish behind Russia's Iron Curtain. Once that happens, it's likely to take more than 15 years to get it back."

The writer used "15 years" as a reference to the surprisingly short time it had taken the Russians to rise to international hockey dominance. Little did he know that the Soviets would dominate hockey's world championships through 1990.

CHAPTER 7

SOVIET AMATEUR HOCKEY DOMINATES THE SIXTIES

> "It's like biology. When a strong tree gets lonely, it dies. So it is with your NHL players. They have no opponents, so they get no stronger."
>
> — *Anatoly Tarasov, former Soviet national coach*

"You Can't Beat The Russians...The Soviet team enjoyed a most successful tour of Canada last winter. They followed this up by capturing the 1963 World Amateur championship in Stockholm, Sweden. They then clobbered the United States national team in three exhibition games in Moscow..."

So blared the headline and beginning of an article in *Hockey Illustrated* late in January of 1964, just before the Russians took their first Olympic gold medal in hockey. The story illuminates how completely the attitude toward the Russians had shifted in North America by the early sixties.

Although Sweden won the 1962 world tourney in Colorado Springs, the Soviets retaliated in 1963 (and would repeat the triumph for the next eight years, consecutively). The Russian team was a veritable steamroller on ice, and the Russian coach, Tarasov, began hinting that the Soviets were now bored with their annual romps over Canadian and American amateur opponents. Lacking a real challenge, Tarasov began to plant another dare — competition on a much higher order — with Canadian observers.

"Why won't the National Hockey League teams play our Russian team?" asked Tarasov of Jock Carroll, who was visiting Moscow for the Montreal Star's *Weekend Magazine* in the fall of 1964.

"You mean you want to play a National Hockey League team?" queried the stunned Carroll.

"Yes," Tarasov quickly responded. "When Mr. [Muzz] Patrick of the New York Rangers was a guest in our hotel room in Stockholm [in 1963], I asked him about playing the New York Rangers.

"He said, first, no one would want to see the game. Second, that we would be beaten 15 to nothing. And anyway, the Rangers could not fit the game into their schedule.

"...If we get beaten 15 to nothing, that is our business...we are just interested to see how our hockey compares with the professional."

Carroll prodded Tarasov further and the Russian coach finally admitted that not only did they wish to play NHL teams, but they would prefer to meet the Toronto Maple Leafs or the Montreal Canadiens — the two dominant teams in the NHL at the time! Furthermore, Tarasov revealed that the Soviet Ice Hockey Federation had actually put a petition before the CAHA to play a Canadian professional team during its 1964 tour of North America.

Weekend checked with Gordon Juckes, secretary-manager of the CAHA, who confirmed that the Russians had requested to play against professional teams. Juckes claimed, though, that no teams had been named, adding that the suggestion had been rejected by the president of the IIHF, A.H. "Bunny" Ahearne. Ahearne had ruled that playing professional teams would be contrary to the IIHF's definition of "amateur."

Nonetheless, the gauntlet had now been thrown, and when the Russian national team made its annual trek to Canada in December of 1964, the hockey world was already abuzz with speculation about a possible USSR-NHL matchup.

Taking a page from the Americans of 1962, who had supplemented their national team with players from other (amateur) leagues — to no avail — the Canadians bolstered their Montreal OHA Junior A Canadiens team of 1964 with six *professional* members of the Quebec Aces (of the American Hockey League). Significantly, all of the added vets had played in the NHL. The Junior Canadiens were joined by goalie Gump Worsley (11 NHL seasons in 586 games), defensemen Doug Harvey (a seven-time Norris Trophy winner and perennial All Star) and Jim Morrison, and forwards Red Berenson (who had met the Russians in the 1959 world championships), Bill Sutherland and Leon Rochefort. Although he hadn't taken a regular turn in the NHL, even Sutherland had played in a couple of NHL playoff games. The six had played a total of 2,336 professional games!

The match between the Junior Canadiens and the Russians took place in the hallowed Montreal Forum on December 11, 1964. The Soviets had just completed a 42-hour trip from Russia and were tired. On the other hand, the pros who had joined the club were tired, too, having played four games in six nights. Accounts of the game described the Russians as skating well, but exhibiting their exhaustion by erratic shooting. The Junior Canadiens, on the other hand, were described as a "bunch of shaky teenagers." The Quebec Aces played the lion's share of the game — as much as 45 minutes of the contest.

The result? The Russians edged the Junior Canadiens 3 2 when the Russian Olympic veteran, 31-year-old Leonid Volkov, jammed the winner past Gump Worsley at 14:04 of the third period (both of the Canadiens' goals were scored by Aces). The Russians had defeated an "amateur" Canadian team well-laced with professionals, albeit still playing by international rules. The rest of the tourney was anti-climactic: they drubbed the Canadian national team 4–0 at Maple Leaf Gardens two nights later, and finished the tour on December 23 in Trail, BC, against the Western International League All-Stars, with an overall record of 7–0–1. The Canadian players and press hastened to rationalize their loss.

"I didn't see an NHL calibre player on the team," said Doug Harvey. "They have a few who might play in the AHL, but there wasn't a Gordie Howe or Bobby Hull out there. On a good night our Quebec team would beat them by five goals."

Gump Worsley credited the Canadian press corps with creating the sudden competence of the Russian squad, as he said, "They're a good intermediate club blown up by you guys. They don't shoot nearly as hard as NHL teams, though they shoot accurately and are good at picking the corners. Our full Quebec club would give them a shellacking."

One of the Canadian game's immortals, Maurice "Rocket" Richard, was on hand for the game, and seemed singularly unimpressed.

"I didn't think the game was too exciting," said the Rocket. "They certainly don't shoot as much as NHL players [each team had shot 26 times...]. No, they wouldn't beat the Canadiens or any other NHL team."

Tarasov, on the other hand, refused to make comparisons, remarking cryptically, "It's like biology. When a strong tree gets lonely, it dies. So it is with your NHL players. They have no opponents, so they get no stronger."

Another challenge had been delivered by the canny Russian coach and the debate over a possible Soviet-NHL meeting heated up considerably. The Russians were described as "mechanical" and lacking the "intuitive" abilities of the Canadian player. It was noted that whenever a Russian play was broken up, the entire squad would retreat behind its own blueline to carefully re-form an attack.

Clarence Campbell, president of the NHL, said, rather snidely, "They play a great heads-down game, those Russians."

Campbell was, of course, referring to the fact the NHL hockey was (and still is) a heads-up game, in which the puck carrier simply asked to be on the receiving end of a fierce bodycheck if he didn't keep his head up at all times. The Russians, old hands at the international rules, which allowed no bodychecking except in a defender's own end of the ice, were prone to getting caught up-ice with their heads down.

In fact, the differences between Russian and Canadian hockey were as great in 1964 as they would ever be. Several observers remarked on the Russian tendency to skate more upright and shoot with their hands high on their sticks, contrary to the Canadian practice of holding one hand low on the stick when shooting. The new slapshot was becoming the predominant shot in the NHL (certain wrist and backhand artists like Gordie Howe being notable exceptions), and a whole generation of young hockey players was learning to simply "play the alley," dump the puck into the opponent's zone and blast slapshots. Puckhandling and passing — the tactics of puck control — were rudimentary compared to the Russian style of play at the time. Furthermore, while the Russians were building a style of play upon total teamwork and the submergence of the individual, the NHL was burgeoning with superstars like Gordie Howe of the Red Wings and Bobby Hull of the Blackhawks, who was beginning his greatest goal-scoring years. It was also a time of superlative NHL goaltending, with the likes of Terry Sawchuk, Glenn Hall and Jacques Plante, while goaltending was a skill the Russians were still working to perfect.

There were many other obstacles to be overcome before the Russians would ever meet an NHL opponent, and differences in the styles of playing hockey were the least of the problems. The debate began to pick at the other dilemmas: for instance, by which rules would such potential games be played? There were three basic differences between NHL and international rules: bodychecking was limited to the defending team in its own ice, there was no legal way to ice the puck (not even when a team was shorthanded), and boarding was not only frowned on (as its more violent forms supposedly were in the NHL, too), but absolutely forbidden in international play.

Significantly, while much was made of the differences in rules, few noted at the time the difference in size between Canadian and international rinks. International rinks were 15 feet wider than standard Canadian rinks (and there was more room behind the nets), and this lateral space accounted a great deal for the Soviet tactics of lateral passing rather than alley play.

Conventional wisdom on the subject said that the NHL would trounce the Russians if "Canadian" rules were employed, even though a small contingent of hockey pundits warned that the Russians learned so fast that they'd adapt within a season or two after playing NHL rules. Even the most chauvinist of Canadian hockey experts had begun to admit by 1964 that the Russians might prevail if international rules were used, although others predicted that the Canadian's ability to improvise would enable him to adapt to international play in a short time.

Behind all the "what-ifs" concerning styles and rules was the reality that a Soviet team would never be able to play an NHL team unless it risked losing its amateur status (and therefore its ability to play in the Olympics with the cream of the Soviet Ice Hockey Federation), or else got approval from the IIHF, the CAHA and the USAHA. Finally, the NHL had to agree to play the Russians.

All the stumbling blocks seemed to be disappearing after the Soviet team's 1964 Canadian tour. Clarence Campbell said in early 1965, "If the Soviet team wants to come to Canada this December, I will recommend that the 1965–66 NHL schedule be drawn up to leave open dates so the Leafs and Canadiens can play them."

David Molson, president of the Montreal Canadiens, hastened to say, "When the Russians were here, I told them if they wanted a game we would be happy to accommodate them. I think it would be good for hockey."

Toronto Maple Leafs president Stafford Smythe was not as ready as Molson, as he counter-proposed, "First I would like them to play my Rochester farm team. Then if they proved themselves, we would be happy to let them play the Leafs." (Meanwhile, the Russians had already rejected both Rochester and Quebec as "unsuitable opponents.")

As for Bunny Ahearne and the IIHF, after years of rejecting any proposed matches between amateurs and professionals, Ahearne said, "Though such a game is against our regulations, I would approve it if our North American affiliated organizations did not object."

The CAHA and USAHA had met in Colorado Springs in December of 1964 and rejected just such a proposal, and CAHA secretary Gordon Juckes said afterwards, "We decided such a game would be detrimental to amateur hockey."

What Juckes had undoubtedly meant was that such a game would be *financially* detrimental to the amateur game, since the Soviet tours meant big profits for Canadian amateur hockey, and a Russian-NHL confrontation could kill any future tours against amateurs.

Stafford Smythe hit closer to home when he admitted that not just Canadian pride, but big dollars would be the final stumbling block: "This is a big deal we could sell on TV all over North America. We can't rush into it. When I bring over the Bolshoi Ballet, I have to deposit the money in a bank in Moscow before they leave. The Russians won't play the Leafs until the right financial arrangements are insured."

Numbers — dollar numbers, body numbers and the number of times the Soviets would win the world amateur hockey title — made the difference in the second half of this decade. First, dollar numbers and body numbers became significant to the NHL for reasons far removed, then, from the Soviets. By 1965 the National Hockey League had a new preoccupation: expansion.

The tight, feudalistic world of the six NHL franchises was being battered by talk of expanding the league, and when the powers-that-be finally realized that expansion could be profitable (first, by potential owners buying into the league, and second, by these same potential owners paying indemnification to existing clubs if they threatened territories), rather than a losing proposition, expansion became inevitable.

Body numbers would then become another preoccupation. While Russia had a population of more than 240 million by the mid-sixties, and more than 150,000 reputedly playing ice hockey, Canada's population was about 20 million. Yet Canada supplied the vast majority of the players, and coaching, managing and consulting personnel for the hockey world outside the Soviet Union!

It would take two seasons of playing with all those numbers to achieve NHL expansion in the 1967–68 season, with the addition of the Philadelphia Flyers, Pittsburgh Penguins, Los Angeles Kings, Minnesota North Stars, St. Louis Blues, and Oakland Seals. By this time the bodies necessary to flesh out six new major league rosters were gleaned from virtually anywhere they could be found: the minors, juniors, seniors. For instance, both Doug Harvey and Gump Worsley of the Quebec Aces would make an NHL comeback with expansion teams. In order to feed the newly-expanded league, it was only a matter of time until the "Canadian" sport would be drawing on the United States' hockey-playing population, as well as Europe.

In the meantime, the Soviet Union was setting a record by taking the world amateur hockey title for the remainder of the decade. But Canada would change the face of amateur hockey forever, as the seventies dawned, by withdrawing from the world championships.

Tired of having their national teams — composed largely of lower-level amateurs who could afford to train and play hockey for several months on a mere $10 per diem — trounced annually by the Russians (and often by the Czechs and Swedes, too), the Canadian hockey world began to push for national teams composed of both amateurs and professionals. It was vehemently argued that the Russian national teams were really professionals, in that the Soviet government paid their way entirely and supplied apartments, cars, jobs outside hockey, etc. When the IIHF refused to budge, Canada pulled out of the world hockey championships in 1970. The country that claimed to have created the game took its marbles and went home, while the Soviet Union dominated the international hockey scene almost completely.

CHAPTER 8

THE SOVIET SECRET WEAPON

> "This is only the appetizer. During the hockey season, we go in for more extensive exercise."
>
> —*Anatoli Tarasov, former Soviet national coach*

The bedrock of Soviet domination in international sports lay in something that the western world is now positively obsessed over, and that is physical fitness and conditioning. The irony lies in the fact that the Russians began a national program of "physical culture" (as they called it well into the sixties) almost immediately after World War II, implemented it on a massive scale and even let the West look openly at what they were doing.

But it took more than two decades for the non-Soviet world to pick up on the fact that they succeeded so incredibly at almost every international sport because of the coaching and physical training programs they evolved for each sport.

As early as Dwight Eisenhower's presidency in the United States (1952–60), sporadic attempts were made to call attention to the woeful physical condition of the American population as a whole, and its youth in particular. When the US found its budding space program with egg on its face as the Russians sent the first successful capsule, "Sputnik", into orbit in 1957, the administration began a national incentive toward more and better science and engineering programs. And when the East

European countries began to arrive at the Olympics every four years with athletes whose physical conditioning made westerners look like blobs, the West began to explore the concept of long-term, year-round conditioning and coaching for its athletes. It was, however, a huge case of catch-up, and without the framework of a nationally-run and funded program, an idea whose time had no hope of coming, at least not yet.

It is crucial to note at this point the huge discrepancies between a state program of coaching and training, in which one system is employed from the very basic, beginning levels of a sport, all the way to the top echelons, and the laissez-faire attitude in a democracy like Canada. As Tarasov pointed out himself, in his works on coaching, a highly structured coaching system does not encourage individual expression, or stars. But then, Tarasov claimed, that was exactly the point of the Soviet system: the teams played almost as units, with interchangeable parts and highly evolved tactics, instead of individual achievement. The rigid standardization of Soviet athletic training could get a little scary: when the NHL's all-star goalie Ken Dryden, who is six feet four inches tall, visited the Moscow Physical Culture Institute in 1972, he was calmly but adamantly told that he would "never have been allowed to be a goaltender, because he was much too long!" Imagine never seeing this Cup-winning goalie in the NHL, because he didn't fit some rigid, absolute notion of what size a goaltender should be! There were obviously ways that a centralized, systematic approach to sports could be ridiculous!

In North America, on the other hand, the coaching and training of athletes was as unique and individualistic as each coach was. In short, there was no system at all. Kids played hockey the way their coach taught it, with the rules of the game being the actual outline for the style of play. Having no set, rigid system of play is marvelous for allowing individual talent to shine through, but poor for instilling a profound sense of teamwork or tactics. In fact, throughout the western hockey world, very little was taught in the way of skills after a certain level. If a youngster reached a good junior team, it was presumed that skating technique, puck carrying and shooting skills had all been learned, and simply had to be honed somewhat. Certainly there were governing bodies — the Canadian Amateur Hockey Association; its US equivalent, USAHA; various senior and minor leagues and the NHL. But as the Soviet Union was perfecting a massive state-run system of training, coaching and conditioning athletes in the sixties, coaching and training with any sort of generally recognized system was at an all-time ebb in the western world.

But, until the Russians had arrived on the scene, hockey's basic "non-system" had worked, and the West, at first, steadfastly refused to actually look at what the Soviets and the East Germans were doing with their athletes and to borrow some of their techniques. Instead, they ignored or rejected East European physical culture programs as the product of rigid, totalitarian, communist doctrine. Whenever western observers would see East European athletes practicing or training, the words "mechanical" and "rigid" would flow from their pens. The occasional heretic might mumble something about "unique" or "impressive," then hasten to praise the great Innovative, Individualistic and Inventive (let's call them the "Three I's"...) talent produced by the West. So the western world stumbled through international athletic competitions militantly maintaining the doctrine of the Three I's as rigidly as Eastern Europe maintained its state-run training programs. The result: international sports became a road show of western-nation individuals scoring personal triumphs (e.g., Peggy Fleming's sole gold medal in figure skating for the US in the Olympics in 1968, or Mark Spitz's four swimming golds in 1972 at Munich), as the East Germans and Russians garnered gold medals by the teamful.

After every Olympics the western press would fill newspapers with rationalizations for why eastern-bloc countries won so often and so much, in almost every sport. They would denigrate state sponsorship on the one hand, then bemoan the fact that the free enterprise system refused to raise sufficient money to support national teams and, better yet, year-round national training programs. Ice hockey was a perfect case in point.

When Jock Carroll visited Moscow in 1964, he was shown the off-season training of Soviet hockey players by coach Anatoli Tarasov, and he described in detail the Soviet "secret weapon," its off-season training program.

"The exercises resumed with a warm-up period of running around the open-air basketball courts. The players ran perhaps half a mile, meanwhile tossing heavy medicine balls back and forth as they ran. As a breather they tossed the medicine balls back and forth across the volleyball net, passing the ball behind their backs or under their legs before returning it. One group stood in a circle, seeing how long they could keep a soccer ball in the air, at one point using only their feet, another time using only their heads.

"...Next Tarasov broke the men into three groups and began a combination of games on three separate basketball courts. On court, two opposing teams played a combination of soccer and basketball simultaneously. They used both a soccer ball and a basketball, and bodychecking was not only permitted, but encouraged. Sometimes a player would find himself dribbling both balls simultaneously, or blocking one ball while trying to pass the other, or just getting set for a shot on the basket when he would be sent sprawling by a stiff bodycheck, or wrestled to the ground."

Carroll went on to describe the Soviet goaltenders juggling tennis balls to improve hand-eye coordination, or the veteran star Anatoly Regulin doing squatting exercises combined with rigorous squat kicks. The players worked out for more than two hours (and this was in midsummer, with no ice in sight!), and then many of them eagerly ran off to play tennis!

"Once you start skating," Carroll queried Tarasov, "will there be as much exercise and calisthenics as this?"

"More," responded Tarasov. "This is only the appetizer. During the hockey season, we go in for much more extensive exercise."

Carroll's wondering response said much for the discrepancies between Russian and Canadian training programs: "Then it's no wonder the Russian teams are in such wonderful condition. I've never seen a Canadian team work out like this."

That was the whole point: there wasn't a team, most likely in any sport and certainly not in hockey, in the western world that had begun to use concentrated year-round training and conditioning techniques. What Canadian hockey players did in the off season was a private decision, and for the most part, that private decision entailed a lot of golf and the search for a career that would substitute for hockey later on. Golf, and to a lesser extent baseball and lacrosse, were considered good sports to maintain some of the muscles used in hockey (especially if a player used the now-rampant slapshot), and that about summed up a Canadian hockey player's attempt to maintain off-season conditioning.

The fact that Anatoli Tarasov ultimately wrote more than 26 books on coaching and conditioning passed virtually without notice outside the Eastern bloc, until long after the Russians had finally faced off against the NHL — none of them were published in the western world until the late seventies.

Each time Russian hockey players would make an appearance in North America through the sixties, writers would marvel and shake their pens at the Soviets' off-ice training antics, sometimes even noting that western athletes might begin to copy their East European counterparts. But the physical fitness craze would not hit the North American professional athlete — nor the amateur, for that matter — for years to come.

There were some NHL players, though, who realized that off-season training of some sort was as essential as on-ice training. One was John Ferguson of the Montreal Canadiens. A player of admittedly limited talents, Ferguson survived in the NHL for eight seasons by dint of his incredible ferocity and drive. Much of that intensity was derived from his off-season and off-ice demeanor. Ferguson refused to socialize, or even speak to, players who were not tattooed with the bleu, blanc et rouge of Les Canadiens — no friendly summer golf tournaments with guys from other teams. Even before he came up to the big leagues, Ferguson spent his summers playing semi-pro lacrosse and working heavy construction. His summer program was a fair facsimile of the conditioning and weight-lifting programs that would become a part of the NHL player's summer repertoire only in the late seventies. And only then as a strong suggestion by management, rather than the rule, as it was in the Soviet Union by the mid-fifties.

Significantly, it would be John Bowie Ferguson whom Harry Sinden would take on as his assistant coach for the initial confrontation between the Russians and the NHL in 1972.

Canadiens' goalie Ken Dryden was disturbed by the inclusion of Ferguson as a member of the Team Canada administration in 1972, largely because Dryden feared that John was there to coach the players in the tactics of intimidation he had excelled in as a player.

"It seems that Fergy has been picked," he said afterward in his book *Face-Off At The Summit* (written with Mark Mulvoy), "strictly to instill an overly aggressive style of play in Team Canada's game. His success in the NHL stemmed largely from his ability to play a rough, vicious game that intimidated his rivals to the point where they began to worry more about their physical safety than the game they were supposed to be playing.

"...I don't think we should use such tactics against the Russians...As our players will find out, the Russians are extremely strong and tend to disdain rough, vicious play, although they are more than capable of playing that way."

It was only later, when the team had begun to work out together, that Dryden guessed at the real reason Ferguson was there.

"I owe John Ferguson an apology," he admitted. "I think I've misunderstood how Fergy used to play. He had an overwhelming drive to win and it manifested itself in an aggressive approach to a game...His inclusion is an attempt to instill this drive to win in our players, though not necessarily by using Fergy's playing style. The more I think about it, the more I understand how he can help us. Peter Mahovlich, for instance, always seems to play better when there is someone around to prod him. In Montreal, Fergy used to chase Peter around the ice during practice — growling all the time — and his gung-ho tactics helped turn Peter from an average player into a 35-goal scorer. Sorry, Fergy."

Dryden also told a story of how he had noted the conditioning techniques of a marathon runner, and he attempted to apply some of this conditioning philosophy to his pre-series training. When Dryden and novelist-turned-chronicler Jack Ludwig (who also wrote about the 1972 series in *The Great Hockey Thaw)* visited the Moscow branch of the national Physical Culture Institute during the 1972 series, Ken tried to explain to Ludwig how he had realized that conditioning was paramount, but had felt he was all alone trying to formulate a program for himself. While the two spoke, they were watching hundreds of Russian children moving through their training paces at the Institute. Ludwig was struck at the grace, ease and "non-mechanical" performances of the children, contrary to what he had heard and read about the rigid, orthodox Russian training methods.

The "Sports Curtain" was slowly being torn from the eyes of western observers, and Soviet methodology and influence in sport was forcing itself into the consciousness of North America. The Team Canada-USSR series in 1972 would open western eyes for good.

CHAPTER 9

TEAM CANADA SHOWS THE SOVIETS

"Sign Language II and Shin Kicking IV weren't the only courses on the curriculum during the Russia-Canada series. Yvan was beginning to learn how to muscle a man off the puck, while Ivan was studying the subtleties of the body jolt, and both sides have profited from the encounter."

— *Ted Blackman, Canadian journalist*

It was 1972 and the moment had finally arrived: the hockey world was going to find out whether the Russian "amateurs" or the National Hockey League professionals were the best hockey players on the planet, whether the Canadian game, played by the undisputed best of North America, was still superior to the upstart Russian brand of hockey.

In order to arrive at the eight-game series between Team Canada and the Soviets, it had been necessary to assure the world that the Soviets would not lose their precious amateur status. From the North American side of the confrontation, it had been necessary to overcome the NHL owners' desire to avoid meeting the Russians because of what were basically promotional values.

Ever since the 1920s, when the NHL annexed the Stanley Cup as its very own, the Cup winner had been recognized as the world champion of hockey, although that winner had never had to face a challenge from any other league or country. The NHL had sold its product as the best in the world. By taking on the Russians, the NHL would be putting its reputation on the line. League governors had always considered the possibility a no-win situation that they militantly attempted to avoid, although former owners had occasionally mouthed interest in the idea. They had done so knowing that scheduling, team composition, financial arrangements and the Soviet amateur status would make it impossible to set up such a series.

But by the end of the sixties public opinion was running against the NHL powers-that-were; and so was a Canadian lawyer named R. Alan Eagleson, the powerful director of the NHL Players Association. Recognizing the value of international contacts between the North American big leaguers and the Europeans, Eagleson bypassed the NHL high command and negotiated with the Soviets as the seventies began. Cutting through the red tape, Eagleson obtained all necessary waivers preserving the Soviets' amateur status, and ultimately hammered out an agreement launching diplomatic relations, at least on the hockey front.

The initial product of the negotiations was the historic eight-game series in 1972, between Team Canada, an all-star aggregation of NHL players (minus four superstars who had just jumped to the rival World Hockey Association), and a similar team from the Soviet Union. The meeting of the world's two big hockey powers was, in theory, only an exhibition series. No financial prizes were at stake, although all parties involved — the Soviet hockey federation, the NHL Players Association, the NHL owners and the NHL players — would all make a hefty profit from the television rights. Nor was the Stanley Cup up for grabs. But the confrontation was treated by the media and the organizations involved as hockey's first genuine world series. For the first time ever, the NHL conducted arduous summer auditions to select the best possible unit to meet the Russians. Similar arrangements were made across the Atlantic.

Despite the relentless improvement in Soviet hockey since World War II and the Russians' triumphs in the amateur world championships in Europe every spring, the NHL was universally acclaimed the favorite in the series, and most critics freely predicted that the North American sextet would capture all eight of the tournament matches, the first four held in Canada and the second four in Moscow.

The voice of hockey for decades, Foster Hewitt, made the prediction echoed by most pundits when he said, “It looks like 8–0 Canada.” Hewitt was describing the game total for the series, not the score of the first contest! The venerable broadcaster’s prediction was seconded by the likes of Gerry Eskenazi of *The New York Times,* ex-NHL referee Red Storey, Fran Rosa of *The Boston Globe,* and countless others.

Some, like Claude Larochelle of *Le Soleil,* respected *Toronto Star* sports columnist Milt Dunnell and Mark Mulvoy of *Sports Illustrated,* graciously ceded one game to the Soviets, usually the first. This was largely because everyone recognized that Team Canada would only have about three weeks to overcome a summer of non-hockey activities and gel into a team. It was only natural to expect that the pros might have a hard time of the first game.

There was one lone voice in Canadian print, however, who spoke dissent. John Robertson, columnist for the *Montreal Star,* stunned Canuck chauvinists by predicting that the Soviets would take the series, six games to two. Robertson so offended some Canadiaphiles that the outspoken journalist was hung in verbal effigy as a “commie pinko” and it was even suggested that he should “return to Russia, where he came from.”

Robertson, though, had watched the Russians train and practice, as well as play. He simply combined what he had seen with what he knew, and came up with the undesirable possibility that the Russians were good, damn good.

So good, in fact, that Team Canada barely managed to win the series on a late third-period score by Paul Henderson (who would become a Canadian hero, still held in reverence today) in the final match of the tourney. The thunderous round of printed applause when Team Canada managed to squeak out a series win obliterated the shocked and amazed reactions that had first appeared as the team left for Moscow behind in the series (Russians: 2–1–1). The reality was, however, that the NHL had won by a single goal after 479 minutes of play!

But the impact of Russian-style hockey finally had left a mark on the NHL, reaching far beyond the series. The Soviets had demonstrated superior skating, passing and technical skills, so impressing North Americans that for the first time coaches, players and tacticians rushed to Europe to *learn,* rather than to teach! Professionals on all levels, from managers through players and trainers, began absorbing European technique into the NHL game.

"Sign Language II and Shin Kicking IV weren't the only courses on the curriculum during the Russia-Canada series," noted *Montreal Gazette* columnist Ted Blackman, "Yvan was beginning to learn how to muscle a man off the puck, while Ivan was studying the subtleties of the body jolt, and both sides have profited from the encounter. There are indeed signs pointing to an overdue improvement in the approach of both [NHL] coaches and players to the game. More teams are attacking the game scientifically, rather than merely throwing their sticks over the boards... Montreal and Buffalo have adopted training techniques (such as assistant coaches) once foreign to [NHL] hockey; Atlanta and Los Angeles are upsetting superior teams by employing a system. Throughout the league, players show as much new respect for their own game as they now have for the Russians."

More than that, the 1972 series generated such interest on both sides of the globe that demands for more such contests were heard throughout the hockey world.

Despite the grass-roots support for more series, the NHL leaders — with the exception of Eagleson — had grave reservations. They feared that a possible Russian triumph the next time around would jeopardize their claim as the world's best. While NHL leaders argued among themselves over whether to continue similar contacts, the World Hockey Association seized the advantage and started its own negotiations with the Russians. The result was a second eight-game series, only this time Team Canada was comprised of the best of the WHA (considered not nearly as good as the 1972 NHL team), which took on the Soviets in 1974. While the series was not as entertaining nor as dramatic as the original match-up (Russians: 4–1–3), the WHA–Soviet series cemented the fact that some kind of Russian-Canadian professional interchange was a must. It further ensured that names such as Vladislav Tretiak (the Soviet Army team goalie) and Aleksander Yakushev (a Soviet Army forward) would become as familiar in Canada and parts of the United States as Guy Lafleur and Bobby Orr.

Stung by the intrusion of the WHA, the NHL moguls reestablished contacts with the Soviets. Under the orchestration of Eagleson, a series of tournaments of various kinds were proposed and approved. In the middle of the 1975–76 season the "Super Series" took place, in which two Russian teams — Soviet Army and Wings of Soviet — played four games each against an assortment of NHL teams in cities throughout North America. By this time Soviet prowess was obvious: Soviet Army opened with a 7–3 trouncing of the New York Rangers, and Soviet Wings walloped the Pittsburgh Penguins 7–4. Although each Russian team was beaten once, their overall quality and professionalism never failed to impress NHL critics.

The next Eagleson-NHL arrangement was dubbed the Canada Cup, 1976: the first time in history six major hockey powers — USSR, Czechoslovakia, Canada, Sweden, Finland and the United States — played a series in which each country's best players competed. Much to everyone's surprise, the Russians failed to reach the two-game final, which pitted host Canada (NHL) against the Czechs. Canada swept the finals, 6–0 and 5–4.

In 1979 the NHL played a three-game Challenge Cup tournament between its all-stars and a visiting Soviet team. The three matches were played at New York's Madison Square Garden, with the implicit understanding that the winner could be considered the world "professional" champion. The teams split two closely contested games, but the Soviets annihilated their hosts 6–0 in the finale. That game, more than any other, firmly placed the Russians at the top of the hockey heap in the eyes of many people.

As the seventies waned, the world of international hockey had undergone a complete transformation. Canada had re-entered the "World Championships" in 1977, with teams that were made up of players from NHL clubs that did not make the playoffs, or those whose teams were eliminated in early playoff rounds. And after endless years of winning the world championships, the Soviets began to show cracks in their armour.

By the 1980s Soviet-NHL meetings were almost commonplace. In the 1984 Canada Cup series, the Russians lost to the NHL in the semi-final game 3–2, and Canada won the series by defeating Sweden in the final game 6–5. Then in 1987 a unique "series" occurred: Rendez–Vous '87, a two-game contest between the Russians and the NHL All-Stars instead of the normal All-Star game. Rendez–Vous '87 was the brainchild of Marcel Aubut, president of the Quebec Nordiques, one of the four WHA teams that had merged with the NHL for the 1979–80 season.

"John Ziegler [now president of the NHL] told me," explained Aubut, "that since Quebec was one of North America's oldest cities, an international city, a winter carnival city, that maybe we should do something special. I said, let me think about it."

Never before had the All-Star event encompassed more than one game, nor had a foreign team ever been invited to participate. When Aubut approached them in February 1986 with a plan for a two-game series against the USSR national team, the NHL board of governors was intrigued, but highly skeptical.

Dealing with skeptics and international complications was nothing to Aubut. He had engineered the defection of the Stastny brothers from Czechoslovakia in August of 1980. Two of the three boys from Bratislava, Peter and Anton, started with the Nordiques in 1980–81, and Peter was still in excellent form, playing with the

New Jersey Devils by the end of the 1989–90 season. Anton and the third brother, Marian, who had arrived for the 1981–82 season, had retired.

Rendez–Vous '87 was timed to coincide with the annual winter carnival in Quebec City, and it became a week-long spectacle that included celebrities, feasts, fashion shows, a parade (featuring floats from every NHL team except the Toronto Maple Leafs, whose owner, Harold Ballard, was protesting the inclusion of the Russians), and concerts (the Soviet Army Band, the Bolshoi Ballet, Paul Anka and Crystal Gayle), culminating with two nights of NHL-Russia hockey games.

The series resulted in a split, with the NHLers winning game number one 4–3, and the Soviets taking game two 5–2, which made nearly everybody happy. More significant was that the total number of games between the NHL and the Russians had now reached 63, and the record stood 37–21–5 in the Russians' favor.

The time was rapidly approaching when the NHL would begin to contemplate a variation on an old adage: instead of "If you can't beat'em, join'em," it would be...If we can't beat'em, let'em join us!

CHAPTER 10

ARE SOVIETS GOOD ENOUGH TO PLAY IN THE NHL?

"Mind you, I don't know how many Canadian players would want to play in Russia, but I sure would like to see a player such as Aleksander Yakushev in the NHL."

—*Alan Eagleson*

By the 1980s, the Russians had gone almost full circle: from complete unknowns in 1954, to total world domination for most of the sixties and seventies, to looking distinctly human and fallible again by the eighties. Anatoli Tarasov was no longer coaching (in fact he crossed the Atlantic several times to act as a consultant to North American teams), and the stewardship of the top Soviet team had been assumed by Victor Tikhonov .

In the 1980 Olympics, Tikhonov's team lost to the US: in 1984 they lost the Canada Cup to the NHL, and in 1986 they lost the Calgary Cup to Czechoslovakia. There were rumors that Soviet players were unhappy with their coach, even word that some players had rebelled (albeit passively) against the drudgery of the year-round training and conditioning.

Most astounding of all, though, was that NHLers had begun whispering about the possibility of Russians eventually playing in the NHL. Slight glimmerings of such heresy had actually surfaced years before. Several seasons before the Russians and the NHL actually met, Larry Regan, the first GM of the NHL expansion club the

Los Angeles Kings admitted, "Los Angeles would certainly be willing to make a trade for Anatoli Firsov [a Soviet veteran and major talent at the time]. We'd give up as many as three good players for him."

Regan was responding to a claim of Firsov's that he had been offered $100,000 to come play with an NHL club. While he denied having offered Firsov the money, Regan admitted that Firsov was on the team's negotiation list. Before the Amateur Draft was officially instituted in the NHL in 1969, the league owners had for years been unofficially divvying up the international crop of bodies among themselves, on "negotiation lists." This meant that if it somehow became acceptable to have European players in the NHL, then each team had such-and-such a number of players from each of the European hockey countries that they could negotiate with. Then, when the "universal" amateur draft began in 1969, the teams would actually name foreign players in the draft, just as they would choose kids from the various Canadian amateur junior leagues, although there was practically none of this done.

In fact, in 1969, the year the amateur draft was begun, there was one European player drafted — a Finn. For four years there were no other European players drafted. Then in 1974 five Swedes and another Finn were drafted. (Being picked in the draft did *not* mean that anyone actually did anything to get you onto an NHL team, or that anyone from an NHL club even spoke to you....) Finally, in 1975, the first Soviet player was picked, by the Philadelphia Flyers. (Viktor Khatulev, picked number 160 out of 217 players drafted.) This was surprising, and indicated how remote the possibility was, at that time, of a Russian player actually arriving in the NHL, because the Snider family who own the Flyers were vehemently anti-Soviet in response to the USSR's terrible treatment of its Jews.

Still, slowly, the concept, if not the fact, of Russian players in the NHL began to look more and more appealing. After one of Alan Eagleson's trips to Moscow (with NHL president John Ziegler) to arrange one of the post-1972 series, Eagleson shocked the media when he admitted that part of the discussions had actually entailed the idea of Russians playing in the NHL some day.

"We took a look at a long-range program with the Soviets," Eagleson said. "We discussed not only a series of games, but also a five-year exchange program involving referees, coaches and, yes, even players. Mind you, I don't know how many Canadian players would want to play in Russia, but I sure would like to see a player such as Aleksander Yakushev in the NHL."

In 1978 Mike Burke, then president of the Madison Square Garden Center, visited Moscow and broached the subject of Russians playing in the NHL, specifically for the New York Rangers.

"They [the Soviet Ice Hockey Federation] seemed much more receptive than I expected them to be," said Burke on his return to the US. He went on to say that the Soviets had also insisted on a procedure being established and cleared through the NHL before specific money terms and personnel could be discussed. "They are very particular about dealing with organizations, rather than individuals such as the Rangers."

Significantly, Burke added, "I think the Russians are very much interested in hard currency these days, and I think they see their hockey players as a source of that currency."

One of the most important reasons that the idea of Russians playing in the NHL had become a possibility was that the NHL was no longer a Canadian league itself, that is, a North American league composed almost exclusively of Canadian personnel. In fact, as soon as the league expanded in 1968, it became obvious that the NHL was going to have to look beyond the Canadian amateur leagues for enough skaters to staff a 12-team league. Only one year later, with the inception of the universal amateur draft, the league drafted 17 players (from a total of 84) from outside the three Canadian junior leagues (the Western Hockey League, the Ontario Hockey League and the Quebec Major Junior Hockey League). Just three years later, when the NHL was confronted with the rival

WHA, it drafted 32 amateurs from outside the Canadian leagues, almost double the 1969 number. As the North American major league rapidly expanded in the seventies, the percentage of amateurs drafted from the international and US college ranks jumped accordingly. By 1978, 32 percent of the amateurs drafted were from the US colleges (something that would have been laughed at as impossible a decade previously), and by the mid-eighties, the NHL annually was drafting as much as 17.6 percent of its amateurs from the international ranks. Finally, by the end of the 1989 amateur draft, a grand total of 45 Soviet players had been drafted by NHL clubs.

The NHL had become so enamored of Soviet hockey players that in 1988 and 1989 they drafted 11 and 18 Soviet players, respectively. But the previous "banner" year had been 1983, and for good reason. In the spring of 1983 the Soviet Union won another of its many world titles, and when the "world" all-star team was chosen, it consisted entirely of Russian players: centre, Igor Larionov; left wing, Vladimir Krutov; right wing, Sergei Makarov; with Viacheslav Fetisov and Aleksei Kasatonov on defense in front of goaltender Vladislav Tretiak. Do these names sound familiar? All five skaters would appear in the NHL in the 1989–90 season. A wild rumor had it that the 38-year-old Tretiak, drafted by Montreal in 1983, would try a comeback with the Canadiens in 1990–91! Fetisov, Kasatonov and Makarov were three-fifths of the Russian players drafted in June of 1983 by the NHL!

It would take almost six more years — of North Americans warming to the idea of Soviet athletes arriving to play, of Gorbachev and glasnost — before those 1983 draftees would begin to skate on NHL ice...in NHL uniforms. But by the beginning of the 1989–90 season, the barriers and walls had toppled, the Soviets had arrived and the NHL world was waiting to see if these "Reds," this band of aging Russian stars (and one defector) could survive, adapt and even thrive...in the milieu of the National Hockey League.

PART 2

CHAPTER 11

OFF AND RUNNING

"The first wave of the Soviet invasion is closer to a flood. The 1989–90 NHL season will forever be remembered as the Year of the Soviet. Glasnost has arrived in the NHL in a big way."
— *Bob McKenzie, Editor of* Hockey News

By the time training camps had closed and the National Hockey League prepared for a season that would open the decade of the 1990s, enthusiasm over the visiting Russians was more intense than for the arrival of any single hockey player — or players — in the long history of the circuit. In the past there had been long vigils for promising stars who had been carefully nurtured in amateur hockey and the minors, but nothing could compare with the fanfare accompanying the Soviet aces.

"I remember a helluva lot of anticipation for Jean Beliveau," recalled Devils vice president Max McNab. "That's when he was playing in Quebec. And there was quite a bit of talk about Bobby Orr long before he arrived in the NHL, while the same thing held for Wayne Gretzky."

Beliveau had been an imposing junior player with the Quebec Citadelles at the turn of the fifties. They called him "Le Gros Bill" when he moved from the junior ranks to the Quebec Senior Hockey League and signed with the Quebec Aces. At the time the Aces, like so many "senior" teams across Canada and in the United States, were a curious amalgam straddling the fence between amateur and professional. The definition of an "amateur" then was anyone who didn't sign a professional contract. Yet the "amateurs" who performed in the QSHL often received more than those in the NHL.

"I remember the Carnegie brothers, Herbie and Ossie, playing for Sherbrooke in the QSHL," said former defenseman Larry Zeidel, a veteran of that league. "Their contracts matched some of the best of the big-leaguers, yet they were listed as amateurs. It was a funny system."

So funny that Beliveau was laughing all the way to the Quebec City banks. "Le Gros Bill" was considered good enough to play for the Montreal Canadiens but he was getting paid so much by the Aces there was no monetary reason for him to leave. "If Big Jean didn't have all that pride," explained Zeidel, "he'd have stayed in Quebec forever."

Beliveau didn't make the jump from the QSHL to the NHL immediately. He indulged in the glory of being the big fish in the Quebec pond for a couple of years; in the meantime a tremendous amount of interest was stirred among NHL fans about this hugely gifted player.

The same held for Bobby Orr, who had been a widely-touted Junior star in Oshawa, Ontario. Orr's rights were held by the Boston Bruins, a truly downtrodden team in the early sixties. Boston rooters knew that Orr would not be available for the NHL until the 1966–67 season but they followed his progress in the Ontario Hockey Association's Junior A League with almost the same intensity they did the Bruins. When it came time for Orr to make his jump, the attention the youngster received was greater than for any previous Beantown prospect.

In Wayne Gretzky's situation there was even more publicity, because he had been discovered earlier than the other Hall of Famers and was signed to a World Hockey Association professional contract when he was only 17. No single player ever received more attention before his NHL debut than Gretzky.

Nevertheless, the spread accorded the Soviet NHL rookies topped anything that either Beliveau, Orr or Gretzky received. It wasn't simply having the Russians on the cover of *Sports Illustrated.* Fetisov, Makarov and comrades made the Soviets the story in every opening season newspaper story and hockey magazine across the continent.

The Toronto-based *Hockey News,* bible of the sport, ran a cover story, "Seeing Red," with an accompanying analysis by its editor-in-chief Bob McKenzie. "The first wave of the Soviet invasion," McKenzie observed, "is closer to a flood. The 1989–90 NHL season will forever be remembered as the Year of the Soviet. Glasnost has arrived in the NHL in a big way."

Hockey News perceived that the Communist invasion, as it were, carried both good and negative aspects with it. "Yes," McKenzie asserted, "it has created a backlash — the Big Red Scare of the 1990s. Are the Soviets taking jobs away from North Americans? Are NHL teams paying exorbitant transfer fees to the Soviet Ice Hockey Federation? Will a 30-year-old Soviet be NHL rookie-of-the-year?

As the league prepared for opening night the questions multiplied. Will a Russian turn into a NHL superstar? How will the Soviets fare as a group? Who won't make the grade? Will Helmut Balderis make as good a comeback as Guy Lafleur? What effect will culture shock have on the players? Who will go out of his way to intimidate them?

"Sergei Makarov will be the best of all of us who came over," predicted Sergei Starikov of the New Jersey Devils.

This was not a minority opinion. Makarov, who signed on with the Calgary Flames, was surrounded by champions and was expected to meld easily with the likes of Doug Gilmour, Joey Mullen and Joe Nieuwendyk. "Makarov is a great one-on-one player, one of the best in the world," said Dave King, coach of Canada's national team. "He will have to learn to be more direct with his plays. He tries to get too cute sometimes, but he's likely to adjust."

McKenzie liked Makarov's "even-tempered approach to the game," but wondered, as many others did, how the excitable Mogilny would make out, and Fetisov, who had worked so hard to leave the Soviet Union to play in the NHL. For some reason — perhaps because he had such a long and distinguished career with the Soviet national team — Fetisov inspired the most attention. "Like Makarov," said King, "Fetisov will have to learn the most direct play is often the best play in the NHL."

Hockey News also considered the question about the Soviet least likely to make the NHL grade and concluded that it would be Fetisov's bulky sidekick, Starikov. The newspaper rated him "a fringe NHLer" whose prime function was to keep Fetisov company during the transitional period. "I wonder at Sergei's ability to handle the physical play in front of the net," said King.

Doubts also were raised about Sergei Mylnikov's ability to withstand the puck flak he would face as goaltender for a defensively weak Quebec Nordiques team. "He's not used to handling the puck," declared King. "He's not used to challenging shooters and he's not used to heavy traffic at the net. I think Pelle Lindbergh was the only European goalie to make an impact here, and that tells you something."

The intimidation factor was raised from the start. Hazing would be attempted by both foe and friend alike. In Vancouver, for example, a number of Canucks wondered whether any teammates would go to bat for Krutov or Larionov when the Soviets got into a jam. "I worry about who is going to be there when they need their teammates," said Rich Sutter, one of the more belligerent Vancouver players. "I know I will. When he's your teammate, you've got to be there. I just hope the others feel the same way."

Across the continent Devils president Lou Lamoriello was expressing a similar sentiment. It was imperative that the New Jersey players welcome Fetisov and Starikov if the Devils were to emerge as contenders and Jim Schoenfeld to retain his job as head coach. "The job Schoenfeld faces this season of coordinating bulldogs like [captain] Kirk Muller and Ken Daneyko with free spirits such as Fetisov and Reijo Ruotsalainen will not be easy," promised Rich Chere of the *Newark Star-Ledger.*

Fetisov's training camp was less than extraordinary, although he did arrest attention with his radar-accurate passes — he seemed to have an all-rink view of player movement. Schoenfeld, one of the brighter hockey minds, allowed that the adjustment required of Starikov and Fetisov was more than the Devils high command had anticipated.

"It's been more of an adjustment for Slava than Sergei," said Schoenfeld as the Devils broke camp prior to the season's premiere in Philadelphia. "Fetisov is a control player used to holding on to the puck and making a spin with someone there to give it to. We haven't had anyone there to take it. We're not used to that yet. He's probably used to a more swinging game and he has more targets. He's waiting for the forwards to be circling. It's an adjustment.

"As for Slava not getting 'up' for exhibition games, all I can say is when a fellow like him is captain of his team, as he was for years, and was competing in world championship games, playing in exhibition games can be a difficult time to get as emotionally charged as he'd normally be. That's just human nature. I played the game, too, and I know how it is. You can't artificially produce it."

The Devils general staff insisted that it was not worried about Fetisov. They believed implicitly that his presence would help make the club's power play among the NHL's best, and his ability to move the puck out of his zone by himself or with a pass would help eliminate one of the club's glaring weaknesses.

His ability to move freely around New York was having a very salutary effect on his nature. In Moscow he could not go home after every practice or game because of Tikhonov. Even though his success and renown as Red Army captain had gained him three apartments, a Mercedes and a Volvo, it could not give him freedom from regimentation. Now he was a prosperous suburbanite who drove home every night from the Devils' South Mountain practice rink in West Orange, New Jersey. "I finally feel like a human being," Fetisov said after a workout in the team's conditioning room.

Starikov rarely made centre stage but when reporters approached him he invariably was amiable and smiling — until questions about his Red Army days were raised. "You sit there," Starikov said, "and you're worrying about your family. Your kids are growing up and you never see them, and all you do is sit around and look at your teammates."

Acceptance of Fetisov and Starikov among the Devils was tentative at first because of the language barrier. Fetisov was the more gregarious of the pair but Starikov certainly was not shunned and did have his share of fans among his new teammates.

"Sergei sits in the dressing room and just giggles," said left wing Brendan Shanahan, one of the younger Devils and known for his outgoing temperament. "He doesn't understand what you're saying, but he finds it all very funny. As for Slava, the other day Jim Korn went up to him and said, 'Hey, Slava. Come on, tell the truth. Are you KGB?' Slava goes, 'No. You CIA?' "

Because of his vast international experience Fetisov had a partial grasp of English and was able to hold passable conversations with teammates. Third-string goalie Roland Melanson sat alongside Fetisov on the green-carpeted clubhouse floor during stretching exercises. "Slava," Melanson explained, "when I go behind the net and leave the puck for you and I see a guy's gonna run you, I'll yell, 'Reverse!' That means move the puck back in the direction you were coming from."

Fetisov momentarily stared at Melanson and then shot back, "In Russia, the goalie doesn't go behind the net."

It was impossible to detect from early training camp workouts how well the Soviets would take to the North American routine and structure. Opinions varied. One professional sports motivational expert who had returned from an international conference reported that the Soviets who had come to North America, "were more interested in partying than playing hockey." Others said it was quite the contrary, that they were determined to prove they were worthy of playing hockey at the highest level. Then, there were those in between.

"To Russian guys, puck is like toy," said Czechoslovakian centre Dusan Pasek of the Minnesota North Stars. "Here, NHL is hard work; puck is not toy."

At times the Devils' Soviet players appeared to toy with the puck the way a youngster plays with a yo-yo. On other occasions, they seemed unable to grasp the ways and means to move the rubber North American-style. It was an issue New Jersey coach Jim Schoenfeld immediately recognized. How to deal with it would prove to be a major problem both for himself and his successor, John Cunniff, who then was Schoenfeld's aide.

"Slava likes to hang on to the puck," said Schoenfeld. "He's going to have to move the puck quicker in the North American game."

The painful aspect both for the Devils and Fetisov personally was the age factor. He was 31 years old when he arrived at camp and looked his age. In many ways he resembled retired New York Islanders captain Denis Potvin. He had grown slightly bulky around the edges — just enough to be noticeable — and was unable to generate the speed that he had in his prime a decade earlier.

"I'm happy I'm here," Fetisov went on, "but obviously it has happened a little later than I would have liked. Soon the time will come when I don't play anymore. Sure, I wish I could have played here three years ago. But I'm going to try to do everything I had done at home."

The attention accorded the Soviets did not go unnoticed in the Devils' locker room nor was it overlooked around the NHL. In Los Angeles, Bernie Nicholls, then a star with the Los Angeles Kings, warned the new Soviets that they had better keep their heads up — or else! Nicholls echoed the sentiments of many NHL players who were bitter because the Soviets would be taking jobs from North Americans. Nicholls predicted that the eight Russians would be in for a rough ride around the league.

Philadelphia Flyers general manager Bob Clarke was the most outspoken of the NHL power brokers to denounce the newcomers. "I think my feelings are in the majority among league general managers," said Clarke, "but I'm probably a vocal minority. Let's face it, two guys who played for the Devils last year aren't going to be here this year."

Devils defenseman Randy Velischek could be forgiven if he felt as though Clarke had pinpointed him. The erudite Montrealer appeared to be one of the odd men out, although he never failed to contribute an honest effort, whether in a scrimmage or regular game. "Yes," Velischek admitted, "I'm worried about my position, but if it wasn't the two Soviets coming here, it might be two Finns or two Swedes or two guys from the minors."

Velischek was not talking hypothetically. The import of the Soviets was only part of a massive shakeup orchestrated by general manager Lou Lamoriello. When he took over the team in 1987, Lamoriello was overseeing a club that often played flawlessly but without the raw talent to break open a game. A mental lapse, a bad pass and the game would be taken by the opposition. This problem lasted through the disappointing 1988–89 campaign, when Lamoriello embarked on his grand plan to revamp the fabric of his club.

In addition to the Russians, he traded once-popular Pat Verbeek to Hartford for Sylvain Turgeon, a French-Canadian who had been a big scorer but had fallen on bad times. Turgeon vowed that he would straighten out his career in Jersey. In another move Lamoriello acquired sharpshooter Walt Poddubny from the Quebec Nordiques.

Poddubny had been reviled by coach Michel Bergeron for what the latter described as laziness and lack of team spirit. At the press conference welcoming him to the Devils, Poddubny denounced Bergeron and called his move to Jersey one of the best things that had ever happened to him. Furthermore, he insisted that he was motivated to have an excellent season just to prove Bergeron wrong.

Then there was Reijo Ruotsalainen. The ex-Ranger and Oiler was to add zest to the power play and scoring to the defense at large. That was the good news. The bad news was that Rexy arrived with a negative reputation as well. He was regarded by his detractors as the ultimate mercenary; a player who cared little for his team or teammates. He betrayed a bit of this streak at camp with his refusal to do interviews and the speed with which he exited the dressing room after a workout.

Once all the hullabaloo over the Russians subsided, training camp began in earnest. Some veteran reporters who had been assigned to the club for several years were not impressed by what they were seeing. "Effort and intensity are lacking," offered Rich Chere of the *Newark Star-Ledger,* one of the most perceptive men on the beat. "If it all clicks, the Devils are good enough to finish near or at the top of the Patrick Division and challenge for the Stanley Cup. If it doesn't fall together, all the talent Lamoriello assembled during the off-season won't mean a thing."

Alex Yannis of *The New York Times* was impressed with Fetisov. "He's a marvel to watch," said Yannis, "especially when he brings the puck out of the Devils' zone and does crafty little things to which his teammates have not yet had time to adjust. His ferocious shot from the right point on the power play is just as frightening to goaltenders as Ruotsalainen's is from the other side." Then, Yannis paused and added a thoughtful postscript. "However, Slava has shown some inconsistency in his defensive play, solving a defensive problem one minute and giving the puck away the next."

The appearance of newcomers Poddubny, Turgeon and Ruotsalainen deflected some attention away from the Russians and added to the optimism of camp. "This is without question the most talented team since I've been here," said Aaron Broten, who had been with the Devils since they moved to New Jersey from Denver in 1982. "The new players give us a chance to execute better than we did in the past."

Broten's point was underlined in their final exhibition game of the season against the New York Islanders at the Meadowlands Arena. New Jersey defeated the Islanders 5–3 and in the process Fetisov teamed with Velischek and the two matched perfectly. "Randy had a settling influence with his steady defensive play," said Chere. "While Fetisov roamed and rocketed several shots just wide of the net, Velischek was solid. Apart from that the Devils have unleashed what could very well be the most devastating power play in the league. A unit which appeared overpowering on paper looks even more intimidating on the ice."

The proof would be in regular season play. As any NHL general manager will attest, exhibition games are revealing to a point but hardly definitive, comparable to the difference between an army recruit's basic training and being on the battlefield with real bullets and shells exploding around you.

Because the Devils were scheduled to open their 80-game schedule at Philadelphia's Spectrum, the reception for Fetisov and Starikov was expected to be unusually hostile. If the Russians felt any fear, it certainly wasn't apparent. "The Flyers are an aggressive team," said Starikov, "but I don't know of any team that plays soft."

Starikov and Fetisov admitted that they had watched on television when the touring Red Army team skated off the ice at the Spectrum in 1975 in disgust over the Flyers' rough play. "I was a young guy then," said Fetisov, "and I saw how dirty they were. Sportsmanlike people don't swing sticks at people's faces."

Fetisov argued that he had played under so many difficult conditions on so many foreign rinks that he was sure he would not experience anything novel from the Flyers. "My philosophy is to play hockey," said Slava, "and whatever happens, happens."

Starikov: "I expect to get hit at any time and I'm not going to let it upset me."

Talking about NHL goon tactics and actually experiencing them are two different things, as the Devils general staff was acutely aware. The debate was how to cope with excessive roughness directed at the Russians. Ken Daneyko, Dave Maley and Jim Korn, the three toughest Devils, indicated that they would support their new teammates — if necessary.

"A lot of people are in for a big surprise if they try to challenge these guys," said Korn, the six foot five, 220-pound enforcer. "Fetisov (six one, 205 pounds) is probably the strongest man on the team. Starikov (five ten, 235 pounds) is built like a bowling ball. These guys are physically strong. I wouldn't be surprised if they initiate stuff themselves."

Fetisov had initiated in an exhibition game against the Rangers. He crosschecked Tomas Sandstrom, sent him sprawling and scored a beautiful goal. Starikov was assertive in front of the Devils net and was equally impressive to this mates. "Sergei really crunched some people," added Korn.

On Wednesday, October 4, 1989, Fetisov, Starikov and the rest of their New Jersey comrades walked through the players' entrance at the Spectrum, along the corridor past the Flyers' executive offices and into the dank walkway to the visitors' dressing room. It was opening night and more than 17,000 Philadelphia fans would jam the oval arena for the historic occasion.

If there was more than a touch of nervousness in the Devils' clubhouse it was understandable. Instead of starting his regular goaltender, Sean Burke, coach Schoenfeld opted for Chris Terreri, a smallish netminder who had been considered an understudy as long as he had been under contract to the team.

Burke had been injured during a pre-training camp exhibition game and underwent arthroscopic knee surgery. He had been considered the backbone of the hockey club and without him the Devils were distinct underdogs.

Some reporters anticipated a bloodbath. The Flyers long had been notorious as a goon hockey club and their roster still had a number of tough players, led by the French-Canadian Craig Berube. Additionally there was Clarke's public dislike for the Russians, and the well-known stand of Flyers owner Ed Snider, the most anti-Soviet of all the NHL club owners.

Yet when the Devils finally took the ice for their pre-game warmups, the visitors looked up to the balcony where a large banner hung over the front-row seats: "VIACHESLAV FETISOV, WELCOME."

There were no visible signs of protest during the pre-game skate. The players seemed at least superficially at ease. "I wasn't nervous," Fetisov later said. "I don't get nervous."

Certainly, he didn't appear ill at ease when the game began. Exactly one minute into the match, Berube was caught roughing by referee Denis Morel and sentenced to two minutes in the penalty box. As expected, Schoenfeld dispatched Fetisov to the right point on the power play for what would be his first major test in a regular NHL game.

Almost immediately the Devils set up their attacking formation inside the Philadelphia zone. Captain Kirk Muller skimmed a pass to Fetisov. Calmly and deliberately, Slava slapped the rubber goalward. It was a hard shot, with more velocity than the average NHL drive, and right on target. Flyers goalie Ken Wregget appeared to have only a partial view of the disk as it bounced off him, hit Jersey's Sylvain Turgeon in the chest and rebounded into the net.

The goal was credited to Turgeon but Fetisov, who organized the play, received an assist. Slava collected his first NHL point just 37 seconds into his NHL career and 1:09 into the game. To a man, the Devils seemed relieved by the breakthrough and resumed their assaults against Wregget. Less than four minutes later Turgeon connected again to give New Jersey a 2–0 lead that held up through the end of the opening period.

Remarkably, the Devils' attacks persisted into the second period. First Janne Ojanen scored, followed by Turgeon again and then John MacLean. By the 14-minute mark of the second period, New Jersey led 5–0.

As for the Soviets, they were holding their own, although each was experiencing difficulties. Following his opening flurry, Fetisov tailed off, alternately looking sluggish and even disgusted but never very much out of place. Starikov's weight problem became apparent whenever speed was necessary, yet for the first half of the game he managed not to do any damage to his club.

Starikov received his first major test at 14 minutes of the second when crafty Mike Bullard of Philadelphia took control of the puck at centre ice. One of the NHL's better puck control artists, Bullard skated at Starikov one-on-one. Normally, a defenseman would concentrate on the puck only until the forward attempts to outflank him. The Soviet committed two blunders; he allowed Bullard to slip the puck between his legs, and he neglected to check the Flyer with his body once Bullard made his end run. As a result, Sergei was left in the embarrassing position of watching Bullard break clear on Terreri. The Flyer had little trouble outfeinting the goalie, and suddenly the Flyers were on the score sheet.

It was 5–1 for New Jersey at the end of the second period. That should have been a comfortable lead but certain breakdowns suggested to Schoenfeld that his advantage was not as secure as it appeared on paper. For one thing, the Flyers had begun working over the Soviets and there was no certainty how Fetisov and Starikov would handle the rough play in the third period. For another, he wasn't certain how Terreri would withstand the pressure, considering that Chris entered the game with a record of no NHL wins, seven losses and three ties.

As for the rough play, Fetisov remained strong. At one point Slava and Flyers pest Keith Acton were penalized. Acton, true to form, unleashed an unending torrent of invective at the Devil. Surprisingly, Slava returned the compliments. "He was always yelling," Fetisov explained, "so I yelled back at him. A little bit in English. I don't need a big vocabulary to yell at him. On ice, I can get by very well."

Early in the third period the Flyers struck again. Rick Tocchet propelled the puck past Terreri on a power play and it appeared that New Jersey might wilt under the pressure. If Schoenfeld was concerned, he didn't show it. Fetisov and Starikov continued to get ice time as the Flyers counterattacked and, at one point, Slava knocked a puck off the goal line and into a pileup with his hand, saving Terreri from what looked like a sure Flyers goal.

Try as they might, the Flyers couldn't fool Terreri again and at 11:37 of the third period Doug Brown relieved the pressure with another Jersey goal. It was 6–2 and the Soviets had, despite occasional and very visible flaws, come through.

With the game out of reach, the Flyers were expected to attempt their traditional late-game goonery. Tocchet rubbed his glove in Fetisov's face at one point, and Brian Propp tripped Slava from behind and his helmet got knocked off in the crease, but nobody challenged the Soviets to fight and the Devils left with a meaningful 6–2 win.

The visitors' locker room at the Spectrum overflowed with media and, fortunately for the Soviets, much of the attention was deflected to Turgeon, who had scored a hat trick. Nevertheless, interpreter Lopuchin had his hands full trying to sort out the questions and Slava's answers.

Had he considered actually dropping his gloves and fighting when he got into a crosschecking rough incident with Acton?

"When I was young," Fetisov explained, "I had to get involved a little more. As I became a veteran, it wasn't required of me. No one would test me."

How did he experience the pressure of his opening game?

"The intensity of the NHL is a lot higher than what we're used to playing in the Soviet Union and in Europe. The long season ahead is going to be quite a task. There's a lot of contact. You have to think on your feet all the time. Situations change very quickly."

And how does he like it?

"It definitely is more interesting."

Starikov was not ignored. A smaller group of reporters cornered the fireplug defenseman and mentioned the Bullard play that had left him helpless. "Every second," Starikov replied, "anything can happen. There's no opportunity, no reason to let up."

The reviews of the Russians were, for the most part, positive. Schoenfeld, who knew well that his coaching job was insecure, offered less than a rave but was enthusiastic.

"Fetisov was certainly good offensively," he said. "We look for him defensively to move the puck a little quicker. I don't think he's used to having people on him so quickly and finishing checks that hard or that frequently as you do in the NHL. But he's an intelligent player, certainly a highly-skilled player. And he'll make that adjustment."

Schoenfeld didn't know it, but his appraisal was remarkably on target, especially the negative critiques. Most of the New Jersey-New York media kept their restraint despite the one-sided result. "Fetisov had a rather uneven game," commented Frank Brown in the New York *Daily News*. "He made some lovely passes, but also put the puck in trouble a few times."

Hugh Delano of the New *York Post:* "Fetisov and Starikov showed they belong in the NHL. Fetisov played smart hockey from beginning to end. Starikov, except when beaten one-on-one by Bullard, played a strong defensive game."

Rich Resnick of the *Hudson* (New Jersey) *Dispatch:* "Both Russians looked steady and confident."

Some observers were not ready to accept the opening night results as definitive. The Flyers, for some reason, were admittedly nervous and committed a number of defensive blunders. Yet the actual play on ice was not nearly as one-sided as the score indicated.

"All over the NHL people are wondering just how these players will be tested by their new peers," noted Rich Hoffmann of the *Philadelphia Daily News*. "The consensus is that they will be marked men early on, required to prove with their fists that they are ready for the rigors of professional hockey over here."

Schoenfeld: "I don't have any worries at all about their capabilities to handle themselves physically. They've played all over the world against good competition and people have always tried to run them. That's part of the game. You have to be able to withstand it. It seems that good players seem to have a knack for knowing when it's coming. They still make the play and get out of the way"

If Fetisov and Starikov enjoyed a rousing opener, it was small potatoes compared with the scenario at Buffalo's venerable Auditorium, known to intimates as The Aud. Alexander Mogilny had been getting the superstar treatment ever since his defection and now the rink was jammed for the home opener against the Quebec Nordiques.

"There isn't a player in the league with Mogilny's breakaway speed," offered Sabres general manager Gerry Meehan, who was not normally given to outrageous praise.

Buffalo is a one-paper town but enough had been written about Mogilny to fill volumes. Now he had suited up and donned his number 89 jersey, the fans were impatiently waiting for the opening night ceremonies to conclude. Mogilny was still in the dressing room lacing his skates when he heard the first cheers. His number 89 was shown on the ice by the laser beam in the pre-game light show. The cheers were louder than for Pierre Turgeon, Mike Ramsey, Mike Foligno or any of the team's traditional heroes. When, at last, Mogilny took the ice, the reverberations were deafening.

"Those who sent up the roars must have known something," said *Buffalo News* sports editor Larry Felser. "Maybe they anticipated something special, some little piece of history."

If history is what they wanted, history is what they got in no time at all. Shortly after the opening faceoff, the Sabres sent the puck behind the Quebec goal. Dave Snuggerud took possession and backhanded a pass to the front of the net. The number 89 uniform seemed to materialize in front of Nordiques goaltender Stephane Fiset as the pass hit the goalie's pads, ricocheted in front and was tapped back into the net. On the twentieth anniversary of the Sabres' franchise, the newest Sabre had scored within 20 seconds of his debut.

When informed of the feat and the fact that he was not the first Soviet to get a point in the 1989–90 season, Slava Fetisov grinned, "Mogilny is younger."

Mogilny did not score again against Quebec but his mates got three more goals and edged the Nordiques 4–3.

The 14,465 onlookers were ecstatic. Many had been around The Aud when an earlier Sabres rookie, Gil Perreault, had dazzled audiences with his footwork. Did the Sabres have another superstar in their midst?

"Mogilny is not to be confused with Perreault for flash and dash," insisted Felser. "Alexander seems to take the shortest route toward the opponent's net and becomes a major menace. There were no end-to-end excursions, no breathtaking blueline-to-blueline dekes. There was just that instant menacing, which translated into, 'Buddy, if you give me one opening, make one mistake with the puck in your end, I'm going to pull the switch on that red light.' "

Others compared him with Danny Gare, a Buffalo hero of yesteryear who developed into one of the most popular and productive Sabres.

"Before the game he didn't seem nervous," said veteran winger Scott Arniel. "He just sat in the corner by himself. You could just sense how confident he was."

But there was one significant off-ice difference between Fetisov and Starikov, and Mogilny. The Devils pair were open. They welcomed interviews and, with the interpreter's help, remained patient and cooperative. By contrast, Mogilny was virtually reclusive, and began on opening night a disturbing trend toward media avoidance.

Not surprisingly, a horde of reporters sought out Mogilny after the game, but he remained well-hidden in an off-limits dressing room while some of his teammates attempted to pinch-hit on his behalf. Defenseman Doug Bodger attempted to make light of the situation, doing an imitation of the Russian while Felser and others attempted to learn something of Mogilny's feelings.

"Shot the puck," explained Bodger, affecting a Russian accent, "it went in. It's only one game. Long season."

When a more aggressive reporter attempted to reach Mogilny both Mike Foligno and Mike Ramsey made a point of barring the way. Even more inexplicable was that Mogilny was left off the post-game list of three stars although his play was among the best. "It was a further case of protection," said Felser. "Once he becomes confident with the English language, Mogilny may not need much protection."

He certainly didn't need a press agent the way his skills were trumpeted by teammates, the media and his coach. "Alex is going to be a start in this league," Rick Dudley predicted. "It may take him a while to get used to the various subtleties in the NHL but he's got a great skill level and he seems to be a proud athlete who wants to excel. Those two things together make you a pretty good shot to be a star at some point in time."

The same words were being used about another Soviet two thousand miles away. While the Sabres were edging Quebec, Sergei Makarov made his Calgary debut against the Detroit Red Wings. The Flames' right winger already had been tabbed "the best of the Soviets" by enough critics to command attention on this night, and he was full value for his notices. Makarov scored a goal and two assists as the Flames opened defense of their Stanley Cup title with a 10–7 victory over the visiting Red Wings.

The Vancouver Canucks were anticipating similar results from Makarov's ex-linemates, Vladimir Krutov and Igor Larionov. Certainly, British Columbia fans had reached a level of enthusiasm for the team unknown since the Canucks reached the 1982 Stanley Cup finals.

"It wasn't an unreasonable feeling of hope," said Brian Burke, Canucks assistant general manager. "We had done well in the 1989 playoffs, taking Calgary to overtime in the seventh game. With the two Russians up front it figured that we'd be a lot better off on the attack."

A clue to how much better would come in the opening game at Pacific Coliseum in Vancouver on October 5, 1989. Canucks promotions people had worked overtime during the summer and had significantly boosted the season ticket base. A crowd of 16,087 jammed the arena, fully expecting the home team to pick up where it had left off in the spring.

"Everybody expected the Canucks to win," said Oilers coach John Muckler, "and the Canucks expected to win. But all that did was put added pressure on them."

The Vancouver media also put unrealistic pressure

on the Canucks with blanket predictions that they would finish ahead of the Oilers in the Smythe Division. The difference, the pundits asserted, would be in the addition of Krutov and Larionov.

However, the results were less than encouraging. More experienced than the Canucks, the Oilers toyed with Vancouver. Edmonton's power play struck for two goals and the penalty-killers limited the Canucks to two shots on Vancouver's first seven power play opportunities. Adding to the embarrassment was the Canucks' inability to capitalize on a five minute power play with six and a half minutes remaining in the game. Vancouver had five harmless shots during the major penalty to Esa Tikkanen.

The Soviets were conspicuous by their failure to generate any meaningful offense. Rich Sutter scored Vancouver's only goal while Krutov and Larionov had popguns on their sticks. Coach Bob McCammon, who was responsible for blending the Soviets into what had been a cohesive team, approached the debacle with his customary candor.

"A lot of people thought the Russians would have a tremendous night," said McCammon in his post-game press conference, "and, quite frankly, they didn't. I'd say this was the toughest game to prepare for since I've been here. There were tremendous expectations from the Russians and from our hockey club."

Expectations were considerably less grandiose for Quebec Nordiques goalie Sergei Mylnikov. For one thing, the Nordiques are almost guaranteed sellout crowds at the Colisée no matter how good or bad the hockey club. Unlike the Canucks, who needed the Russians to boost their gate, the Nordiques needed a good goalie and weren't particularly concerned whether he was Russian, Serbian or a native of the Cocos Islands.

Coach Michel Bergeron had hoped to satisfy the French-Canadian audience with a francophone goalie, but Stephane Fiset wasn't ready, nor were any of the other young netminders in the Nordiques system. By default, Bergeron was compelled to insert Mylnikov into the lineup. The date was Thursday, October 26, 1989. The site: Boston Garden.

"It was the worst place in the world for a new goalie to play his first NHL goal," said ex-Quebec captain Peter Stastny. "The rink is so small [smaller than the NHL average] and the fans are so vocal."

In any event Mylnikov moved between the pipes as the audience rose for "O Canada" and then "The Star Spangled Banner." Sergei's propensity for chubbiness immediately caught the eye of *Boston Herald* columnist Charles Pierce. At five foot ten and 175 pounds, Mylnikov was not your everyday advertisement for physical fitness.

"Mylnikov is nothing if not a splendid advertisement for 'la haute cuisine of la belle province,' " chuckled Pierce. "This is a tub, this one, whose odd style is not going to satisfy many purists."

Mylnikov's propensity for playing far back in his net immediately raised eyebrows, as well as the fact that he flopped more than a seal. Sergei also revealed an inordinate problem handling rebounds. Still, with all his faults, Mylnikov held the Bruins to only one goal through the first half of the game. It was 1–1 until Andy Brickley tipped in a Glen Wesley blast, and eventually the Bruins put four pucks behind Sergei to win the game 4–2. On the fourth goal Cam Neely swooped in from the left side. Normally an NHL goaltender would have moved several feet out of his net to cut down the angle, but Mylnikov seemed riveted to the goal post. His opposite, Andy Moog of the Bruins, explained that the larger European rinks inspire goaltender to remain close to the net.

"You put any goaltender on one of those big rinks and you see how far he wanders out," said Moog. "All the Russian goalies play right there on the goal line because there's so much room. Even when I played over there, I stayed, not on the goal line, but a lot closer to it than I would here. It's too easy for people to go right around you."

Mylnikov certainly did not disgrace himself. He faced a total of 35 shots and had 31 saves. His team had been completely dominated by a Boston club that would eventually finish with the best overall record in the league. Perhaps the most accurate assessment of Mylnikov was provided by Pierce.

"Beaten goaltenders look pretty much like beaten goaltenders, regardless of race, creed, national origin or ideology. Mylnikov after Neely's goal looked pretty much like Moog did after Guy Lafleur beat him on a blast that came from 1978. The only thing conspicuously red about Sergei Mylnikov was that bothersome light that kept going off behind him."

Most of the Bruins gave Mylnikov passing grades. "He gave up four goals," said Ray Bourque, "but they all weren't his fault. Quebec lost no matter who was in goal."

Notorious for his impatience, Bergeron insisted that he had no compunction about playing the Russian in Boston Garden. "It's time he played," said the Nordiques coach. "Mylnikov came here to play, not practice, and it was time to give him a shot."

All of the Soviets had their first shots. The reviews overall were positive, with a few raves and a few knocks. "If there was one conclusion to draw from opening night," said Devils vice president Max McNab, "it was that it was much too soon to make any definitive judgements. We just have to wait and see what happens in the weeks and months to come. But it will be interesting to see what happens between opening night and Christmas."

CHAPTER 12

RUMBLINGS OF DISCONTENT

"I used to hate the Russians, I was brought up that way...Now we have to live with them...You're a team and you do whatever it takes for each other."

— *Mike Foligno, Buffalo Sabres*

It didn't take very long for rivalries to develop. Tomas Sandstrom, then with the New York Rangers, was notorious for his needling and frequently took a fist in the face for his barbs. One look at Slava Fetisov on the ice and Sandstrom opined, "I don't think he's that good like everybody says. You've got to keep in mind when he played in Europe he played with some good guys like Aleksei Kasatonov, Vladimir Krutov, Igor Larionov and Sergei Makarov."

Fetisov shrugged when informed of Sandstrom's appraisal and reminded the reporter that the two had nearly carved each other up with their sticks during international play. "I could say the same thing about Sandstrom," Fetisov replied, and left it at that.

Larionov was the first Soviet to be physically victimized by an NHL player when he was crosschecked by Quebec's Lucien DeBlois. "There wasn't even a penalty called on the play," complained Canucks coach Bob McCammon after learning that Igor had suffered bruised ribs. Larionov shrugged off the injury and donned a flak jacket so that he could return for the following game. "I told him he could take the next game off," McCammon recalled, "but he insisted, 'Oh no, I'm playing.' He's a tough little guy."

The Kings' Bernie Nicholls, one of the foremost mouthpieces in the NHL, took due note of Larionov's wounds and said not to worry, he got what he deserved. "We play 80 games here and we take the body," Nicholls asserted. "That's a long grind. Guys like Larionov are great players and to slow down great players, you've got to take the body. If you've watched hockey, you know what Mike Bossy and Jari Kurri had to put up with. I've never played a game where the other team didn't try to slow me down. If you let a great offensive player free-wheel, he'll do damage. Our way is to use the body. The Russians' way is to use the stick."

In the opening games, there was no reason to test the code of teamsmanship. None of the Russians were jumped, mugged or otherwise molested by the foe, but their teammates knew that at some point the Soviets might be unnecessarily attacked and then the response would be carefully studied by NHL analysts. Mike Foligno, who captained Alexander Mogilny's Buffalo Sabres, was acutely aware of the dilemma.

"I used to hate the Russians," Foligno confessed. "I was brought up that way. I hated their way of life and what they stood for. Now we have to live with them and win with them. Now there are nineteen guys on this team who are a member of Alex's family...If someone hurts a family member, you take it personally. You do something about it. He's not alone here. He's one of nineteen. You're a team and you do whatever it takes for each other."

Wayne Gretzky was critical, but in a fiscal sense. Hockey's premier spokesman still could not figure out why the Soviet federation was receiving so much NHL money when it was the Russian players who were aching to play in North America.

"It doesn't make sense that we pay their federation $700,000 a player when they want to play in our league as badly as we want them," Gretzky reasoned. "Nobody knocked on my door to pay my mother $700,000 for me to play hockey. Parents in Canada struggle to their last penny to put their kids in proper equipment so they can play."

The criticism began to abate once the season unfolded and everyone could concentrate on the visitors' ability to make the necessary adjustment. By far the most impressive of the lot was the Flames' Makarov, and that didn't surprise many. After all, Sergei had been the Soviet scoring champion for six consecutive years before leaving for North America.

In the Flames' first road game, at New Jersey's Byrne Arena, Makarov's puck movement was so nimble on Gary Roberts' killer fourth goal, Roberts insisted that the Russian get not one but *two* assists on the play. "He deserved them, too," said Roberts. "First Sergei passed the puck to me, and then, just as I was shooting, he whacked down the knob of [goalie] Sean Burke's stick, so the blade bounced up off the ice and my shot went underneath the bottom. Two assists, see?"

The Flames won 4–2, in a game that pitted Fetisov against Makarov for the first time. At one point Slava forgot himself and the color of Sergei's jersey and inadvertently passed him the puck. "Then, too late, I remember," Slava explained. "It seems like we had played sixty or seventy years together!"

After eight games the Flames were lukewarm (4–2–2) but Makarov remained red hot. He had an average of two points per game on the strength of two goals and 14 assists. At that pace, he would produce a league-leading 160 points over an 80-game season. Coach Crisp was tickled, yet befuddled by his gifted rookie.

"Sergei keeps going out there and doing his job," he explained, "but, I'll tell you, getting a smile out of him has been one hell of a chore. He's a stoneface. I can never tell what he's thinking."

Others in the Flames high command were thinking that Makarov, despite his rash of points, still had to work on aspects of his game, other than offense. Assistant coach Tom Watt, one of the NHL's more insightful tacticians, was concerned about Makarov's defensive game. Watt noticed that when Makarov chased an opponent, the Calgary defense was as far as he chose to skate. It was as if he had reached a barrier and would turn back. Watt pointed out that Sergei was expected to carry on through the Flames' defense, if necessary. Makarov countered that once the puck reached the Calgary defense, it was up to the Flames defensemen and the centreman to do the job. That, Sergei explained, was the way he did it in the Soviet Union.

Watt was dedicated to changing Makarov's thinking, a fact that did not elude reporters following the team. One day Red Fisher of the Montreal *Gazette* asked Watt, "Have you straightened him out on it?"

The Flames aide wore a puzzled look. "Are you ever straightened out on anything until after the last game?"

Makarov's teammates, Gary Roberts and Joe Nieuwendyk, were not complaining. By the Flames' fourteenth game Roberts had 12 goals, and this despite an obvious communication gap between the North American and the Russian. "We were missing quite a bit because of the language barrier," said Roberts. "We weren't really communicating. We'd finish a shift, come back to the bench and Sergei would just sit there and say nothing. But it's really something playing on a line with him. I feel the same way about Sergei as I do about Wayne Gretzky. He's just so dominant. I can't say what it's like to play on a line with Gretzky because I've never done it. But I'd definitely argue the point that it could be any better than playing with Sergei. I sure can't see where Makarov is that far behind."

Spectators at Calgary's Saddledome are among the most reserved in the NHL, not unlike those in Edmonton, Winnipeg and Vancouver. But when the line of Makarov, Roberts and Nieuwendyk would clamber over the boards, the rink would echo with applause. Pretty soon Makarov could be heard as well; a dialogue opened between Sergei, Gary and Joe.

"Sergei used to sit and say nothing on the bench, stare down between his skates and not really say anything," Roberts observed. "By the start of November he was talking a lot more. We'd get in a two-on-one situation that might not work and we'd discuss it. Once we'd get to the bench, he'd say 'get it to me' or 'I'll get it across' or whatever. And when we did something right, he'd tell us right away. He'd say 'nice play' or something. I finally began to feel that he was understanding."

Makarov's European influence became evident on the ice. The Roberts-Nieuwendyk-Makarov line employed crossing patterns in the offensive zone that were rare among traditional NHL units. "They'll also play a lot more against the flow," noted Winnipeg Jets assistant coach Clare Drake, who had vast experience with international hockey. "They'll take drop passes as they come back. And that can be really effective, especially if the defense gets backed in too far and the forwards aren't coming back deep enough to pick it up. They read it so well. They get you coming deep and going one way, then they'll drop the puck and have the speedy winger coming the other way across the flow. They're tough."

Nieuwendyk: "Playing with Makarov, you've got to get yourself moving because he's always looking to make passes and you want to get yourself in the open. We got some pretty good chemistry going."

Makarov's first taste of a disputed NHL play occurred in Montreal. Trailing 2–1 at 10:23 of the third period, the Flames mounted a siege of the Canadiens' net. Doug Gilmour, who now was on Makarov's line, kicked the puck goalward. If the puck had gone in, it would have been disallowed, but Sergei thrust his stick at the rubber and appeared to make contact before it passed over the red goal line.

The red light never went on and the referee waved off the apparent score on the grounds that Makarov failed to touch the puck before it crossed the line, therefore it was a kicked goal and illegal. Uncharacteristically livid, Makarov didn't even wait for his interpreter to join in the media conversation after the game.

"I first, I first," demanded Sergei, after interrupting his interpreter. "I see it. I put it in!" Then he shrugged sarcastically. "But maybe my eyes no good. Maybe I'm getting old."

Actually, Makarov was displaying some good old NHL frenzy, which is not always consonant with the facts.

A check of the video replay clearly indicated that the puck had passed over the goal line before his stick made contact. Makarov's burst of bluster was arresting but it could not conceal the obvious: the goal correctly was disallowed.

Sergei wasn't frowning for long. He revelled in the NHL play and was intrigued by the boisterous behavior of Canadian fans. During a game at Quebec's Colisée, he watched in astonishment as play was interrupted on three separate occasions by fan shenanigans. "In Russia," he laughed, "the home team would get a two-minute penalty for that."

When the Flames visited Capital Center, home of the Washington Capitals, he watched a buxom young lady arrive in a raincoat. Underneath she had on only a G-string.

He was no less surprised when Capitals defenseman Neil Sheehy, a graduate of Harvard, approached him and mentioned that he bought one of Sergei's CCCP national team sweaters when he was in Moscow on tour. He paid $40 to the Russian trainer.

"From the first time I saw Makarov, I thought he was a great player," said Sheehy. "I still do, obviously. So much so that I wanted the guy's sweater."

Sometimes Makarov seemed too good for his own good, or at least for his teammate's sense of self-esteem. At times he did not appreciate — or at least understand — that Roberts and Nieuwendyk lacked some of his own special skills. Kevin Allen, hockey writer for *USA Today*, observed, "Makarov is intolerant when his new Calgary Flames teammates can't match his ability."

An episode that illustrated the point developed during a Flames power play. "I made a pass through four guys," said Roberts. "I thought I made a helluva pass, but Sergei was upset because it was in his skates. He wanted it right on the tape of his stick. I told him in plain English, 'Sergei, I'm not that good.' "

Makarov came to realize soon enough that NHL defenses weren't that good either, especially when two teams decide to have a shoot-out. Sergei's first experience with that all-offense game unfolded early in the season at Quebec when the Flames staged a furious third period rally to tie the Nordiques 8–8. When it was over a reporter asked Makarov what his former Soviet national coach Viktor Tikhonov would say about an undisciplined game like that. "Twenty Soviet players would go like this," said Makarov, making a slashing sign across his throat.

While Sergei was having a very positive effect on Nieuwendyk and Roberts, one Calgary player suffered by his presence, and that was New York-born Joey Mullen, who had been one of the Flames' foremost scorers until the start of the 1989-90 campaign. After fourteen games Mullen had recorded only four goals and five assists; Makarov was considered responsible, in part, for Mullen's lowered production.

The reasoning went this way: late in the 1988–89 Cup-winning season, the Flames had their lines playing longer shifts. The practice was continued after Makarov joined the team but, as it happened, Mullen's line always would follow Sergei's onto the ice. Unfortunately for Joey, Makarov invariably would remain on the ice twenty seconds or longer than Nieuwendyk and Roberts. This automatically put Mullen at a disadvantage. Mullen was traded after the season.

Makarov was at no disadvantage communicating with his fans. As his popularity rose, so did demands for his time. He soon was treated like other Calgary heroes such as Mike Vernon and Jamie Macoun. In no time at all he was asked to make promotional appearances, and did his first during an autograph session at a Ford dealership.

One of those waiting in line for Sergei's signature was 53-year-old Yuri Goldberg, a native of Moscow, who was clutching his camera and pictures of Makarov. Goldberg had been granted an exit visa in 1980 and moved to Calgary, where he worked first as a geologist and then an interpreter for a company that does business in the Soviet Union.

"I've never seen anything like this before in Russia," said Goldberg. "Back home nobody actually has a chance to communicate with hockey players like people do here in Canada."

Makarov was accompanied by his son Artem — already known as Tom in Calgary — and had little difficulty speaking English with most fans. Mostly he said "Hi" and "Thank you." He had no problem understanding requests. A few, like Goldberg and Mary Conklin, the daughter of Russian-born parents, spoke to him in his native tongue. Nobody was more thrilled than Goldberg.

"I was always a hockey fan," he explained. "I know Sergei's team in Russia very well. It's interesting to see how these guys like Makarov, Fetisov and Larionov are playing in the NHL. It seems that Sergei is adjusting pretty well."

The most outspoken voice of dissent belonged to Don (Grapes) Cherry, former NHL coach and one who had long been critical of Europeans playing in the NHL. "Makarov," Cherry insisted, "won't score twenty goals in the National Hockey League."

In a sense Cherry had a point. Makarov was more a playmaker than a shooter. At times he passed the puck when it appeared that he might have scored had he taken the shot himself. It exasperated many Flames fans, including a Calgary *Sun* columnist who commented, "I have this nightmare: Makarov swoops toward the net, has the goaltender at his mercy, but, instead of shooting, makes a nifty drop-pass — on a PENALTY SHOT!"

Makarov's problems were considerably fewer than those of his former linemate Vladimir (The Tank) Krutov. Unlike Makarov or their other comrade, Igor Larionov, Krutov never was particularly obsessed about coming to North America and finally was persuaded by Igor. Shortly after the instant fuss and fanfare over his arrival, Krutov went into a deep funk. His family still was in Moscow and Krutov obviously was terribly depressed by his isolation. "For six weeks," said Canucks assistant general manager Brian Burke, "all Krutov did was mope."

The sooner the Canucks could expedite the arrival of Vladimir's family, the better the chance of improving his play, which had been conspicuously disappointing compared with Larionov's.

Of course, it was much easier for Igor for two reasons: he really *wanted* to play in Vancouver and he spoke fluent English. Because of his communication advantage he was way ahead of Krutov. Larionov's easy dialogue with reporters gave him an instant public relations advantage with the media and, from the start, he was the favored Russian.

The reaction of influential Vancouver *Province* columnist Jim Taylor is a case in point. Rather than pressure the Soviet as the New York-New Jersey writers were already doing with Fetisov and Starikov, Taylor took a completely different route and pleaded patience.

"The Canucks must be congratulated, particularly by those of us who've laughed at their Soviet soaper from the day the first bubble was blown," said Taylor. "Ideally, Canucks fans should view Larionov as another rookie trying to find a spot on the team. He will not tear the NHL apart. If he scores 25 goals and has an 85- or 90-point season, the customers should be dancing in the streets."

By mid-October the Krutov family situation was approaching the critical level. When he had arrived in Vancouver on September 15, he was told his wife and two sons would be able to join him in a month. This did not happen and it appeared that just when the Canucks needed him most — on a road trip to the East Coast — he was ready to return to Moscow to facilitate his family's move.

"There's a snag," Brian Burke revealed, "and we believe it hinges on his full release from the military. Apparently, Vladimir has to be present in Moscow when his family finally gets its papers. If the papers are processed, it's possible he might not miss many games."

Meanwhile, Krutov stayed at Larionov's house. "Every day," said Igor, "he calls Moscow to ask, 'When are you coming?' " Larionov then shook his head disgustedly and muttered, "Bureaucracy!"

Finally, Krutov received word that he had to return home. He had been scheduled to play against the Islanders at Nassau Coliseum. Instead, his name was removed from the Vancouver lineup and a bulletin was issued to the press: "Vladimir Krutov will not play in tonight's game. He is returning to Moscow to attend to a personal matter. The length of his stay in Moscow is undetermined."

At first there were rumblings that Krutov would never return, that he was turned off by his reception in Vancouver and didn't particularly enjoy his NHL experience, limited though it was. The Canucks waited expectantly for word from Moscow hoping they wouldn't lose the coveted Tank. At last Krutov phoned with the good word: "I have been released from the army and we have our visas. There are other difficulties but everything is to be resolved and I will be back soon. The only difficulty I have had since I came to Vancouver has been with my family situation. Now I have told them about the lifestyle we will have in North America and they are looking forward to it."

Krutov was true to his word and returned quickly to Vancouver. In truth, he had not been missed. The Canucks by the end of October had a decent enough record (6–5–1) and held down second place in the Smythe Division, three points behind the Stanley Cup-champion Flames. Larionov was not playing as well as Makarov but Vancouver fans were willing to be patient.

"When I played for the Soviet national team," Larionov explained, "I played Russian-style hockey. I'm in the NHL now so I must play NHL-style."

Igor was asked if he was having fun.

"Fun? That's a difficult question. It's fun when we win."

When he was asked to compare Soviet coach Viktor Tikhonov to Canucks coach Bob McCammon, Larionov laughed.

"Every city I go to, people ask me that same question. They're very different."

Igor then affected a thoughtful pose with his arms folded. Without further ado, he went right into his Bob McCammon impersonation: "Igor, just dump the puck in, wind it around, and get off!"

The listener asked Larionov whether he was complaining.

"I take 25-second shifts and then I'm off. I can do that. That's easy."

Larionov was told that his former teammate, Fetisov, found an answer, NHL-style, to the shorter North American shifts: Slava doesn't look at the bench until he's ready to come off the ice. To that, Igor just laughed.

McCammon only occasionally smiled over his immigrant forwards. "It's like having two Quebec kids here who don't speak English," the coach said. "But at least the French are used to our ways."

Why McCammon chose to overlook the fact that Larionov's English was first-rate is a matter of conjecture but it had already become apparent that the coach realized that the Soviet pair, in their own way, would be a vexing problem for the next five months.

In Buffalo, Sabres rookie coach Rick Dudley knew the feeling. Despite Alexander Mogilny's flashy opening night, the young forward already was sending subtly negative signals to the team. It wasn't something anyone could really put his finger on because the season was too young and even his teammates had not yet grown to understand him, but the signs were there nonetheless.

To begin with there was the case of the missed bus. The Sabres had a midweek game at Maple Leaf Gardens in Toronto and normally take a chartered bus from Buffalo. For some reason Mogilny showed up at a parking lot in Cheektowaga and missed the bus. The team left without him amid reports that Mogilny was missing and had not been seen by the Sabres for a day.

Fears were calmed after Mogilny caught a ride to Toronto and showed up at Maple Leaf Gardens in plenty of time for the pre-game warmup. In a sense, the incident was symbolic of the zig-zag efforts of Mogilny on NHL ice.

Dudley had placed Mogilny on a line with the veteran Rick Vaive, one of the NHL's top scorers, and Christian Ruuttu, a Finn who had gone to school in the United States and was one of the speedier and more artistic Buffalo players. Playing against Toronto, Mogilny frequently had press box observers on the edge of their seats with his dazzling movements below.

On one shift Alexander skated one-on-one against tall, hulking Toronto defenseman Brian Curran. A clumsy skater, Curran was at Mogilny's mercy as he backed off the blueline. The Sabres rookie dashed to the right as if going on an end run and then, just as quickly, shifted to the left (inside), leaving Curran a twisted, useless hulk. Mogilny swooped in on goal and, typically, fired the puck wide.

"That," wrote Jim Kelley of the *Buffalo News,* "was the story of Mogilny's first 13 games in the National Hockey League. They've been a baker's dozen of delights. A delicious blend of speed, power, grace and a tremendous variety of shots, but lacking one essential ingredient — goals."

In 12 games, the youngster with the boundless potential had only one goal since his home opener. The high command was baffled, as were his teammates and Mogilny himself. "I don't know," he replied to questions about his scoring drought. "I think I have to play more. No, not more, just better."

Those covering the team realized that Mogilny was sensitive to questions about his slump. It was the first time in his career that he was not one of the team's most productive players. Not that the Sabres were complaining. They were a solid second in the Adams Division, well over the .500 mark and only a point behind first-place Montreal, but if Mogilny had been clicking on all cylinders, Buffalo could be on top.

"Alex has had his problems," said assistant coach Don Lever. "There was a time earlier in the season where I thought he might be a little bit homesick, but he seems to have overcome that. He also seems to try to use his shot a little bit too much. Instead of doing some things with his skating or just dumping it in and making them turn it over, he likes to create his chances with his shot."

His shooting had placed Mogilny among the team leaders in shots taken and near the top of the list among NHL rookies. "We keep stats on chances," added Lever, "and Alex leads the team in creating scoring chances, not just for himself, but for the team. We didn't realize it ourselves until we saw the computer printouts. One of his problems is that the league is tougher than he had imagined. A lot of good players come in and think they can move through it doing the same things that got them here, but it isn't that easy. It's hard to get your goals in this league. No matter how much talent you have, you still have to learn how it's done."

Mogilny allowed that he had a lot to learn and that perhaps he was rushing his shot, as he had on the play where he had beaten Curran. Like so many of the Soviets, he leaned toward the chessboard-style passing plays that constantly create opportunities. It was not his nature to merely dump the puck into the corner — automatically giving up possession — in the hope that a teammate would get there first.

"I don't like to shoot it around the boards," Mogilny confessed. "I try to play for my partners, but sometimes it doesn't work. The coaches tell me to shoot it in more, but I'm not used to that. I need time. It's different."

The Sabres coaches were hardly depressed over Mogilny's showing. They had learned to be patient with high draft-pick Pierre Turgeon and now the nimble French-Canadian was leading the Sabres in scoring. Lever believed that peer pressure was involved with Turgeon's development and the same would happen with Mogilny.

"First," Lever explained, "there's a period of adjustment and then there's the peer pressure of having to keep up with what the other players can do. As much as he has to get used to us, we have to get used to him, too. He's very quick to pick things up and he's very smart, but there's also a lot we haven't seen yet. We have to get used to that."

Nobody understood Mogilny's situation more than Montreal Canadiens defenseman Petr Svoboda, who escaped from then communist-controlled Czechoslovakia at the age of 18 to play in the NHL. "Mogilny's adaptation could be even harder than mine was," said Svoboda. "It's day and night between the lifestyle in the Soviet Union and North America. I wouldn't be surprised if Mogilny gets homesick in the course of the winter.

"People don't have the slightest idea how difficult it is for a hockey player like him who might never see his family or friends again. That's the way I felt until my parents came to Montreal and joined me two years ago. Another thing is Mogilny won't feel at ease until he masters English. I'll never forget my first year in Montreal. After taking intensive English classes for a few months, I understood the new language but I still couldn't express what I felt. I kept everything inside and it was very frustrating."

Svoboda's teammate, Guy Carbonneau, already had seen Mogilny in action and was impressed by his style if not his substance. "He's going to need time to get used to the smaller ice rinks," said Carbonneau, "but that's only one out of a lot of things that's new to him. He's suddenly found that his pockets are full of money. He's discovering fame, women and bars. We'll see how he reacts after that."

His reactions were positive at first and Alexander indicated as much during the few interviews that he granted to non-Buffalo journalists. He would show his visa to everyone because it meant something special to him, like a birth certificate to the West. "I want to play here," Mogilny reiterated while on a trip to Hartford for a game against the Whalers. "NHL best league in the world. Make money. Make my life. Russian system, I didn't see a future in my life. This is good life. People very friendly."

They certainly were at Buffalo's Auditorium. The Aud rocked with a 30-second standing ovation when the Canucks were in town. Mogilny had decked four Canucks and, this time, put the puck into the net, not wide of the target.

"Talent-wise, he reminds me of Kent Nilsson when Nilsson was in his NHL prime," said Ruuttu. "Alex already is a helluva player and he can be a superstar."

Teammate Turgeon, who had played against Mogilny when they were 16-year-olds competing in an international tournament, insisted that Mogilny was having the same adjustment problems that he had experienced because of culture shock. "I understand what Alexander's going through," said the French-Canadian. "I didn't speak any English when I came to Buffalo either. But once you see his talent, his speed, and the way his vision on the ice is so good, you'll see why he'll be great. He's starting to talk to the guys without any problem. It must have been very difficult for him to leave his home, his parents. And this league is even stronger than he expected. The game is so fast. He had to adjust to a smaller ice surface than he's used to, and in Buffalo the ice is even smaller still."

Pierre Dorion, a player analyst with the NHL's Central Scouting Bureau, watched Mogilny from the start of training camp and offered this appraisal. "He's the best prospect I've seen in ten years and that includes Mario Lemieux. The only possible drawbacks are that he's the biggest hot dog I've seen and there are twenty things that could happen to him on the way to the rink."

Dudley understood that he had a distinct advantage over coaches such as Jim Schoenfeld, Bob McCammon and others with Soviet players, because Mogilny was in Buffalo to stay, whereas the others eventually would return to the Soviet Union.

"Alex is maturing faster than we thought he would," said Dudley. "He didn't know what to expect because of the new culture and language but he's grasping it very quickly. He thought he would be scoring easier than he has, but I simply told him to do his best. He knew that he'd be playing some, but not a lot. As the season progresses, he'll play more and we're hopeful he'll be a major part of this club.

"He's a bright kid who understands what works and what doesn't work in this league. He uses his gifts well, especially his speed. Defensively, he'll progress as the season continues."

Progress was somewhat slower for 37-year-old Helmut Balderis, who seemed more adroit with the media than with the opposition. When someone asked him if he expected to play as well as Wayne Gretzky, Helmut shot back, "Not exactly. He is younger. But if the other defensemen are going to be as gentle against me as they are against him, then I'll be pretty close to Gretzky's caliber."

With Balderis in tow, the North Stars jumped off to a 5–0–1 start before losing a game, and ranked among the most surprising teams of the early going. Helmut was not a regular but he had made the big team. Sergei Mylnikov was virtually ignored by Quebec coach Michel Bergeron, who preferred Stephane Fiset and Ron Tugnutt, neither of whom displayed any particular puckstopping prowess.

Mylnikov was understandably frustrated and critical of Bergeron. "Michel shows a lot of energy," said Mylnikov, "and you see him standing up on the bench yelling and moving around and arguing with the referees. But Bergeron never comes up with new ideas and, as a result, this team is playing under its potential. Serge Aubry, the goaltending coach, isn't doing a good job trying to change my style. He forgets that I'm over 30 and I've been through a lot of competitions."

It was clear that as long as Bergeron remained coach, Mylnikov would be a non-person on the Nordiques roster. In time the Nordiques described a steady descent to the bottom of the Adams Division, Bergeron became a hopeless figure behind the bench, but Mylnikov remained in the doghouse, no matter how many games Quebec lost.

By contrast, the Devils' future in 1989–90 appeared bright over the long haul, if not cloudy after the opening night win in Philadelphia, when Fetisov launched the barrage with his blistering shot that enabled Sylvain Turgeon to score. The relatively easy win at the Spectrum already had some New Jersey journalists projecting a first place finish, with Slava choreographing both the attack and defense in the manner of Bobby Orr with the Stanley Cup-winning Boston Bruins of 1970 and 1972.

The enthusiasm was braked after the Devils returned to East Rutherford for their premiere against Mario Lemieux and the Pittsburgh Penguins. The 4–4 tie was less than satisfying, and it was followed with a major test against the defending champion Flames. The game's evolution over 60 minutes of play would be terribly revealing for the Devils, not just for the night, but for the entire season and playoffs as well.

New Jersey's David Maley scored two minutes into the game and the Devils nursed a 1–0 lead into the second period. Fetisov displayed none of the jump he had shown in Philadelphia. The Flames refused to allow him to move freely into the play as the fourth attacker, as he had done in the Soviet Union.

"We'd heard all the reports of him moving into the attack," said Calgary goalie Mike Vernon, "but we just wouldn't allow him the room. Our guys were right on top of him. Guys like Sergei Makarov were on top of him deep early and held him up."

With Fetisov stymied, the Flames counterattacked with four consecutive goals in the second period. Patrik Sundstrom added one for New Jersey early in the third period, but the Devils could muster little else in the way of an attack after that. Slava caused a stir once when he whacked little Joe Mullen of Calgary into the boards well after the whistle.

"I'd just stopped skating," Mullen explained "and was cruising. All of a sudden he takes me into the boards and then gets his stick up around my face. I didn't do anything to provoke it." A brief melee followed but no damage was done, and the Flames proceeded to wrap up a 4–2 win.

The Devils could alibi the loss by noting that their opponents were the defending Stanley Cup-holders, but that excuse didn't wash. Shortly after, the Flames visited Madison Square Garden and were beaten by the rival Rangers. To those close to the Devils scene, it had become apparent that the addition of the two Russians had created a glut of defensemen, and management had yet to sort out the top-liners from those who would be benched, or perhaps traded.

Ken Daneyko, who had been the club's toughest and most intense defenseman over the previous two years, was scratched at the start.

Craig Wolanin, a number-one draft choice who had been earmarked for stardom, turned into a question mark. Tom Kurvers, who was esteemed for his offensive abilities and led Devils defensemen in scoring, found himself watching games from The Halo, Byrne Arena's press box near the roof.

Fetisov and Starikov were guaranteed starting assignments during the early games along with Bruce Driver, a veteran who had missed a large portion of the previous season with a severe leg injury. Tommy Albelin, the Swedish-born back-liner, also was given a starting berth while coach Schoenfeld attempted to determine how to fit the fleet Finn Reijo Ruotsalainen into the lineup.

The Devils continued their erratic play, as did Fetisov. "He may not have as much petro in the tank," said former NHL coach Harry Neale, who had become a Canadian television commentator. By now Starikov was being mocked for his weight. When someone asked McCammon when he expected Sergei to get down to his proper playing weight, the Canucks coach replied, "I don't think his contract is that long!"

Meanwhile, the benched Devils defensemen remained restless, complaining in confidence to the media. On October 16, Lamoriello defused the tension somewhat when he announced that Kurvers had been traded to the Toronto Maple Leafs for a first-round draft pick in 1991. The news was greeted with jubilation in East Rutherford and dismay in Toronto. Critics on both sides of the border agreed that it was a steal for the Devils. Kurvers had goofed on a late game play in one of his few appearances — he dressed against the Edmonton Oilers at home — and was considered disposable. A first-round pick was regarded as a rare prize, particularly since the Devils still appeared overloaded with defenders.

The assumption, of course, was that Fetisov and Starikov would establish themselves as top-of-the-line defenders, or average at the very least. Obviously, Fetisov was the key and in his first spate of games he established himself as an enigma. "His inconsistency is baffling," commented Kevin Allen in *USA Today.* "His play has been ingenious at times, but at other times his talent reserve seemed bankrupt."

Still to be determined was his ability to withstand the heavy checking. Slava was treated with no undue violence in his early games, but heavy flak was sure to come. "He'll get hit," said Guy Carbonneau of the Canadiens, "because some players see him as a job-stealer. The thing is for him to get past his first thirty games. After that he won't be treated any different from the others."

For Viacheslav Fetisov it would be game nine of the 1989–90 season when he would learn first-hand about NHL violence and it would be a lesson that would have reverberations for the rest of the campaign and the play-offs as well.

CHAPTER 13

FETISOV–CLARK, ROUND ONE

"I'm mad at myself I wasn't better prepared for these things. I reacted much too calmly to what happened to me, but I will change that in the future."
— *Slava Fetisov, New Jersey Devils*

Doug Carpenter did not like the New Jersey Devils. How could he? College-educated, self-assured, the red-headed career coach was certain he had finally steered owner John McMullen's franchise in the right direction by the 1987–88 NHL season, after several frustrating years of being eliminated from playoff competition. But by the middle of the season — following a humiliating defeat at Madison Square Garden — president Lou Lamoriello decided to replace the prideful Carpenter with Jim Schoenfeld.

Within months Schoenfeld had become lionized as a miracle-maker. The Devils beat out the despised New York Rangers to clinch a playoff berth on the final night of the schedule and then upset both the Islanders and Capitals before losing to Boston in a pulsating seven-game series. It all tended to make Carpenter look bad, since Schoenfeld had succeeded where he had failed.

After a season coaching in the American Hockey League, Carpenter got another chance to prove his worth in the NHL when he was hired to run the downtrodden Toronto Maple Leafs. Notorious for his Captain Bligh demeanor, Carpenter received mixed reviews when he moved into Maple Leaf Gardens. The local media, which had been disenchanted with the John Brophy and then

George Armstrong regimes, was hopeful about the change to a man who seemed qualified and dedicated. But others, who had worked with Carpenter in the past, were quick to denounce him.

"He's not a nice man," said one former NHL aide. "By Christmas every player on the team will hate him."

Sure enough, there were reports of an uprising within the Maple Leafs dressing room shortly after the season began. Carpenter managed to quell the dissidents and keep his club competitive, if not overwhelming. One of his major assets was the team's aggressiveness, an NHL euphemism for quasi-dirty play.

General manager Floyd Smith had accumulated some of the roughest — if not talented — hombres on skates. Tall Brian Curran was a veteran gunslinger who had worked for the Bruins and Islanders before being obtained by Toronto. A poor skater with limited skills, Curran was fast and loose with his fists, although he rarely won his fights because of poor skating balance. In John Kordic, Smith employed one of the NHL's true goons, an unpredictable, uncontrollable "hit man" whose talents were even more limited than Curran's.

When the Capitals decided that Lou Franceschetti was no longer needed, Smith signed the forward who had long developed a reputation as a vicious checker with a number of victims hospitalized with injuries. Unlike Kordic and Curran, Franceschetti also had some scoring talents, which would be evident early in the season.

Most fearsome of all, however, was one of the more gifted skaters on the team, Wendel Clark. A defenseman when he played junior hockey in Saskatoon, Clark betrayed a mean streak that had become feared throughout the league. Although he was relatively small (five eleven, 194 pounds), Clark had fought some of the biggest players in the league and often dominated with his ferocity.

With the likes of Curran, Kordic, Franceschetti and Clark in the lineup, as well as heavy checkers such as Brad Marsh and Rob Ramage, the Maple Leafs iced a team that was as intimidating as any in the league. Adding to this factor was Carpenter who, in the minds of many who knew him, revelled in the rough play. This was the team Slava Fetisov would skate against on the night of October 23, 1989, in Toronto.

The game opened innocently enough with no incidents until New Jersey defenseman Ken Daneyko took a two-minute interference penalty at 2:39 of the first period. Six seconds before Daneyko's penalty expired, Clark had put Toronto ahead, 1–0. Just over a minute later, the Devils counterattacked and tied the score on John MacLean's goal. The visitors added two more goals before the period had ended, and in the second period extended their lead to 5–2 before it was half over.

At this point the Maple Leafs' game plan abruptly changed as if Carpenter merely pushed the "violence" button, and explosions erupted all over the rink. The first collision involved Toronto centre Dan Daoust and Devils goalie Sean Burke. As the bodies made contact, Burke lifted an elbow that creased the smallish Maple Leaf. Daoust immediately retaliated with a crosscheck and players from both teams sped to the scene like bees to honey.

Inexplicably, Toronto goalie Mark Laforest felt inspired to leave his crease 190 feet away from the melee and skated the length of the ice to engage his fellow goalie, Burke, in combat. The goaltenders briefly battled and peace seemed to have been restored. Burke returned to his net and Laforest was enroute to his crease when Burke motioned to Laforest. "He waved me to come down," Laforest explained, "so I went down."

Laforest accepted the invitation and headed directly for Burke, who met him in the Devils' zone and pummelled the Maple Leaf netminder. "The first time I was surprised that he had come all the way down the ice," said Burke. "I just turned around and there he was. The second time I told him he was a little smaller than me and I really didn't want to be in this. He said something about me not being very tough and I told him that even though he had played with Ron Hextall in Philadelphia, he wasn't quite in that category."

When the two padded players finally were separated by linesmen Jerry Pateman and Gerard Gauthier, referee Terry Gregson ejected both of them from the game. "It didn't enter my mind that I could get tossed out," Burke allowed. "If I had known, I would have avoided it if I could."

Toronto's aggression continued through the end of the period and produced a late goal by Tom Fergus against substitute Jersey goalie Chris Terreri. "It was pretty obvious," noted Devils forward Mark Johnson, "that they were coming at us physically."

The pounding continued into the third period and appeared to be focused on Fetisov. Daoust, who normally is not known for his hitting, had run Slava into the boards in the first period, inflicting a bump that would require a postgame ice pack. But that was nothing compared to subsequent events. Daoust kept hitting and then Clark rumbled after Fetisov when Slava went behind his net.

On the surface it looked to be a normal confrontation. Slava certainly was not expecting any further aggression and had no intentions of pursuing the matter. As he later pointed out, he had not had a fight in ten years and didn't believe in fighting for the sake of fighting. Reared on the robust Canadian prairie, Clark thought just the opposite and was encouraged by his coach's general policy.

Suddenly, and without provocation, Clark rained blows on Fetisov, knocking off his helmet and pressing the attack although it was evident that Fetisov wanted no part of the bout.

"When Clark hit me," Fetisov explained, "I was not prepared for it and it threw me off."

Mercilessly, Clark continued slugging the Soviet until linesmen intervened. To the utter astonishment of the Devils' bench, Fetisov was penalized two minutes for "roughing." The aggressor, Clark, received a pair of roughing penalties, totalling four minutes.

"I'm mad at myself that I wasn't better prepared for these things," Fetisov added. "I reacted much too calmly to what happened to me, but I will change that in the future."

Coach Schoenfeld wasn't worried about the future; he was concerned about the present. His club looked ready to fold after holding a three-goal lead and he was concerned about the pounding that Slava and Starikov were taking.

After Clark's penalty, Carpenter revved up Toronto's

attack once more and they poured over the blueline with impunity. Only Terreri's adroit goaltending allowed New Jersey to nurse its one-goal lead. With ten minutes left in the third period, Schoenfeld benched both Soviet players and for the remainder of the game, his defense hung tough, enabling the Devils to escape with a 5–4 win.

Having retreated to the sanctity of the dressing room, Fetisov had a few minutes to pull himself together before the media hordes entered and pumped him with questions. The final ten-minute benching irritated him no end and when the reporters arrived, Slava ventilated his anger.

"It's the first time I ever did not play in the last ten minutes of a game," he said. "I don't know why it happened. I was upset by it."

Schoenfeld wasted no time producing an explanation. "It certainly wasn't anything out of the ordinary in an 80-game season," he said. "With all the penalties from the fights, we were playing with a shortened bench. Two of our defensemen, Randy Velischek and Ken Daneyko, had sat out 10-minute misconducts, which meant the Soviets had played a great deal in the first half of the third period. Besides, it was our fourth game in six nights and Fetisov has played a great deal of hockey for us — excellently, too. He had been dinged by the Daoust hit and looked just a bit tired."

Across the ice in the home team dressing room, Clark was doing some explaining himself. "Thirty seconds before the fight," Clark insisted, "Fetisov had given me his stick. Then he was looking right at me. He was looking for it."

Clark's statement was fatuous to say the least. What Fetisov was looking for was a way to escape his zone with the puck. He certainly did not high-stick Clark, as the Leaf asserted. "It was not the most pretty version of the game of hockey," Slava concluded before leaving Maple Leaf Gardens.

It is unlikely that Slava could have anticipated the media reception he would receive in the next day's papers. COMRADES FIND LEAF HOCKEY NOT VERY PRETTY, observed the *Toronto Star*.

Columnist Frank Orr, appreciated for his humorous bent, opened his essay by twitting the Russians: "The rumor was denied by all concerned that while the Maple Leafs and Devils were doing their World Wrestling Federation giant tag-team special, a couple of Soviet lads, Viacheslav Fetisov and Sergei Starikov, had a little chat on the Devils bench. 'You know, Sergei, maybe Viktor Tikhonov was not such a bad guy after all,' Fetisov reportedly said, which was later denied. Perhaps on nights like these, the Fetisov view of curmudgeon Viktor might be softened just a little. Seldom in the big league back home did Viacheslav absorb the pounding he took from the Maple Leafs."

Jim O'Leary of the *Toronto Sun* wrote a parody of a conversation between Fetisov and former teammate Aleksei Kasatonov, who still was in the Soviet Union. "We told you to keep your head up over there," said Kasatonov, laughing. "What were you doing anyway? Looking for a message on the scoreboard?"

Not surprisingly, the unkindest cut of all came from Don Cherry, the opinionated and influential commentator for "Hockey Night In Canada." Cherry was incensed at the feckless behavior of Fetisov. "Wendel didn't want to hurt him," chortled Cherry, "just punch him a couple of times."

New York Times columnist Ira Berkow was astonished at Cherry's remark. "This is intriguing," wrote Berkow in rebuttal, "because in most cases that I've heard about, when someone throws a punch at someone's face, the intent is not as of throwing a kiss. It is more to cause welts, or dismantle teeth, and the like."

The Fetisov-Clark confrontation was viewed by countless New York and New Jersey hockey fans. Not only was the event featured on SportsChannel, the cable system that carries most of the Devils' games, but it received top play on local newscasts. One broadcaster, after showing video of Clark's assault, cried, "Look at this! He doesn't want to fight!"

Unfortunately for Fetisov, it was an issue that would not die. Two days after the episode in Toronto the most stinging rebuke of all appeared in the New York *Post* under Hugh Delano's byline. A former Marine, Delano had been covering hockey for more than two decades and had been known as a diligent reporter who happened to be employed by a newspaper given to sensationalism. Like other staff members, Delano jazzed up his copy whenever possible and the Clark-Slava incident was ideal for a followup.

On Wednesday, October 25, Delano opened his story, "Fetisov had better learn to defend himself with his fists, not his stick, or word will quickly spread throughout the NHL that he may just be a red Devil with a yellow belly. The former Russian army major may have lost some respect for refusing to accept Clark's challenge to duke it out."

Devils president Lamoriello was said to be furious over Delano's article, as were Schoenfeld and, of course, Fetisov. In addition, several of Delano's journalistic colleagues took exception to his verbal assault.

"Anyone who questions the courage or manhood of Slava Fetisov or any of the Soviets in the NHL should examine himself and let us know what his true agenda is, because it certainly isn't honest reporting," snapped Larry Brooks, hockey analyst for WABC Radio, which carried the Devils' games.

Sports media critic Steve Hanks added, "Delano reached such a low point in New York sports writing that even the late Dick Young would have been outraged. Even if you agree with Delano that the Soviets shouldn't play in the NHL — and why on earth not? — he is being gratuitous, mean-spirited and reactionary."

Soft-spoken and genial, Delano seemed somewhat taken aback by the fuss made about his story. "I'm not a great believer in the Soviets in the league," he said by way of explanation during a pre-game conversation in the Byrne Arena press room. Asked about the "yellow" slur against the Russian, Delano defended himself. "I used it kiddingly. I tended to believe that Fetisov was not prepared for Clark's assault."

The Devils general staff decided to remain relatively mum on the issue. "Fetisov can speak for himself," said Lamoriello, when pressed for a rebuttal to Delano. "We don't have to defend his character whatsoever."

Not long after he returned to New Jersey, Slava asked teammate Jim Korn for some pugilistic tips. Fetisov said it wasn't that he had never had a fight on skates in the Soviet Union, but it had been a while. He needed to brush up. "I haven't had a fight in ten years," he admitted, "not since the world Juniors and my first three years on the Soviet national team. I forgot some things. Now I remember them."

Somebody even sent Fetisov a photo of the Clark fight that ran on page one of the *Toronto Sun*. In the picture, Clark is grabbing Slava's jersey with his left hand and ready to land a punch with his right. The headline read, "Good night Glasnost." Fetisov decided to use the photo as inspiration. "I have it hanging over my bed."

Schoenfeld was less amused. "The prejudice against the Russians is really starting to annoy me," he said. "If another hockey player who wasn't Russian had been caught off guard like that, we wouldn't be hearing about how he isn't willing to fight. Fighting is overrated. The only time you lose is if it changes your game. It won't happen with this guy. He's had better players than Wendel Clark take a run at him."

When the dust had cleared, a clear division — pro and con Fetisov — was apparent among the media. Jingoists such as Cherry ("The Russians don't want to fight; they don't know how.") maintained their macho offensive.

On the flip side were columnists such as *The Times'* Berkow, who railed at the NHL for permitting hooliganism of the Wendel Clark variety. "What Cherry was saying, of course, is that it's all part of the game. But it is apparently a different sort of game than Fetisov is familiar with. Fetisov says that he doesn't think fighting — the dropping of gloves and sticks and the yanking at suspenders — is sportsmanlike. 'The beauty of the game is to play hockey,' he said.

"Incredible statement, since everyone who follows professional hockey in North America knows that the beauty is when the game stops to allow a bunch of guys on ice skates to try to pull one another's hair out. As for the Soviet players' lack of ability or desire to fight, tell that to those who, for example, in the siege of Stalingrad fought off the Nazi panzer divisions for five months, and defeated them, turning the tide of World War II in the East. Tell that to the partisans who fought in the woods. And don't tell that to Napoleon, who burned part of Moscow before he got a boot in the derriere."

A boot in the derriere was precisely what Schoenfeld was trying to avoid in the coaching department. Try as he might, the club's leader could not regain the magic of 1988, nor could he shake off the trauma of the Toronto game. When the Devils visited Calgary on Saturday, November 4, Fetisov looked forward to playing against his old pal Makarov, in a game that would be beamed back to the Soviet Union. He was stunned when informed that he had been benched for the entire match, along with Starikov.

Delano went after them again. "The heat is on Lou Lamoriello," he warned in the November 6 edition of the *Post*. "The Russian 'supermen' the Devils g.m. brought to America are playing more like Lois Lane and Jimmy Olson than the Man of Steel. Fetisov is upset with Schoenfeld's decision to bench him."

As the newspaper was being distributed, Lamoriello was huddling with his public relations director David Freed. They were preparing a press release on the firing of Schoenfeld. After only fourteen games of the young season, the Devils were in second place with a 6–6–2 record, although recently they had been braked by a 0–2–1 mini-slump. It hardly seemed time enough to judge the coach on the campaign, but Lamoriello argued that he couldn't wait any longer.

"I felt our team was headed in the wrong direction and it was better to make the change now," said Lamoriello. "Things were not working well with our team. There was inconsistency in our type of play. We were going in the wrong dircction. It's better to react now."

But this was more than a case of a coach being fired for not winning enough games. A headline in the *Post* linked Fetisov and Starikov to the dismissal: RED DEVILS WIN OUT — BENCHING OF SOVIET STARS COSTS SCHOENFELD HIS JOB.

Delano wasted no time explaining the sacking. "Schoenfeld's decision to bench Fetisov and Starikov for bad play may have helped cost him his job. That's how it looks. It could be a reason why Lamoriello pushed the panic button and replaced Schoenfeld with assistant coach John Cunniff."

Lamoriello emphatically denied the charges. "Absolutely not," he shot back. "Whether Fetisov was not in the lineup was not a factor. Anyone who thinks that does not have respect for me; that would be a total fallacy."

Others took potshots at Lamoriello for what they considered the sacrifice of Schoenfeld for the Russians. "My guess is that Jim didn't want to put up with the Russians' bull," said Rangers defenseman Lindy Ruff. "The Devils paid so much money for these guys to come over, and now they wonder how he can sit guys out. Fetisov and Starikov have not played well at all. Starikov can't play in this league and Fetisov is playing like an average defenseman."

The Devils convened at their South Mountain practice rink that same day. Only this time the scrimmage was conducted by the stoic Cunniff. When the workout was over, reporters huddled around Fetisov in the training room.

"For me," Slava explained, "this is just new. This is the first time my coach has been changed since the Soviet Union team changed from a good coach to Tikhonov."

It was pointed out to Slava that several published accounts of Schoenfeld's firing blamed his handling of Fetisov; specifically the benching late in two games and his sitting out in Calgary. Did Slava believe those reports? He shook his head. No!

"The Devils play fourteen games and Fetisov doesn't play one," he said. "That's why coach goes? That's crazy. These are not my questions. They are questions for the general manager. Right now the Devils [6–6–2] are not playing so good. Last season the Devils didn't play so good. Maybe that's why Lou Lamoriello wants the team to play better.

"I am not used to losing at all. I played on a team where only one loss was cause to be upset. No, I am not happy Jim was fired. I haven't been here long enough to cause any problems. Usually when you're around for a short time, you can only say good things."

In fact, good things were being consistently said about only one Soviet, Sergei Makarov, and even he had his detractors.

Sergei Priakin, one of the least publicized Russians, eyes the puck for the Flames.

Igor Larianov was less than the scoring threat Canucks fans had expected.

Although many believed that Sergei Makarov was too old to qualify, Makarov nevertheless won the Calder Trophy in 1990.

Helmut Balderis played briefly for the Minnesota North Stars during the 1989 – 90 campaign.

The "problem child" among the imports was defector Alexander Mogilny, whose difficulties included a fear of flying. The Sabre forward had no trouble here flying past Kelly Kisio of the Rangers.

The Soviets became renowned for their slick offensive play around the enemy net. Rod Langway of Team USA moves in too late.

Who says the Russians don't hit?

Vladimir Krutov (left) had all the ingredients for success but he was sadly lacking in motivation. Here he checks John Ogrodnick of the Rangers.

The most famous Russian goalie was Viacheslav Tretiak, depicted here in an exhibition game against the New York Rangers at Madison Square Garden during the 1975 – 76 season.

More crafty than most NHL forwards, Sergei Makarov stickhandles through a wall of Rangers.

Aleksei Kasatonov wraps his arms around Oleg Mikulchik of the visiting Soviet Wings during an exhibition game in January, 1990.

From time to time Sergei Starikov showed flashes of defensive excellence on the Devils' defense, as when he levelled Andrew McBain of the Pittsburgh Penguins early in the 1989 – 90 season

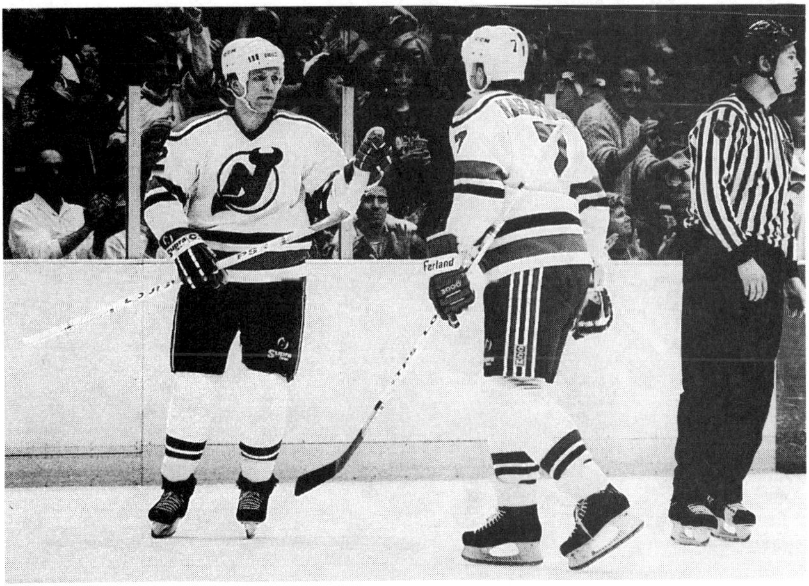

Normally, Slava Fetisov would not talk with teammate Aleksei Kasatonov because of differences dating back to their playing days in Russia. But they made an exception when Slava scored. Here, Fetisov accepts congratulations from his defensive partner at Byrne Arena.

The players' wives were just as happy to be in America as their husbands. Lada Fetisov (left) and Irene Starikov are with their spouses at their first press conference in New Jersey.

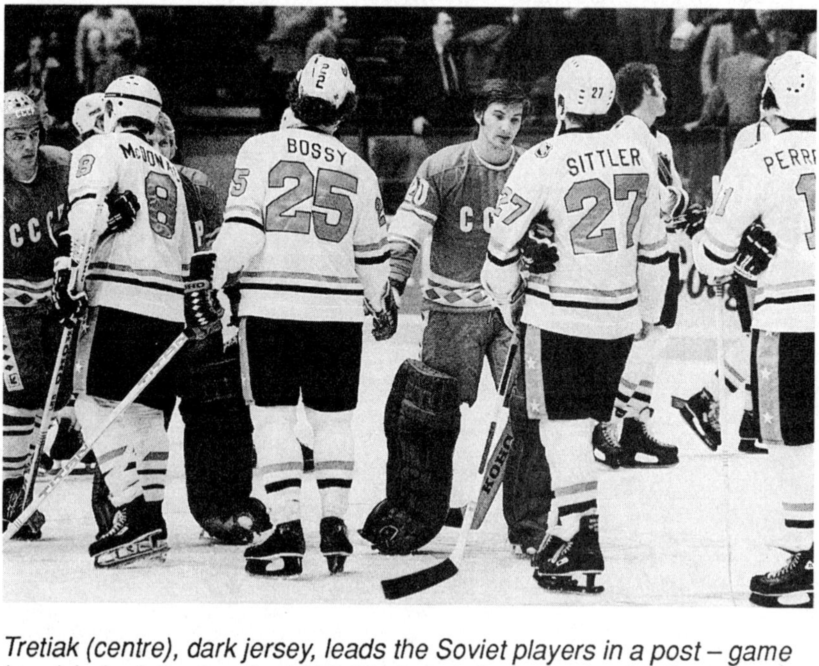

Tretiak (centre), dark jersey, leads the Soviet players in a post – game handshake following the 1979 Challenge Cup, won by the Soviets, at Madison Square Garden.

CHAPTER 14

DUMPING ON MAKAROV

"By rule, the Calder goes to the player selected the most proficient in his first year...in the NHL, period. Not a word about thirtysomething Russians."

—*Keith Gave,* Detroit Free Press

Nobody had to tell the Calgary Flames how difficult it would be to win a second straight Stanley Cup, least of all ebullient coach Terry Crisp.

"A week after we had won the Cup," Crisp remembered, "I was down in the Co-op, shopping at our grocery store. Everyone was congratulating me on a job well done and telling me I'm going to win it again in 1990. I had exactly one week to enjoy the 1989 win. That's all they would allow me; one week to enjoy the Stanley Cup, then it was back to the business of trying to win it again in 1990."

It would not be an easy business. Mighty as they appeared from a superficial viewpoint, the Flames suffered a few cracks in their armor. Lanny McDonald, the inspirational leader of the club for many years, finally retired, while Hakan Loob, the speedy Swedish star, returned permanently to his homeland. In addition, experienced defenseman Rob Ramage was traded to Toronto and assistant coach Doug Risebrough moved up to the front office.

This hardly was cause for panic among the Flames general staff, as there was still a nucleus of dependable veterans and some rookies, such as Paul Ranheim, who displayed enormous promise. Most of all, there was Sergei

Makarov, acclaimed as the finest of the active Soviet players and the one most critics guaranteed would be an NHL impact player.

Crisp understood that integrating Makarov into the Flames lineup would not be as easy as snapping his fingers. "To begin with," Crisp said, "when we were on our Soviet tour in September 1989, I made a point of spending an afternoon with the great Russian coach Anatoli Tarasov. I went over to his place with my assistant coaches Tom Watt and Doug Risebrough. We got as much as we could out of him. At one point, I asked, 'Mr. Tarasov, who are the best players you have ever had in Russia?'

"He picked Vladimir Krutov and Makarov, even over Vladislav Tretiak. So I asked, 'How do you coach them?' He said, 'They play, they play. You let them play.' Now it's well and good to say let them play, but we have 19 other guys who we've got to keep happy, too. So we decided that we were getting a world-class player and it would not be wise to make him something that he doesn't want to be.

"We agreed that for the first 40 games we would play the guy come hell or high water. We found a spot for him with Gary Roberts and Joe Nieuwendyk and we talked a lot with them."

Makarov started off like gangbusters and then levelled off, but displayed superior talents if not astronomical numbers. After 40 games, Makarov was averaging just over a point a game with ten goals and 33 assists. The high command had mixed emotions over his play.

"Sergei had done some things that we weren't happy with," added Crisp, "and we had done some things that he wasn't happy with. After the 40 games I called him into my office with his interpreter. I said to the interpreter, 'I want this verbatim. Word for word what I say, and I want word for word what he says back to me — good, bad or indifferent.'

"It was interesting because he had never had the opportunity to talk to a coach, and in the Soviet Union you don't talk back. Well, he got a lot off his chest and it was neat. Lots of his points were very valid from his point of view. For example, in the Soviet Union he was used to getting so much more ice time than we were giving him. And in Russia they don't match lines the way we do. We watch Wayne Gretzky, Mario Lemieux and Pat LaFontaine. We'll pull a guy off with two minutes to go and put our best checking line out to hold them down. He wasn't used to being pulled off in the last two minutes so I could put out our best checking line."

Crisp quickly discovered that his Soviet shooter had been withholding some of his feelings about the coach's strategy and the manner in which he was being handled.

Crisp: "He told me a good story. He said, 'You must learn to call time out at the right time.' When I asked him what he meant, he explained that players get tired. 'You have to change. Call time out. It's your job.' I said, 'Okay, that's fine.' A week later we were up at Edmonton and winning 3–2. The clock was counting down and we had about a minute and 20 seconds left. Makarov was on the ice and turned around and said to me, 'Time out.' I said, 'Okay, Sergei, we'll get a time out for you. No problem.'At that moment, the whistle blew and — what do you know — the Oilers' coach John Muckler called a time out. Sergei looked down at their bench and then looked back at me and said, 'Smart coach!'"

Smart manager, is what opponents were saying about Cliff Fletcher, mostly because of Makarov's excellence. "Sergei is the undeniable star of the nine-person Soviet delegation," commented Kevin Allen in *USA Today*.

Not only was Makarov a star, he also inadvertently became a cause célèbre; as controversy swirled around him, the better he played. It all centred on a question that would be bruited about from the first quarter of the season until the final 1989–90 NHL awards were presented in June — should Makarov be eligible for the Calder Trophy as NHL rookie of the year?

The award, named in honor of the NHL's original president, Frank Calder, was first presented in 1937 and has been awarded every year since. League rules clearly stipulate that the Calder is "An annual award to the player selected as the most proficient in his first year of competition in the National Hockey League." Nowhere does it say anything about age or previous playing experience.

While there always has been a suggestion that the Calder be awarded to a young player, many previous winners had extensive experience or were up in their twenties when they took the trophy. These include Jimmy McFadden of the Detroit Red Wings, who won it in 1948, Kent Douglas of the Toronto Maple Leafs in 1963, and recently Peter Stastny of the Quebec Nordiques, in 1981.

Stastny was a 24-year-old international star when he defected to Canada. He had played for the Slovan team in Bratislava and was a member of the Czech Olympic team. As Stastny displayed more and more prowess in his rookie NHL season, 1981–82, opposition developed against his eligibility for the rookie of the year prize. Opponents said that he should be ineligible because of his vast international playing experience, which gave him a significant edge over youngsters who were breaking into the league. Peter played in 77 games and finished with 39 goals and 70 assists for 109 points, a commendable total for any All-Star. When the votes were in Stastny was on top.

"This much I can tell you," Stastny said, "I don't think I would have won the Calder if I wasn't ahead by so many points. That's why I could sympathize with Makarov. He wound up in a very controversial position just because he was a good player."

The controversy began flaming at mid-season when it became apparent that Makarov was for real and, on talent alone, would be the top candidate for the Calder. He also would be 32 years old at the time of the voting by 68 electors from the Professional Hockey Writers' Association. This infuriated players such as Wayne Gretzky and Guy Lafleur.

"A rookie," said Lafleur, "is a guy who gets drafted at 18 or 19, not someone 30. The young guys don't have a chance to catch up. It's not fair. The Europeans should come here at 18 or 19 and play in the league like the rest of us."

While there was considerable logic to the anti-Makarov stance, there also was an unmistakable smell of pro-Canadian bias and anti-European prejudice, masked by the reason: "I don't think a guy who's played ten years at the world level should be eligible," as Gretzky added.

Some thought Gretzky was unnecessarily peevish toward Makarov because Wayne was deemed ineligible for the Calder in 1980, when he played *his* first NHL season. At that time, he had played 80 games in the World Hockey Association. The qualification for rookie is "a player cannot have played more than 25 games in any single preceding season nor in more than six games in each of any two preceding seasons in any major professional league." In 1980 the WHA had been classified as a major professional league, and therefore Gretzky was ineligible.

Gretzky and Lafleur were not the only personalities speaking out against Makarov. Several teams had begun to mount campaigns of their own for purely selfish reasons. The winning of the Calder had become an achievement of considerable significance to team publicists, who would use their top rookies as vehicles to ticket sales in the upcoming seasons. During the 1988–89 season, for example, the Rangers spent considerable money in their drive to win the Calder for one of their two freshmen aces, Brian Leetch and Tony Granato. The club went so far as to publish elaborate brochures for each player. These were widely distributed to members of the media. As it happened, Leetch won the trophy.

Several public relations directors believed that they had a potential Calder winner on their club in 1989–90 and the only obstacle, in their estimation, was Makarov. Sergei's competitors included:

- Mike Modano, 19, the Minnesota North Stars first pick in the 1988 draft and one of the key factors in the club's renaissance.
- Jeremy Roenick, 20, Chicago's first pick, eighth overall in the 1988 draft. Under Mike Keenan's severe tutelage, Roenick was blossoming into a star with the Blackhawks.

- Mark Recchi, 22, Pittsburgh's fourth pick, 67 overall in the 1988 draft; overshadowed by the Penguins' megastar Mario Lemieux, but getting notices by the quarter-point in the campaign thanks to notable goals.
- Darren Turcotte, 22, the Rangers' fifth pick, 114 overall in the 1986 draft; developed into an offensive force. His laser-like shot helped the New Yorkers climb to the top of the Patrick Division early in the season.
- Rod Brind'Amour, 19, the St. Louis Blues' first pick, ninth overall in the 1988 draft and favorably compared with Islanders' future Hall-of-Famer Bryan Trottier. Some observers said that Brind'Amour's problem was playing in St. Louis, where hockey does not get the attention it does in other centres such as Toronto and Montreal.
- Paul Ranheim, 24, Calgary's third pick and 38 overall in the 1984 draft; speed and a good shot were his principal assets. The Flames were not about to have a competition between Makarov and Ranheim, so the points would do the talking.

In a decision based on points alone, it would be no contest. Makarov moved ahead of all his competition early on and appeared fully capable of retaining his lead through the finish line. He would soon discover it was not merely a matter of artistry alone. In fact public relations would be as much a factor as goals and assists, particularly when members of the PHWA were involved.

"I can't consider Makarov a rookie," said PHWA member Walt MacPeek of the *Newark Star-Ledger*. "Even Viacheslav Fetisov openly admits that he's not an NHL rookie, so why should Makarov be considered one?"

Former goalie John Davidson, who had become a television hockey analyst, was another who disparaged Makarov's accomplishments. "Sergei stepped into an ideal situation playing on a line with Joe Nieuwendyk and Gary Roberts," said Davidson, "and he was given a spot on the power play right away. It bothers me to think he'll win the rookie vote because he has 500 games of international experience. The NHL was unprepared for this and should have changed the rule last summer. It's really too bad because Turcotte, Modano, Roenick, Brind'Amour and Recchi have all had rookie of the year-type seasons."

Francis Rosa, venerable Boston *Globe* hockey analyst, agreed that the NHL was caught by surprise. "The league could have prevented all the controversy very easily," Rosa suggested. "All it had to do was classify the European leagues as major professional."

Makarov was not without his supporters within the PHWA, some very vocal about the matter. Keith Gave of the Detroit *Free Press* was one of them. "Whether a veteran of many years of world-class competition should win the Calder is no longer an issue," stated Gave. "By rule, the Calder goes 'to the player selected the most proficient in his first year...in the NHL.' Period. Not a word about thirtysomething Russians. Now anybody who doesn't agree that Makarov is the best first-year player has taken too many pucks to the melon. Mind you, even Makarov said he doesn't consider himself a rookie.

"But he doesn't get to vote. Writers vote for the award, but they can't redefine it."

Gave's position was underlined by colleagues such as Jim Kelley of the *Buffalo News*. "I'm going to vote for Makarov," Kelley asserted. "This decision does put me at odds with a great many hockey people. The league itself considered a rule change to exclude such veteran performers, and in a fit of wisdom it voted against the change.

"I, for one, think it's a simple case. The rookie award goes to the best rookie. Anyone who doesn't think Makarov is the best rookie has smoked too many Gorbchows."

The Flames stayed out of the fray and merely hoped that Makarov would beef up his goal-scoring to balance his superb playmaking skills. "With all due respect to Wayne Gretzky," said Makarov's linemate, Gary Roberts, "Sergei sees the ice as well as anyone in the world. He finds me in places I don't expect to get the puck. He's had to do some adjusting and has been great. It's not just a Russian, it's any new guy on a hockey team, and you earn respect by showing you can play. Sergei can."

No backlash was apparent in the Flames boisterous dressing room. By Christmas 1989, Makarov had become integrated enough into the team to appear in the eyes of outsiders to be one of the boys. The process had been accelerated by the pre-season trip to the Soviet Union. Just by being in Russia, the Canadian and American-born Flames were better able to understand Makarov and what made him tick.

"The trip gave our players an appreciation of Sergei's way of life and our way of life," said Flames assistant GM Doug Risebrough. "Good or bad, they saw it with their own eyes. Instead of Makarov coming here and guys asking him stupid questions like, 'Do you have colored buses in your country?', they can talk to him about important things. It brought a certain normalcy to his being here."

Normalcy at the Calgary Saddledome also meant being the target of coach Terry Crisp's invective. The rookie and the coach enjoyed their own form of glasnost until the club's 32-game mark. By this time Crisp had found enough flaws in Makarov's play to feel obliged to let him have it, and he did. For one thing, he wanted his Soviet to concentrate more on defensive play and to accept the fact that he would see less ice time than he had enjoyed earlier.

Makarov hollered at Crisp and the coach did likewise with his rookie. "I told him I want him to be Sergei Makarov," said Crisp, "but I also said that he has to be willing to give a little. I can't have other players coming to me, saying, 'Geez, coach, what about him not playing defense?' Everybody has to accept our defensive style or it's not fair to the other players. We know it takes time but he has certain responsibilities, certain duties. We don't want Sergei telling us how they did it in Russia. Sergei knows what has to be done. He's not a dummy."

The Bruins made that discovery during a game at Boston Garden on January 18, 1990. With the game just six minutes old, Bruins' giant defenseman Gord Kluzak brought the puck out of his zone. With a move that only the superior player can make, Sergei read the play perfectly as Kluzak floated a soft pass toward Bobby Gould. Makarov easily intercepted the pass, slammed on the brakes and turned back toward the Bruins goal. In a trice, the Soviet had created a three-on-one break against the foe. He skated a few strides and then dished a pass to linemate Nieuwendyk in the right circle. Nieuwendyk easily slipped the puck past goalie Reggie Lemelin.

"Occasionally," kidded Crisp after the game, "I have to remind Sergei that his linemates aren't Larionov and Krutov anymore. But he's adapting well."

The better he adapted, the more a hue and cry rose over his right to win the Calder Trophy. For the most part, the other rookies kept their thoughts to themselves in the early going, but once the season had reached its mid-point and it was obvious that Makarov would not be overtaken in the points race, the jealousy surfaced and youngsters began popping off.

"I'd sooner see Jeremy Roenick win it than Makarov," said Brind'Amour. "Or even Mike Modano."

Roenick, himself, was quoted as disparaging Makarov but then backtracked shortly thereafter when it appeared to be sour grapes. Asked again about Makarov winning the trophy, Roenick was more diplomatic the second time around. "It's touchy," he said. "But if people think that was what was expected from Makarov at his age in the NHL, that he did better than was expected, then so be it and give it to him. If they feel that he deserves it, I have no problem with that."

Roenick's boss, Chicago general manager Bob Pulford, was more explicit. "I hope sportswriters don't vote for Makarov," said Pulford. "I hope they see that the kids are catching Makarov now that the season has heated up. The vote should come down to Roenick and Modano."

The vote was not tallied until after the season had ended. The winner was Sergei Makarov.

CHAPTER 15

GOING AND COMING

"We know he's Russian but we don't really care. When you look at him, he's not Starikov the Russian, he's Starikov the Utica Devil...Starikov the friend."

— Dave Marcinyshyn, Utica Devils

Makarov often was pestered by reporters who invariably pressed him about the Calder fuss. "I don't care," he would say. "I play, you vote on that."

And play he did. On a visit to Edmonton for a game against the Flames' traditional rivals, the Oilers, Makarov was taken to the enormous West Edmonton Mall, an enclosed amusement park-permanent fair that boasts, among other metabolism-movers, rides called The Mindbender and The Drop of Doom.

Sergei played the tourist and kidded a friend who asked him if he had any other motives for "spying" on Edmonton. "Russian secret," clucked Makarov. "Special tactic — spending day in enemy territory."

When he returned to Northlands Coliseum to face the Oilers, Makarov was full of hockey secrets that baffled his foe. Less than five minutes into the game he finished off a two-on-one break with Al MacInnis, scoring off goalie Pokie Reddick.

That was Makarov's only point of the first period but he burst the dam in period two and finished the game — a 10–4 Calgary rout — with two goals and five assists, breaking the club record of six points in a game.

Ironically, the record had been held by the man who helped Sergei considerably against Edmonton, Gary Roberts.

"If Makarov was young enough, or stayed here long enough, he'd hold all the records this team could dream up," said Roberts. "He's a wizard. I wasn't around when Kent Nilsson was performing his magic here, but it's tough to think of him, or anybody else, being a much better offensive player than Sergei."

What made Makarov's production even more impressive was that many referees — perhaps because of some conscious or subconscious anti-Soviet feelings — had ignored countless fouls committed against him. The assaults came in the form of high sticks, spears and the usual clutch-and-grab techniques employed by less skilled opponents. If the Russian was disturbed by the tactics he did a remarkable job of concealing his displeasure until pressed.

"I knew at first the referees would do nothing," he said. "Players could hit me, slash me — because I'm a Russian. At first I was mad about this, but I've quit paying attention to it. I'm used to it."

His teammates were getting used to Sergei, especially those playing on his line. Roberts, for one, was having a career year. "If you had told me at the beginning of the season that I'd have 30 goals before February was over [as he eventually did], I'd have said, 'Thanks very much' and walked away happy. The way Makarov is playing, if you didn't get goals, you'd start wondering about yourself."

As Makarov's play improved, so did his English. On the ice, however, he talked to himself in Russian, and when he felt obliged to berate an official he did so in his native tongue. Once Sergei was so exasperated with referee Terry Gregson's failure to call a penalty against an opponent who had offended him, Makarov withered him with some choice x-rated Russian expletives.

Gregson turned to Makarov and shouted, "Why don't you speak English?" To which Makarov replied, "Fuck you! Is that English enough?" It must have been;

Gregson gave Sergei a ten-minute misconduct. Disturbed as he was over the episode, Makarov managed to overcome his momentary trauma and return to the winning groove. Whenever he felt depressed or lonely or bothered by the rough NHL play, he merely thought about his good fortune and how difficult it was playing under Viktor Tikhonov. After he had helped Calgary score five goals in the last five minutes against the Nordiques — including two shorthanded goals — Sergei was asked if he had ever been in a game like that back home.

He laughed. "In Soviet Union, we play game like this..." finishing the sentence by running his finger across his throat in a neck-cutting move. Yes, there was pressure in the NHL. More games, more travel and certainly more media, but Makarov found it more enjoyable than the grind of hockey back home.

"When I play for my own country," he explained, "there is more pressure. This is a job they pay you for. The other is for patriotism. Me, I'm lucky to be playing on a team as good as this, the Stanley Cup champions. It is easy to adapt because my teammates help a lot."

"My situation is different from Krutov, Larionov, Fetisov and the others. I can't say anything about them because I can't be in their skins. I don't know about their problems."

In the case of Alexander Mogilny, his problem was capsulized by an incident at Nassau Coliseum early in December. His Sabres were to play the Islanders and, not surprisingly, a large contingent of the New York media had come to see the highly-touted Russian. During the pre-game workout Mogilny was accidentally hit on the leg by an errant shot, left the ice and was deemed incapable of playing. He watched the Sabres lose, in civilian clothes in the press box.

Following the match, some reporters attempted to interview Mogilny but were rebuffed. Alexander spoke at length to a Soviet journalist but would not deal with the English-speaking media. "The policy was established by the Sabres," explained Mogilny's agent, Toronto-based Don Meehan. "It's not the best situation and it's something we hope to work out later on in the season."

The Sabres high command remained annoyingly vague about their decision to shield Mogilny from the media. Meehan promised one television reporter friend that he would definitely arrange an interview with Mogilny after the New Year. One of the most media-conscious of all the agents, Meehan apparently meant what he said, but the interview was never consummated.

Nor were the hopes for Mogilny. After a dazzling start, the Sabres' momentum began slipping as the club approached the mid-point of the season. They settled into second place and Mogilny settled into an average mode of play. His game had deteriorated since the one-month mark, when Kevin Allen of *USA Today* gave him a B rating in an overall grading of the Soviets.

Makarov was the only Russian to win an A — Allen: "He's already an NHL star." Larionov received the second-highest mark, B-plus, and the comment, "an elite offensive player."

Curiously, the Canucks had no idea that Larionov had been suffering from an eye deficiency when they obtained him and only later did they give him an optical test and provide corrective measures. Larionov explained that the Soviets' idea of a physical was, "How are you feeling, Igor?"

Helmut Balderis and Viacheslav Fetisov each received a C grade. Although he saw only spot duty, Balderis had become something of an eccentric favorite because of his age and knack for providing the journalists with the quotable quote. "I used to be a Soviet gladiator. Now I work for Helmut Balderis." The lowest grades were for Vladimir Krutov, C-plus, Sergei Mylnikov, D-plus, Sergei Starikov, D, and Sergei Priakin, who received an inconclusive mark because he still had not broken into the Flames' lineup.

The *USA Today* report was the earliest of the overall ratings of the Soviets. At that time most of the teams with Russians — with the singular exception of Quebec, which rarely used Mylnikov anyway — were playing average to superior hockey. The Flames dangled between first and second in the Smythe Division. Minnesota did likewise in the Norris after a sensational start. Vancouver was in the playoff hunt, as was New Jersey, while the Sabres appeared good enough to finish first in the Adams Division.

But just a few weeks after the *USA Today* report card appeared, the Russians collectively began to slip, although some individuals continued to excel. "Larionov has for sure lived up to our expectations," said Brian Burke, Vancouver's director of hockey operations. "From the blueline in, he and Krutov are deadly."

Larionov made an easy adjustment to the western lifestyle. He dressed western, had no trouble making his way across a disco dance floor and easily won the hearts of Pacific Coliseum fans who chanted "Igor, Igor" when he touched the puck.

Krutov was another story, and an increasingly unpleasant one for the Canucks. For starters, there was his weight problem. Vladimir had never met a menu he didn't like and it had become apparent as he went from city to city. His nickname, Tank, became a source of ridicule around the league, and after watching Krutov give some half-hearted efforts, Edmonton *Journal* columnist Jim Matheson observed, "I never knew that tanks could float!"

According to teenagers' lexicon Vladimir had "an attitude." Conservatively speaking, it could be said that Krutov displayed a negative charisma quotient. "I ask him if he's happy," said Canucks' coach Bob McCammon. "He says yes. I ask him if he wants to be here. He nods. That's about all I get. It's frustrating. We all have a lot of compassion for the guy."

Sports Illustrated writer Jay Greenberg, who jetted to Vancouver for a mid-season review of the Russians, took due note of the Krutov enigma. "McCammon looks into Krutov's eyes and tries to find some light, a glimmer, a sense of motivation. He finds only a wall. Krutov will open up only in his own time, at his own pace, if he ever does at all."

Neither Krutov nor his teammate, Larionov, could — or would — find the knack for playing the NHL checking game, particularly the backchecking variety and the part that involved physical play. In this sense they were not unusual among the Russians. "They occupy the passing lanes and think they are playing defense," said Burke. "We play man-to-man, stick around the waist, and they aren't used to that."

Interestingly, it seemed that whenever possible the Soviets would bring up stories about Tikhonov's oppressive behavior. Late in November, Fetisov suffered a knee injury after a collision with John Cullen of the Penguins. Slava said he originally damaged cartilage in the knee at Quebec City during the three-game Rendez-Vous '87 series. "First game injured, second game play," Fetisov explained sarcastically. "Doctor Tikhonov says to me, 'Go play.' Coach...trainer...doctor Tikhonov," Fetisov added disgustedly.

Slava remained a baffling case to those who had been expecting to see a Russian Bobby Orr. Though he was an innocent victim of the Wendel Clark assault at Maple Leaf Gardens, Fetisov emerged from the attack as an unsympathetic figure, the butt of wisecracks. "We learned," noted Kevin Allen, "that Fetisov needs a boxing coach."

John Dellapina, who covered the Devils for New Jersey's *Bergen Record,* gave Fetisov a B-plus on his report card. "He has been disappointing as a scorer and defender," said Dellapina. "The reasons: adaptation period, conditioning problems, teammates unfamiliar with his style, unrealistic expectations. But he also does many terrific things that go unnoticed and is capable of a big second half."

According to a European player on another NHL club, Fetisov was suffering from the shock of not getting the puck back after he gave it up. "In Europe, Slava would run the show," the player said. "But now he passes the puck, waits for it to come back to him and the play is already way up the ice. It's different."

Fetisov was not unaware of his dilemma, nor was he the sole cause of the Devils' failure to play to their advance notices. Turgeon sputtered through his first 15 games, despite an opening night hat trick, and was hardly a dominating scorer. Ruotsalainen contributed little while being shuttled in and out of the lineup and on and off the power play. He seemed lost in the locker room. Injuries and lines that were set while he was injured kept Poddubny from contributing. Had they made points in the manner expected, much of the heat would have been diverted from Slava.

It also would have helped if Starikov had done more. Sergei had looked bulky when he made his first appearance before the media early in the summer of 1989. At the time it was suggested that he was built like such renowned "fireplug" NHL defensemen as Bill (The Beast) Juzda and Leo Boivin, each of whom was a bodychecking threat.

Starikov was a threat as a balloon. His discovery of the free enterprise supermarket caused his weight to climb from 212 pounds to 235. "What we've learned about Starikov," added Kevin Allen, "is that he needs Weight Watchers."

Thanks to Schoenfeld and then Cunniff, Sergei was doing plenty of watching. Starikov's woes started with Schoenfeld, who simply could not abide the Russian's tortoise-like skating. "Sergei has to react quicker to defensive situations than he's reacting right now," said Schoenfeld. "He's a good passer; he's moving the puck well, but what I'd like to see him improve is playing the man instead of the puck."

Schoenfeld waited in vain. Before Starikov had time to shape up, the coach was fired. Cunniff was to experience the same reaction to the round Russian. After 18 games he had been benched eight times; and this a player receiving $250,000 a year. And while he spoke little English, Starikov was aware of what his critics were saying about his sub-par performances.

"It's not pleasant to hear but I try not to pay attention to that," Starikov said through translator Dimitri Lopuchin. "I try to think of the positive things rather than dwell on the negative."

His most positive efforts came against the

normally tough Philadelphia Flyers and when he was teamed with Fetisov. Still, Cunniff wasn't sure about Sergei, and often he would be seen stalking through the Byrne Arena corridors heading for the elevator to The Halo, where he would watch most of the games.

"NHL hockey," Starikov explained, "is at a higher level more consistently than in the Soviet Union. Here, all the games are difficult. When we play in international hockey or in the Soviet Union and a team is down 3–2 with a minute left, people consider that game over. Here, they still think you have a chance to win. The game is never over.

"The best thing about hockey here is you can't let up at all. A game can be won or lost in a matter of seconds. The intensity here reminds me of world championship games. The pressure is the same. I also know that the game is harder for defensemen because we have the potential to have a lot more blame on us if we don't play well. I know I got confused at the start because of the English terminology in hockey, particularly in the heat of battle, but I got over that problem and I feel better.

"What bothers me most is the fighting. There's so much more physical contact here and the game is more explosive compared with the style in Europe. The players are always fighting."

By mid-December, Starikov knew he was fighting for his NHL job. Because of the excruciatingly tight Patrick Division race, Cunniff did not have the luxury of playing Starikov just to make the deal for the Russian look good. He had to go with his best skaters and Sergei was not one of them.

The ultimate confirmation of his status occurred the day after Christmas when he was given a one-way bus ticket to Utica, New York, home of the Devils' American Hockey League farm team. His NHL totals said plenty: 16 games, no goals, one assist, one point.

It is noteworthy that Starikov took his demotion with a smile. He was welcomed by coach Tom McVie, a gravel-voiced veteran of NHL and minor league coaching, and made the adjustment to NHL hockey with elan. "He's a hell of a player," said McVie, after watching Starikov work out with his forces. "He doesn't make a bad play. His skill level is outstanding."

Despite his English shortcomings, Starikov became fast friends with the rookies and over-the-hill gang that comprised the minor league club. On the trip to Newmarket, Ontario, a few players took Sergei to a topless bar, something he had never seen before. "He sat there with a grin on his face," said Dave Marcinyshyn, captain of the Utica club. "I'm sure he wasn't used to it. So many things are new to him, but he picks up on everything. He's an observant guy."

Starikov settled in comfortably, buying blue jeans, sweatshirts, leather jackets, a Walkman, and he even rented an Oldsmobile 88. "Much power," said Sergei, sounding like an auto salesman. "Very fast!"

McVie turned Starikov into one of his power defensemen and Sergei responded exactly the way he had not played in the NHL. He scored regularly, became a playmaker and impressed critics such as Herb Zurkowsky of the Montreal *Gazette,* who watched Starikov score the winning goal in a 4–2 victory over the Sherbrooke Canadiens at the Palais des Sports in Sherbrooke.

"Starikov impressed many with his on-ice habits," Zurkowsky observed. "His teammates consider him smart, patient, a skilled passer and the possessor of a low, accurate shot."

Perhaps Sergei believed that eventually the Devils would recall him to New Jersey; he left his wife Irena and his two children at their home in Caldwell, New Jersey, while he lived alone at a Utica hotel. "Management and players went out of their way to make his time a memorable one," said Zurkowsky. "He is treated like one of the guys and is included in all activities. And no one has complained of a communication problem. When words are not understood, gesticulations take over."

When Starikov moved into the upstate New York city of 70,000 he was provided with a part-time interpreter who attended practices and home games. McVie decided that it would be in the player's best interest if the interpreter was released and Starikov placed on his own. This meant that the players would have to pitch in and be cooperative. To the Utica team's credit, they made life easier for their foreign friend.

"We know he's Russian," said Marcinyshyn, "but we don't really care. When you look at him, he's not Starikov the Russian, he's Starikov the Utica Devil...Starikov the friend."

McVie saw to it that Sergei had a different roommate on every road trip. "He was never late for practice, the bus or a team meal," said McVie. "He must understand me or someone's telling him — and no one speaks Russian. He's always smiling. And he has a favorite phrase — 'No problem.'"

Zurkowsky noted that he quickly learned the custom of at least one bottle of beer after a game. "After game," added Starikov, "two, three bottles."

The hope of every minor leaguer is to get a crack at the majors. Several of Starikov's teammates already had been in the bigs, including Pat Conacher, Peter Sundstrom and Neil Brady. Sergei still was hopeful that he would get a return bus ticket to East Rutherford. "I think I play...I want to play," he concluded. "Yes, I happy. For now, no problem."

Starikov may not have known it, but there was a problem barring his return to the NHL, and his name was Aleksei Kasatonov.

CHAPTER 16

SUPER SERIES 89–90

> "This series wasn't about elite hockey. It's about laying a business foundation, about working toward the day when one can see officially licensed *bleu, blanc et rouge* sweaters on Soviet backs in Red Square. In three words: cash and carry."
>
> —*Rich Hoffman,*
> Philadelphia Daily News

In the midst of the 1989–90 season, only a few days before Kasatonov secretly signed with the New Jersey Devils on December 11, 1989, Super Series 1989–90 was begun. This 21-game confrontation between four Soviet teams and the entire National Hockey League roster marked the seventh time since 1975–76 (the first so-called Super Series) that Soviet clubs had come to North America to face off against NHL clubs. It was also the most extensive tour yet: the first time that every NHL club would play a Soviet team, in one series.

There were other firsts about this Super Series: most notable, of course, was that the four Soviet teams would actually play against their former teammates and countrymen. It was also the first time that a Soviet team other than Soviet Army, Dynamo, Wings or Spartak would face off against the NHL, as Khimik Voszkresensk joined the Russian road show and kicked the series off in Los Angeles on December 4. Khimik was the Soviet opponent in all of the first six games of the series. The entire series would be played by NHL rules (meaning there would be regulation overtime if necessary), and one of the Soviet clubs, Dynamo, had stipulated that they would only play the Buffalo Sabres if the lone Soviet defector, Alexander Mogilny, did *not* play (he didn't).

After defeating Los Angeles in the opener, Khimik went on to Edmonton (losing to the Oilers 6–2), Calgary (another loss, 6–3), Detroit (a bloodbath Khimik won 4–2), Washington (one of the few near-sellouts, which saw Khimik lose to the Caps 5–2) and finally St. Louis (they whipped a tired Blues team 6–3).

The entire Super Series was notable for two factors: the number of regular NHL veterans who were "rested" for the game their club played against a Soviet team; and the number of fans who didn't show up, even though many of the NHL teams had tied the games into their season-ticket packages. In the first game, for instance, between the Kings and Khimik, Wayne Gretzky hardly played and Kelly Hrudey, Tom Laidlaw, Dave Taylor, John Tonelli and Larry Robinson didn't take a single turn around the ice. Even coach Tom Webster took the night off, sitting in the press box while his assistants Cap Raeder and Rick Wilson ran the bench.

The crowd, considerably less than capacity (13,513), offered only a polite ripple of applause as the Soviet players were introduced before the game began, with one exception. When Alexander Smirnov skated out on the ice, the crowd gave him a hearty cheer, and the poor Russian was completely nonplussed until it was explained to him that the fans were simply reacting to the name of America's best-known vodka!

The Kings' Mikko Makela, a Finn who had played the Russians many times in his early career, summed up the feelings of many NHLers about the series when he said, "It's really tough — we shouldn't have games like these. It was more like a practice than a game."

Ironically, Makela scored the first Los Angeles goal in the second period, after Khimik had charged to a 3–0 lead. It was the first goal Makela had scored since

November 2. And despite the Kings' obvious attempt to play the whole game at considerably less than full tilt, Steve Kasper was injured by a high stick in the first period and was out the remainder of the game.

Despite perestroika and glasnost, it was noted that Khimik had the old-fashioned battery of dark-suited Soviet security types in tow. The unsmiling, mute escort traipsed with the team to watch the Kings play the Rangers, as well as following the 35-man unit to Hollywood and Marina del Rey.

Khimik Voszkresensk had on its roster two players who had been drafted by the NHL: Roman Oksyuta (by the New York Rangers in 1989, in the tenth round, 202 overall), and Igor Viazmikin (the last player drafted in 1987, by the Edmonton Oilers). Viazmikin had been a member of the Soviet Army team then, but allegedly had severe alcohol problems, was dropped from the team, and rumor even had it that he had been a cabbie and luggage handler in Moscow before being given a second chance with the Khimik team.

"That is a joke. Nonsense," said Vladimir Vasiliev, the Khimik coach, after being asked about Viazmikin's reputed problems. "I wouldn't say he drank too much. His game went down because his life changed altogether."

Khimik next trekked north to Edmonton, where they played a lethargic game, allowing the Oilers to romp to a 6–2 win before the smallest crowd, 6,804, ever recorded in Northlands Coliseum. "We didn't care what the Soviets did," said coach John Muckler. "We just wanted to keep our good habits. It was better than practising. It's always interesting to play somebody different. I don't know where Khimik is, though."

Esa Tikkanen, another Finn, who had played the Russians many times before his NHL career, set up three of the Oilers' goals, but presented a more positive attitude about playing an exhibition game against the Soviets in the middle of a grueling 80-game season: "We're on a really good streak right now and nobody wants to take a day off. It's a big win anytime you beat the Russians. Every time you play against the Russians, it's great."

Khimik's third game against an NHL team was the first episode of Russian against Russian-NHL'er, as the Calgary Flames defeated Khimik 6–3, aided by two goals from former Soviet Army star Sergei Makarov, one on a power play and the other on a breakaway. Once again the fans showed up in underwhelming numbers, as only 11,873 came to the Olympic Saddledome to offer mild applause.

As for game four against Detroit, on December 11, someone apparently forgot to tell both teams about the thaw in the Cold War, as the teams battled repeatedly. When the ice chips had cleared, Khimik had won 4–2, but four Red Wings — Steve Yzerman, John Chabot, Dennis Holland and Dave Barr — required stitches after the game.

"I'm just glad the damn thing's over," snorted Red Wings coach Jacques Demers after the game. "They wouldn't last very long in the National Hockey League, cutting like that."

Washington, DC, would present Khimik with its only near-sellout crowd and another defeat, 5–2, on December 14. "I think there has been more excitement in our area because of the trip the Caps took in September," said Lew Strudler, Caps' vice president of marketing. "I think people have been asking themselves, 'What made it so important for the Caps to pack up their entire training camp and move 8,000 miles to the Soviet Union?' A lot of publicity came out of the trip, and I think people wanted to see a Russian club."

In St. Louis, although the game had again been tied in with the season ticket package, only 8,827 fans arrived to watch Khimik trounce the Blues 6–3. The scoring was initiated by Igor Viazmikin — he who was alleged to be former alcohol and discipline problem — only 37 seconds into the first period against the Blues' rookie goaltender, Guy Hebert. St. Louis came back and played their entire game in the remainder of the first period, ending the initial stanza with a 3–1 lead. To show how little effort the Blues put forth for the rest of the night, the most notable moment for St. Louis in the second period was when newly-acquired defenseman Jeff Brown blasted the puck into the Khimik bench and nearly decapitated coach Vasiliev! The win against the Blues meant that Khimik Voszkresensk finished its six-game part of the Super Series with a .500 mark, 3–3–0.

The remainder of the Super Series was executed by Wings, Soviet Army (which, ironically, still had Aleksei Kasatonov listed on its roster until a few days before facing off against the NHL) and Dynamo, and was basically an opportunity for several clubs to watch potential Russian NHL'ers play. The Winnipeg Jets faced off against Red Army (December 27; Jets win, 4–1), which boasted two players the Jets had drafted: Pavel Kostichkin (eleventh round, 199 overall, 1988, who scored Army's only goal against the Jets) and Evgeny Davidov (twelfth round, 235 overall, 1989).

After the game Davidov was approached by the press and was asked, "How did your team play tonight?"

"Which team?" shot back Davidov through an interpreter, with a grin that needed no interpretation. Davidov flashed a Jets pin and added, "Now I have a three-year contract with CSKA Red Army team...but, I would try to play [for the Jets]. I hope so."

Jets coach Bob Murdoch hoped so too: "I think both of them are world class athletes and great hockey players. I would love to see them in Winnipeg Jets uniforms."

Altogether there were 19 NHL draft picks skating for the four Soviet teams, ten with Red Army, six with Dynamo, two with Khimik and one with Wings. Quebec led the NHL with four Soviet could-be NHLers — all from Red Army, including longtime star Valeri Kamensky. Edmonton and Winnipeg each had three Russian draft picks: Edmonton with two from Dynamo and the now-infamous Viazmikin of Khimik; Winnipeg with the two already mentioned from Red Army and Sergei Kharin on Soviet Wings. Detroit and New Jersey each had two Russian draft picks playing for Soviet teams in the Super Series, while Washington, Calgary, Vancouver, the Islanders and the Rangers each had drafted one player currently on the roster of a Soviet team in Super Series.

Another factor NHL-watchers got to observe in Super Series 1989–90 was the Russian style of play. Some were shocked to discover that the Soviets, once classified as "corner-shy" and leery of the NHL's physical style of play, were giving as good as they got.

Furthermore, the classic European (mostly Soviet) style of pass, pass, criss-cross was yielding to a more familiar technique.

"The Soviet Army squad we watched," said Winnipeg columnist Scott Taylor, "...has players with slapshots as hard as Al MacInnis'. They dump and chase it with as much success as the sixties Toronto Maple Leafs did. They aren't afraid to hack and chop in the corners. ...The Soviet players we are seeing...are an awful lot like the Canadian players we watch."

Mike Smith, GM of the Jets, happens to have a doctorate in Russian studies, and he, too, noticed the "North Americanization" of Russian hockey. "The Soviet game actually started to change on the ice as early as the mid-seventies. I first noticed it one night in Hartford when a Soviet defenseman named Bilyaletidnov took four roughing penalties against the Whalers. For the first time the Soviets had a player who said, 'Yeah, try me!'

"They see the slapshot and they pick it up. They're more relaxed, and they play that way. In the past 12 years they've picked up as much from us as we have from them. North American hockey has picked up three things from the Soviet Union: skill level, conditioning and coaching."

Red Army went from defeat at the hands of the Jets to blanking the Vancouver Canucks two nights later, preventing former teammates Igor Larionov and Vladimir Krutov from appearing on the scoreboard. On January 2 they beat the Minnesota North Stars 4–2; on January 7 the Chicago Blackhawks yielded, 6–4, and on January 9 Red Army finished its five games by edging past the Flyers 5–4. Their 4–1–0 record proved to be the best of the four Soviet teams.

The Flyers-Red Army game bears mentioning because it was one of the few sold-out games and because it was an almost-placid antithesis to the pounding, pelting Phillie-Soviet games of the past. Several Flyers sat out the game — Rick Tocchet, Mike Bullard, Murray Craven and Jay Wells — and the only Flyer who seemed to put his entire body and heart into the contest was Tony Horacek, who was trying to skate and bang his way back into the line-up after being scratched for several games. With only 4:38 left in the third period and the Flyers on a power play that looked as though it might produce the game-tying goal, Horacek crosschecked Alexei Gusarov. For one moment it appeared as though echoes of January 11, 1976, might reverberate through the Spectrum. On that date Ed Van Impe (who was sitting in the stands this night) had violently cross-checked Valeri Kharlamov, but no penalty was called. The Soviets, incensed, marched off the ice and refused to return for 18 minutes.

But on this night, 14 years later, Horacek's infraction was promptly whistled, nobody lodged a protest, and Red Army finished the winner. Red Army coach Viktor Tikhonov tried his best to be diplomatic afterwards: "Tonight Philadelphia outplayed us in the third period. I think if we had played four periods, Philadelphia would have won."

The Soviet team Dynamo scored victories against Pittsburgh, Boston and Toronto (where Russian-hater Harold Ballard had threatened to schedule the game for 2:30 a.m. and charge $50 per ticket to keep people away!). They lost to Buffalo (minus not only Mogilny, but veterans Phil Housley, Mike Ramsey, Pierre Turgeon, Mike Foligno and Scott Arniel) and the New Jersey Devils, to finish with a record of 3–2–0. The Devils game took place on January 6, and the newly-arrived Kasatonov scored a goal and an assist to help New Jersey defeat his former compatriots (Fetisov was scratched for the night, along with five of New Jersey's top scorers).

Finally, Soviet Wings posted the only losing record of the four Russian teams. The New York

Islanders were playing well at the moment (and would briefly lead the Patrick Division) and played their full roster before a crowd of less than 6,000 at Nassau Coliseum, to defeat Wings 5–4. Hartford sold out the Civic Center and defeated Wings 4–3 in overtime, while the basement-dwelling Quebec Nordiques (who did not put their roly-poly goaltender, Mylnikov, between the pipes) managed to squeak out the only tie of the Super Series, 4–4. Wings earned their only victory against the New York Rangers (who were in the midst of a lengthy losing streak) on New Year's Day, 3–1, before another miniscule crowd of less than 6,000, then finished their five games by losing to Montreal two days later, 2–1.

The final tally for the four Soviet teams was 11–9–1, and now the post-mortems began.

"All-star competition still is viable," said Rich Hoffman in the *Philadelphia Daily News,* "between the NHL and Soviets: the Canada Cup always has been a fine show. But this series wasn't about elite hockey. It's about laying a business foundation, about working toward the day when one can see officially licensed *bleu, blanc et rouge* sweaters on Soviet backs in Red Square. In three words: cash and carry.

"The Soviet Hockey Federation received transfer payments in exchange for allowing most of the Soviet players to come to the NHL. The Soviet Hockey Federation receives a cut from the gate receipts from this series, along with the NHL Players Association and the teams themselves. That is where these exhibition games fit in. They make money. They further the business relationship. But they sure aren't very exciting."

Detroit general manager Jim Devellano called the series "an unnecessary nuisance." Flyers owner Jay Snider said, "This game was forced down our throats." Pittsburgh defenseman Paul Coffey said, "The novelty has worn off." Islanders forward Don Maloney suggested, "Maybe a year or two of not seeing them might do more good than anything else." Boston's Andy Brickley said, "It seems like we're playing Russians all the time anyway."

And indeed, Brickley was right. Whether familiarity would breed the death of Super Series at some point in the near future, there was no doubt but NHL teams were "playing Russians all the time," as the NHL Soviets struggled to adapt to their new league.

CHAPTER 17

THE NHL'S ODD COUPLE

"I knew what to expect from Slava when I came. I was very concerned about the situation between us before I came over, how we would get along. But the main thing was that I really wanted to play for New Jersey."

— *Aleksei Kasatonov, New Jersey Devils*

Even before Sergei Starikov got his walking papers from the New Jersey Devils, there was talk that yet another Soviet player would be emigrating from Russia and heading for the Meadowlands. His name was Aleksei Kasatonov and, like Fetisov, Makarov, Larionov and Krutov, he had been a star in Moscow for a number of years. The Devils had the perspicacity to draft him in 1983, but it was a bit of bookkeeping that generally had been overlooked in the media.

Now, suddenly, it was big news. Word came from the Byrne Arena press room that Kasatonov would be the latest Russian added to the Devils' roster.

This should have been good news to Fetisov, who needed all the help he could get. Slava simply was not cutting the mustard in the manner expected of him. *Sports Illustrated*'s mid-season report card was hardly encouraging — a C-minus for Slava with the accompanying report:

"As he holds on to the puck, waiting to begin the attack with a drop pass, the rest of the Devils head up-ice, leaving him alone to get creamed by a forechecker. Fetisov, who was not intimidated by a fistic beating administered by Toronto's Wendel Clark earlier in the season, rolls off the checks nicely and threads outlet passes that 90% of

NHL players make only in their dreams. But it may take more years than he has left as a player to get him to jump up into the play and put his wonderful offensive skills to work. On the power play, in which he figured to be deadly, he looks like a mannequin, standing idly by while his roommate, Bruce Driver, runs the offense from the point."

Devils general manager Lou Lamoriello had hoped that the coaching change from Jim Schoenfeld to John Cunniff would have a positive effect on Fetisov. In Slava's eyes, Schoenfeld couldn't control his emotions, whereas Cunniff was less demonstrative and considered a more stabilizing influence. "Hockey is a game first," Fetisov explained. "Everyone was skating and playing under Schoenfeld, but not playing as a game." Translated, it meant that it was difficult to have fun playing for a coach who was too high after victories and too low after defeats.

Those unfamiliar with Fetisov's relationship with Kasatonov thought that Slava would be kite-high over the impending signing of his onetime Soviet defensemate. Instead, reporters were greeted by a glum and slightly stunned Fetisov. "No," Slava asserted, "I'm not happy about his coming here. The situation with the team may be tense."

The surprise generated by Fetisov's remark sent journalists scurrying for details and in no time at all they had gotten to the roots of the rivalry. Slava and Igor Larionov had been the most vehement critics of Soviet national coach Viktor Tikhonov and eventually won the right to complete their hockey lives in the NHL. The pair had hoped that Kasatonov would support their cause, but were dismayed when Aleksei remained true to the coach. In Fetisov's eyes, Kasatonov had betrayed the rebels and left them vulnerable to criticism and possible punishment.

The depth of Fetisov's open displeasure with Kasatonov was difficult to calculate, but it certainly did not deter Lamoriello from pursuing the Soviet ace. Quite the contrary, as Devils officials crowed over the possibility of landing yet another experienced defenseman in mid-season. "You have to give [owner] John McMullen the credit for drafting him," said Devils vice president Max McNab. "We needed defensive help back in 1983 and two days before the draft he asked where the best defensemen were. We said Russia, and he suggested very strongly that we draft them. He felt that something would happen that would allow us to sign them."

True enough, but the Kasatonov scenario was 180 degrees removed from Fetisov's, principally because of the total lack of advance hype. Aleksei's name was never mentioned by the press corps as a possible addition to the Devils' roster until just before his arrival in New York.

Once it had become apparent that Kasatonov would be wearing a New Jersey uniform the purveyors of "good news-bad news" moved out in force. The negativists proclaimed that the last thing the Devils needed was another Soviet defenseman who was likely to sow the seeds of dissension in the dressing room and provide a good excuse for Fetisov not to play up to his standard. The positive thinkers noted that the 30-year-old Kasatonov was an eight-time Soviet league all-star who was known to be as strong defensively as he was offensively.

The Devils officially signed Kasatonov in late December 1989, and immediately assigned him to their Utica farm team in the AHL. Lamoriello said he wanted Kasatonov to get into better shape and thought a short period in the minors would help him get accustomed to North American-style hockey.

The first thing he had to learn about was a post-game ritual where journalists select the three stars of the contest. When each of the three names are mentioned, the selected player takes a step or two on the ice and then returns to the dressing room. Kasatonov, an instant star in Utica, received such a selection and went out to take his bows. Apparently, nobody had told him how it was done. Instead of a simple step on and off the ice, Kasatonov skated an entire lap around the rink, waving to the fans as if he had been voted player of the year. Meanwhile, the fans — knowing what the ritual really was like — kept encouraging him, and Kasatonov kept waving and skating until teammate Jeff Madill skated after him and turned him around.

During Kasatonov's basic training, the Devils were attempting to make good on their coaching change.

Cunniff appeared to have the players' support and on December 26 they showed commendable resiliency, fighting from behind to tie the New York Rangers 4–4 at Madison Square Garden. Kirk Muller got the tying goal with only 25 seconds remaining. The Jersey general staff did not overlook the fact that the Rangers had taken a 4–3 lead with 5:40 to play in the third period when Ulf Dahlen skated past Fetisov to set up the goal.

Lamoriello waited until the new year before summoning Kasatonov and when Cunniff was informed he was delighted. "He's big, he's strong and he's tough," said the coach, "and he's gonna help us." Fetisov merely grunted. His displeasure was there to see and Slava did not have to embellish his feelings with more words. Unfortunately for Slava, he had no choice.

Kasatonov would make his NHL debut on Thursday, January 4, 1990, at Byrne Arena. The opponents would be Wayne Gretzky and the Los Angeles Kings. Because the megastar called The Great One was in town an unusually large media contingent descended on the Meadowlands. They attended the pre-game skate and then followed the players to the locker room.

Tall and surprisingly lean, Kasatonov was an impressive figure on the Devils' defense. "He *looks* like a hockey player," remarked SportsChannel associate producer Roland Dratch. "There's a certain style — even his facial expressions — that tells you he's a pure NHL type."

If Kasatonov was nervous about his American premiere he betrayed no such emotions, skating as if he had been with the Devils for years. "It would be nice if he could speak English," one of the stickboys remarked, "then we'd know what the guy is thinking."

Following the workout, Aleksei made himself available in the dressing room, with translator Dmitri Lopuchin at his side. His new defense partner, the affable Craig Wolanin, dressed nearby. "He's a good one," Wolanin winked. "You can tell he can skate and instinctively he makes the right moves. We can't communicate that well because of his poor English but he knows what to do and I'm working with him."

When Fetisov emerged from the shower he, too, was surrounded by the Fourth Estate and reiterated his displeasure over Kasatonov's arrival. Obviously, this was a gnawing sore for the Soviet veteran and he was making no bones about it; teamsmanship be damned.

Some reporters were hesitant to bring up the irritating relationship but Fetisov was not reluctant to discuss the matter, although in the most limited terms. He wore a frown as the television cameras moved in after the print media moved out. His answers were the same and the frown remained, although he never turned hostile on a questioner. "This is not what I wanted," Slava concluded, but added that it would not affect his play. The first test would come that night against the Kings.

Working with Wolanin, Kasatonov never missed a step. He played impeccably in his own end of the rink and displayed a knack for leaping into offensive holes when the occasion demanded. "At both ends of the ice Kasatonov looked comfortable," said *Hudson Dispatch* reporter Rich Resnick, "maybe more so than his more famous compatriot, Viacheslav Fetisov."

One theory had it that Kasatonov's presence would lift Fetisov's game, that Slava's competitive nature would be tested and that he would play better simply trying to outshine his rival. On the evidence, this seemed to be the case. Fetisov played one of his better games and the Devils skated off with a 4–2 victory. But the story was Kasatonov, and this was demonstrated by the crowds surrounding him in the winners' dressing room.

"Kasatonov was impressive," said John Dellapina in the *Bergen Record*. "He played well at even strength, drawing duty on the power play and killing penalties. He's strong, quick and skillful. He made several rushes into the offensive zone and almost picked up his first NHL point when his pass led to a near-goal by Muller midway through the second period."

A more critical NHL scout tracked Kasatonov from the beginning to the end of the game and filed this report:

First period: "Took five shifts. On first shift was caught eyeing King right-winger and gave up scoring chance on left side, but goalie Burke made the save on a slapshot. Constantly goes with puck-carrier to middle of ice and leaves his right side open. Not afraid to use his body at every chance. Not a bad first period in NHL!"

Second period: "Took seven shifts, paired both with Craig Wolanin and Tommy Albelin. Played some time on the point of the power play and did some effective penalty-killing. He was point man on Devils' power play goal and involved in melee afterwards. Showed smart hockey in his own zone but chased man with puck behind net on Kings' power play, leaving his side wide open."

Third period: "Took three shifts and nearly allowed third Kings' goal by not blocking slapshot and screening Burke."

Conclusion: "He had five giveaways over the entire game and, all in all, played not badly. He must work on staying in position and not roaming toward the man with the puck."

Cunniff made his usual appearance in the post-game conference room but appeared more effervescent than usual. Kasatonov's surprisingly upbeat performance in his debut was a tonic. "He's big, strong and excellent on the one-on-ones," said the coach. "My main concern about him is his conditioning. He hasn't played that much and I'm hoping that he can keep up. Right now, I'm optimistic. He's a smart player and he worked well together with our other players."

Dressed in a brown suit with a gold-and-black print tie, Kasatonov patiently held court until the last reporter departed. "I feel very confident," he concluded.

Just a cubicle away, Wolanin adjusted his tie. He looked over at Kasatonov, knowing that the Soviet had become an instant regular and that meant only one thing: yet another Devil defenseman would be history. "I guess," said Wolanin, "this is my swan song."

Lamoriello was cautious. "We know that Aleksei is a world-class player," the president advised, "and he could help our team significantly. But at the same time under no circumstances will we upset the present chemistry of the club."

If anything, Kasatonov enhanced the Devils' potential as a playoff team while creating a glut in the club's used-defenseman lot. Randy Velischek and Reijo Ruotsalainen were regularly scratched from the lineup, and Wolanin became a player to be showcased for possible trade. "Combine Rexi [Ruotsalainen] and Craig," said Cunniff, "and that's Alex. He's got that offensive movement and size."

Wolanin was playing with Kasatonov regularly — and worrying overtime. "You wonder if you're playing because they want to keep you here to perform for them or if they want to showcase you," said Wolanin. "There have been rumors mentioning me all year. We all realize there are eight defensemen here and more than likely one will go. You try not to think about it, but at one time or another, it enters your mind."

In addition to the Devils' eight defensemen, the club believed that Eric Weinrich, then with Utica, was ready to play in the NHL. Velischek, who often had been the unsung hero of the Devils' blueline corps, was equally despondent. "With the arrival of Alex," added Velischek, "the handwriting is on the wall. I can see my ice time diminishing with each passing game. In addition to being a quality player, Alex is a penalty killer. That was my role at one time, sort of, my ace in the hole. It's no longer my ace.

"I don't wonder why I'm the guy whose playing time has dropped. I look at it from the coach's perspective. He's got Slava and Bruce Driver, two good offensive defensemen, and Tommy Albelin and Ken Daneyko, his two top defense pairings. The fifth guy is Alex. No wonder at all to me that I'm the odd man out. Realistically, I don't do enough things well. The five guys ahead of me deserve to be there. They're all quality hockey players."

Cunniff's preference was to find a regular partner for Kasatonov. Wolanin, no matter how well he played, apparently was a stopgap until a satisfactory deal could be made for him. The coach didn't have to be told he had many egos to soothe. "We might make a trade," he conceded, "but we don't want to give anyone away. It's hard for Craig, Randy and Rexi."

If Lamoriello was worried about his club's chemistry because of potential dissension, he need not have been concerned. Wolanin, Velischek and Ruotsalainen all maintained a teamwork decorum. "They reacted with class and surprising restraint to the arrival of Kasatonov, a player who has virtually stolen their ice time," said Rich Chere of the *Newark Star-Ledger.*

It would have been difficult for Wolanin, Velischek and Ruotsalainen to dispute the Lamoriello-Cunniff lineup. With Kasatonov finding his groove, the team loomed as a winner; at least in the eyes of the media. DEVILS ARE DEVELOPING INTO A WINNING TEAM, blared a headline in *Newsday,* a daily that had given the Jerseyites only scant coverage in the past, but had discovered them with the arrival of the Soviets. "It took half a season," noted columnist Jim Smith, "but the Devils appear to have solidified into a team that could win its first Patrick Division title. Their only lingering problem is one that most teams would love to have: too many defensemen."

As far as Fetisov was concerned, there was only one too many on the roster and that was his compatriot — but hardly his comrade — Kasatonov. In Slava's view, teamsmanship went out the window when it came to Aleksei. There was no forgiving Kasatonov's alleged indiscretion — according to Fetisov — in the Soviet Union, and simply because Kasatonov was now wearing the same jersey was not cause enough for Slava to thaw their personal cold war.

Teammates were amazed by their frigid byplay. When Fetisov saw Kasatonov for the first time in six months, the greeting was limited to nods on both sides. Now that they were playing together, the greeting remained as distant. Those close to both understood that the enmity was generated by Slava and that Aleksei, if anything, would love to have an entente cordiale, but also realized that it was not about to happen.

"I knew what to expect from Slava when I came," Kasatonov said. "I was very concerned about the situation between us before I came over, how we would get along, but the main thing was that I really wanted to play for New Jersey."

The fascinating buffer between them was Devils' strength-coach turned interpreter, Dmitri Lopuchin. In many ways the mustachioed native of Nyack, New York, was one of the most important members of the organization and certainly a pivotal force in cushioning the culture shock for Fetisov, Starikov and, most recently, Kasatonov.

For the first five years of his Devils stewardship, Lopuchin had been an offstage character, aloof from the media but extremely well-liked by players and management for his tireless dedication to the team.

The moment he accepted Lou Lamoriello's offer to act as team interpreter for the Soviets, Dmitri leaped to centre stage, and became an object of curiosity to both home and visiting media.

Unlike other NHL clubs that employed Russian interpreters, the Devils were unique in that their man, Lopuchin, had been on staff for years and was considered an integral part of the hockey club. He had learned Russian from his parents, who emigrated from the Soviet Union after World War II.

"Since my parents were immigrants," Dmitri explained, "it was natural for them to speak Russian in the house all the time. When I was young, English was discouraged in our house. I was supposed to speak Russian. But my parents will verify that I was not a very enthusiastic Russian student. Where I grew up, there was a Russian Orthodox church where they taught language, history and culture. But the classes were on Saturday, which interfered with Little League and all the other things you want to do when you're a kid."

Lopuchin obtained a master's degree in sports science from Indiana University in western Pennsylvania, and began working with the Devils in 1984 through the Sports Training Institute in West Orange, New Jersey. He was named full-time strength coach in 1987.

His first opportunity as an interpreter developed during the 1984–85 season when Petr Kopta, a young Czech centre, tried out with the club. Kopta's English was weak but he could speak a bit of Russian and Dmitri proved an effective intermediary.

That experience, however, was small potatoes compared with what he was required to do once Fetisov and Starikov arrived. Lopuchin took them to the motor vehicle bureau for their licences. He took the players and their wives to supermarkets to show them where and how to shop. He helped them buy appliances, showed them how to use their credit cards, balance their checkbooks and even supervised the installation of cable television at their homes.

Lopuchin's most important function was acting as liaison between the Soviet players and the media, as well as providing a link between the players and coaching staff. "I would say I'm very functional," said Lopuchin of his command of the language. "Fluent means you can zip through War and Peace and talk at high-level political meetings at the United Nations. I can speak Russian well, I've learned how 'in tune' you have to be with the language, but I speak better English."

From the very first "meet the press" gathering in the summer of 1989, Lopuchin always could be found in the vicinity of Fetisov and Starikov. When Kasatonov arrived, Dmitri always was available to help the newcomer.

"They're not used to dealing with the media diplomatically like the players here are taught," Dmitri asserted. "Russian people — and I've been accused of it, too — are stonefaces until you get to know them. They're not used to smiling or showing any emotion. That's not the Russian way. It's difficult for them."

Similarly, it was difficult for Dmitri. He and his wife Teresa had a young son, Alex, but Dmitri's time with his family became sharply diminished. There were days when he seemed to spend more time with the families of Fetisov and Kasatonov.

"When Slava settled into his house in Jersey," Lopuchin recalled, "I took his wife, Lada, grocery shopping. I was in a hurry but it took us three hours. That was frightening. The same thing happened to every other Russian player's wife who came over.

"Over there, whenever you see anything on the shelf, you buy as much of it as you can because you know it won't be there tomorrow. Here you can't tell them when they go into a Pathmark that this is all going to be here tomorrow. They don't believe you, until they've been here and come back a second day and see it still there.

"There was just no way I could convince her because she knew in her mind it couldn't possibly be there tomorrow. She bought a lot of stuff. They were stocked."

One of the highlights of his rapport with the new players was the opportunity to bring them to visit his father, Nikolai. Fetisov was exceptionally curious about how the elder Lopuchin happened to emigrate from the Soviet Union following the Second World War.

"If you're Russian," Dmitri explained, "whether you're here and have relatives over there or you grew up there, everybody's life was affected by World War II. Everybody has World War II stories. Fetisov told me about relatives he learned were killed during the war. That's common ground between all Russian people. Meanwhile, my father wanted to know what was going on there now. It was a good time for them."

Dmitri startled Fetisov and Kasatonov when he revealed that his family roots are traceable to Peter the Great, whose first wife was a Lopuchin. He impressed the media with his courtly demeanor, his constant calm under deadline pressure and his overall grace in the interpreter's role. While Dmitri insisted that his command of Russian was "middle of the road," the players disagreed, suggesting that it was first-rate.

"The guys have been good," Lopuchin concluded. "They say my Russian is better than some of the official interpreters they've had." Certainly, nobody among the journalistic corps complained about Dmitri's work, especially after Kasatonov arrived and the added element of his disagreement with Fetisov became a central issue through the heart of the season.

The more obvious the feud became, the more the journalists pressed Fetisov for an explanation. He finally allowed that he developed a dislike for Kasatonov in the winter of 1988–89 when the top Soviet players were disputing with the Soviet authorities and coach Tikhonov in an effort to be allowed to play in the NHL. "We four were together," Fetisov said, alluding to Igor Larionov, Sergei Makarov and Vladimir Krutov. "Aleksei became Tikhonov's boy."

Fetisov pointed out that when the four players joined the NHL at the beginning of the 1989–90 season, Kasatonov chose to remain in the Soviet Union. But Aleksei was quick to offer a rebuttal that made sense to many listeners.

"A lot of players left the Red Army team at the end of last year, and they asked me if I could stay a little longer to help the young players get some confidence," Kasatonov explained. "They wanted me to stay for a whole year, but I told them I wanted to leave before the winter break."

Kasatonov and his wife found a house in West Orange, New Jersey, not far from the Devils' South Mountain Arena training base and close to where the Fetisovs lived, yet the players remained far apart.

As Aleksei became acclimatized to NHL life, he expected to be tested by league bullies just as Fetisov had been in his encounter with Wendel Clark of the Maple Leafs. He survived his professional initiation into the world of North American pro hockey goonery during his three-game American League tuneup and even was involved in a fight with Maine's Louie Crawford. When the Devils would ask him about it, Kasatonov minimized the bout's significance. "What's to tell? It was a situation on the ice where he pushed me and I pushed back. I'm not very comfortable giving blow-by-blow descriptions. But I am ready for such things. I talked with Lou Lamoriello and he told me what to expect. I knew what I had to do. That's the biggest adaptation for Soviet players — the physical contact."

In no time at all, Aleksei had become "one of the boys," in the words of teammate David Maley. "He has a great sense of humor," Maley added, "although it's obvious we don't understand everything he says."

Aleksei merely was concerned about fitting in with his new mates. "The big thing for me," the ruddy-faced Russian confessed, "is that things go fairly well for the team and for me to keep my spot. I know that some of the other defensemen feel uneasy about me taking their jobs. The team is together and I may be looked at as a disruptive influence.

"As for Slava, we spoke briefly and we agreed everything we do we have to do for the team. I knew I was coming and I knew what to expect from him. It's more Slava's problem than it is mine. But as far as the work relationship, everything is clear. No problem."

Inadvertently cast in the middle of the intra-Soviet feud was coach Cunniff. He understood that he had to tread carefully between the two and not make it appear that he was taking sides. Most of all he did not want to disturb what appeared to be a team on the rise.

"They'll put any differences behind them," assured Cunniff. "We've already talked to them about it. They're teammates. On the ice is where you have to be close."

At first Fetisov hardly acknowledged Kasatonov either on the bench, in the dressing room or on the ice. Aleksei went to great pains pointing out that his relationship in Utica with Starikov was completely different than it was with Fetisov in New Jersey. Starikov not only welcomed him but showed him whatever one could in the short time that Kasatonov remained in the AHL.

"Sergei and I have a good relationship," said Aleksei. "I played with him for 15 years and we played together the short time I was in Utica. He was able to help me, not just with the game but getting accustomed to life here. I would like to have a normal relationship with Slava. The last time we were on friendly terms was when we were in New Jersey a year earlier during the Soviet-NHL Super Series."

Cunniff continued to separate the Soviets on the ice except for brief periods when they would work together on special teams, killing penalties or working the power play. They remained separated through the early part of 1990. On January 12, the Devils played host to the Canadiens. An NHL scout filed the following report, which gives an insight into the quality of their play at the time.

First period: "Fetisov had five shifts and Kasatonov three. Aleksei was really using his size in the corners.

Slava seemed to be obsessed about passing up the middle. Fetisov had one giveaway and Kasatonov three. Slava was paired with Bruce Driver; Aleksei with Tommy Albelin."

Second period: "Each had five shifts. Fetisov was rushing the puck up the ice more than usual and showed exceptional playmaking abilities. He had two giveaways, as did Kasatonov. Aleksei was bothering Montreal captain Guy Carbonneau with his stick in the corner and with solid checks. He had a great period."

Third period: "Fetisov had seven shifts and Kasatonov six. Slava had three giveaways to two for Aleksei. Kasatonov took a hooking penalty at a bad time. Carbonneau scored at 14:50 and it turned out to be game-winner. Fetisov has a bad habit of chasing players behind the net, leaving the slot open."

Conclusion: "Although he was the goat, in a sense, Kasatonov appears to be an all-round solid defenseman. Fetisov had a good game but often appears tired and slow."

It was a fair assessment. Kasatonov, despite his late start in the middle of the NHL season, fitted into his new league like a perfectly-meshed gear. Fetisov played in spurts; at times he was outstanding and as speedy as some of the better NHL skaters, while on other occasions he appeared slow and preoccupied. Some critics insisted that Slava was showing his 31 years but Aleksei disagreed.

"The question is of adaptation and not whether he is too old," said Kasatonov. "I didn't have any doubts about Makarov with his physical capabilities. He's at a high level of physical development. I thought Slava would adapt faster than he did. That's probably why they sent me to Utica. I still feel I have the physical attributes that will allow me to play at high levels."

A turning point of sorts occurred on February 6, against Edmonton. Cunniff, who was only mildly pleased with his defense pairing, decided to unite Fetisov and Kasatonov for the first time on the same regular unit. In the first period they each took seven shifts and killed penalties four times. Fetisov pokechecked opponents instead of using his body. On one occasion it cost Kasatonov, as his man stepped around him and scored. In the second period Fetisov impressed with his offensive passing, once setting up Ruotsalainen with a neat feed on the fly. His shot also was very effective from the point. While having a propensity for getting caught in ahead of the play, Kasatonov was caught short and as a result, Edmonton had several two-on-one opportunities.

In the third period both appeared to be running out of steam, but hung in through the sudden-death overtime. Fetisov logged a total of 22:30 minutes while Kasatonov was on for 24:45. Cunniff was pleased with the results. "I put them on together," he explained, "because I wanted to put them against Mark Messier's line. I wanted Alex and Slava to read off each other, and they did. They played well as a pair."

So well, in fact, that Cunniff decided to keep them together through the rest of the regular schedule — barring some defensive calamity — even if Fetisov continued his cold war against Kasatonov. Cunniff insisted that the feud had not been a problem up until now and he didn't foresee it as an obstacle in the future. "I haven't seen it affect the team," he added. "But I don't see a change for the better coming either. I've known North Americans on the same team who didn't talk to each other."

After 42 games of an 80-game schedule the Devils had a record of 20–18–4 and occupied first place in the Patrick Division. It was a fragile lead. Each time Cunniff hoped to put a long winning streak together, the team invariably would take a few steps backward. If Fetisov was miffed over Kasatonov's appearance on the team, it didn't show in his relationship with other teammates. Once, when the team was playing in Edmonton, defenseman Ken Daneyko and forward Troy Crowder slept through their wakeup call and missed the flight back to New York. When the pair failed to show up at the airport, their teammates wondered aloud what had happened to them. Without blinking an eyelash, Fetisov exclaimed, "I think they defected!"

With the home stretch looming, Fetisov and Kasatonov played well enough to remain a cohesive defensive unit. Aleksei was the more consistent but every so often Slava would play the brand of two-way hockey that confirmed Lamoriello's decision to pursue him. One game in particular showed Slava at his world class best.

The Devils were visiting Mario Lemieux and the Penguins at Pittsburgh's Civic Arena. It was a Patrick Division matchup with major ramifications, since only four of the six teams gain a playoff berth, and the Penguins loomed as one club the Devils would have to surmount. On this night John MacLean scored two goals — one short-handed — while Doug Brown and Patrik Sundstrom added scores in the 4–2 New Jersey win, but the night really belonged to Fetisov. He assisted on two goals, blocked two shots and was on the ice for all the Devils' goals. Even his arch-critic, Hugh Delano, went out of his way to laud the Russian.

"Slava gained tremendous respect for withstanding a brutal cheap-shot hit into the corner boards by Lemieux," said Delano. "And he did a terrific job checking Lemieux."

There was 11:49 remaining in the second period when Lemieux blasted Fetisov with a blindside check so hard that it rattled the boards and made the crowd of 16,236 gasp. Mario did it behind the play and deserved a charging penalty, but referee Terry Gregson apparently didn't see it. Teammates immediately came to the aid of Fetisov, who had to be restrained by a linesman from going after the Pittsburgh superstar.

Chewing on a wad of gum after the game, Fetisov was unfazed over the incident. He merely smiled and shrugged when asked if he considered it a cheap shot by Lemieux, but teammate Tommy Albelin was less reluctant to talk. "Slava is a big, strong guy," said Albelin. "He can take it."

Cunniff agreed. However, the coach was wondering how many of Slava's giveaways he could take without running for the aspirin bottle. It was a cogent point because the Devils now knew they were in an excruciating race for a playoff berth and Fetisov would be a major player down the stretch.

CHAPTER 18

BUILDUP TO A LETDOWN

> "Everything here in the NHL is different from the Soviet Union. Life is different; there's a different style on the ice. NHL play is much more physical, much more difficult every night. Everybody wants to hit the Russians."
>
> — *Igor Larionov, Vancouver Canucks*

Despite their obvious differences, Slava Fetisov and Aleksei Kasatonov emerged as the Devils' best defense pairing and the most pivotal element in their drive for a playoff berth. "They may be the best two players we have on the team now," said WABC Radio broadcaster Larry Brooks, who handled the analysis for the Devils' games. "Alex is proving to be a world class defenseman."

While the Sabres had slipped to second place in the Smythe Division at the far turn in the race, they still were performing admirably enough to boast the second-best record of the 21 teams (33–22–6), right behind the Adams Division-leading Boston Bruins. Alexander Mogilny obviously was not hurting their cause.

The team with great expectations — and, conversely, an awful record — that literally died by the three-quarter pole was Vancouver's Canucks, who had counted so heavily on the Russians. Every player on the team knew that management was paying Krutov $750,000 a season over three years — split evenly between Vladimir and the Soviet federation — and each Canuck could see before their eyes what a poor deal it was for Vancouver hockey fans, let alone the team.

In the entire month of December, when other Smythe Division teams were solidifying their positions, the Canucks won only twice and Krutov might as well have remained in Moscow for all the good he was doing. Just what effect Krutov had on his teammates is a moot point. A year earlier Paul Reinhart was the Canucks' catalyst and one of the NHL's best defensemen. This time around, he was middle-of-the-pack at best and usually worse than that. Listening to Reinhart, reporters knew that he was just short of fed up with Krutov.

"When we get traded," said Reinhart, "we all believe we need time to get used to new teammates, new surroundings, new systems. Add language and lifestyle to that, and you understand what Vladimir is going through. At the same time, we're under the gun to win hockey games, and it's a lot easier to be patient when you win. Krutov is the typical Russian, not very emotional or talkative. If you accept that as a cultural difference, then fine, but there are guys on the team who don't understand that. They reach out to try to make him feel at home and after a while expect him to reach back. Nobody's turned away. But some are nearing that point."

They got closer to that point in the final two months. The Canucks were firmly in last (fifth) place in the Smythe with 18–35–10, which translated to 20th worst in the NHL. By comparison, the Flames were just tickled with Sergei Makarov, and they could afford to be. The Stanley Cup champions were at the opposite end of the Smythe standings, sitting in first place — third overall in the league — with a solid 29–19–13 record, primed for another run at the championship. Unlike the disliked Krutov, Makarov continued scoring at a merry pace and continued to stir commotion over his good work.

By the beginning of March, newsmen belonging to the Professional Hockey Writers' Association began preparing to vote for rookie of the year, for the Calder Trophy. Had Makarov slipped significantly in the scoring statistics by this time, they would have no choice but to ignore him because of his advanced hockey age. But there was

Sergei, not slowing down a bit and way ahead of his competitors. What to do?

Lloyd McLachlan of the *Windsor Star* counselled his co-writers with one bit of advice: vote for Makarov. "His 52 assists are testimony to an unselfish attitude and superb playmaking ability," said McLachlan. "Skeptics [among the voters] are still lurking out there. They call themselves purists. They wail loudly about the injustice of a 31-year-old veteran, a three-time Soviet player of the year, being classified as a novice. But if the central issue is fairness then nobody else but him is more deserving under the current set of rules."

NHL director of communications Gary Meagher acknowledged that the arguments around Makarov were unusual to say the least. "There's not been a trophy as controversial over the years," said Meagher.

Next the league's legal counsel, Gil Stein, got into the act. "The rule is very clear," said Stein. "I'll quote from the yearbook: 'An annual award to the player selected as the most proficient in his first year of competition in the National Hockey League'. It can't be any clearer than that."

Many reporters were convinced that some of their colleagues would vote against Makarov simply because they wanted to be different, because they wanted to cause controversy. "The Calder Trophy race will tell you how many members of the PHWA are interested in making the news, as opposed to reporting it," said Tim Campbell of the *Winnipeg Free Press*. "The way the rules stand and the way the players have played, I believe Makarov should be the winner. You may not agree with the rules of eligibility, but as they stand, he is the winner.

"But among the writers, there's a considerable movement afoot to take matters into their own hands. There's a large contingent ready to be the news instead of the medium to deliver it."

When the Blackhawks fired another public relations salvo in favor of their 20-year-old sharpshooter Jeremy Roenick, Calgary's vice president in charge of hockey operations Al MacNeil fired right back. "Roenick's too young," chuckled MacNeil. "He's not even old enough to appreciate such an award. We shouldn't let 20-year-olds win it. It's not fair!"

Some in the Vancouver dressing room whispered that it was unfair to lump Larionov in on the media abuse being heaped on Krutov. Igor's play overall had been acceptable to say the least and superior at other times. "Everything here in the NHL is different from the Soviet Union," Larionov explained. "Life is different; there's a different style on the ice. NHL play is much more physical, much more difficult every night. Everybody wants to hit the Russians."

Sports Illustrated's evaluation of the Soviets' progress offered a perceptive insight into why Larionov was acclimatizing better than Krutov. "Igor had campaigned for years for the opportunity to play in the NHL," the magazine explained. "His wife, Lena, a former figure skater who had travelled extensively outside the Soviet Union, is embracing all aspects of North American life."

Larionov added, "It will be most difficult for me to go back to Russia. Here, there are no problems. There, there are many problems."

Yes, there were problems on the ice as they would develop in the last two months. After an exuberant run carried them to first place, the Flames inexplicably sputtered in the stretch. Makarov, though he still had the points in his favor, was quietly accused of being a floater, a player who only gives one hundred percent when the spirit moves him and at other times floats or cruises in low to middle gear. Coach Terry Crisp became fed up with Makarov's endlessly long shifts that disrupted his club's flow.

"I let the long shifts go during the first 40 games because Sergei hadn't been used to coming off when the line broke," said Crisp. "He believed in the Russian concept that possession is nine-tenths of the law. And I love it. But we sometimes have a different style of hockey that the Russians can't quite grasp and one we used that would kill them. They won't dump-and-chase. And Makarov wouldn't dump. There were times when there was no way he was getting into the open and nobody knew where to go when he was doing his thing. There have been little things that he's done his whole career that we had to adjust to and some of our players had to adjust."

Unfortunately for the Flames, the adjustment left something to be desired. In Makarov's case, the buildup was turning into a bit of a letdown. In Fetisov's case, the pairing with Kasatonov was not working out as neatly as it had appeared in the first weeks of their reunion.

Where first place once appeared a good bet, the on-again-off-again Devils now had the wobbly look of a club that would be fortunate to even make the playoffs. "We're self-destructing," said coach Cunniff, "killing ourselves with unforced errors, slowly destroying ourselves, beating ourselves."

He didn't have to look beyond a dreadful 4–2 home loss to the Winnipeg Jets, although New Jersey outshot the visitors 16–1 well into the first period. In a situation like that the team carrying the play must beware of a critical mistake that could quickly turn the tide in favor of the retreating team. Here, again, Fetisov was the culprit, resorting to a tactic that might have worked in the Soviet Union but, time and again, proved vulnerable in the NHL.

Although he had control of the puck and ample time to make a safe, accurate advance, Fetisov made a ridiculous pass into the slot. It was promptly picked off by Jets defenseman Dave Ellett who flicked the rubber past goalie Sean Burke. "It was a crazy pass," said the ever-candid Cunniff, "and one that Slava should not have made."

But Slava kept making them at the most unpredictable times, while Cunniff appeared to be maintaining a laissez-faire attitude toward the Soviet star, hoping that he would get his act together in time. "The hard thing with our defensemen," the coach explained, "is that we have only one guy — Kenny Daneyko — who plays the North American-style game. Slava, Alex, Tommy Albelin and Bruce Driver are all more finesse players. The Soviets are big and strong and can pin guys on the boards, but they're not going to bang guys around in front of the net.

"What teams are doing to us is going hard to the net. With Sean Burke in goal, that's not so bad because he's big enough to whack them when they get in there. But with Chris Terreri, teams take advantage."

Complicating matters for Slava was his awareness that the Devils suddenly found themselves immersed in an extraordinarily close Patrick Division race. Any one of the six teams — Rangers, Islanders, Penguins, Flyers, Capitals or Devils — could finish on the bottom of the division, which meant that it was imperative that New Jersey put together a winning streak, even a modest one. Then there was the media pressure. The C-minus rating Fetisov obtained from *Sports Illustrated* got continent-wide attention and merely accentuated the letdown in relation to his pre-season buildup.

"I don't think Slava thought he would come over here and dominate," countered Lamoriello. "But a lot was said about it and whenever you have high expectations then maybe self-inflicted pressure takes over. I don't believe there is any other kind of pressure. No matter what Slava does, people will have expected much more. I have total confidence he'll be the player we feel he is. I have no problem with that. I don't feel any different now about what his abilities can do for this team."

Fetisov had never played an 80-game schedule and never was involved with two or sometimes three airplane flights a week across a country. As the games became more important, so the hitting become more severe. "In principle," said Fetisov, "it's more difficult than I had anticipated."

Devils captain Kirk Muller had observed his Soviet teammate closely. "I get the feeling," said Muller, "that Slava's biggest adjustment is how you have to go every day — the mental part. You have to be ready to go the next night and even the next morning for practice. We're a hard-working team even in practice. Obviously, he has the talent, but he hasn't adjusted to the grind yet. That's what makes Wayne Gretzky so great. He does it night after night and he knows when he can take it easy and conserve. Then he turns it on."

Mark Johnson, the Devils forward who had played against Fetisov in the 1980 Olympics, was another who was fascinated with the Soviet's evolution in the NHL, particularly now that the club had reached the heavy point in the campaign. "All of a sudden," said Johnson, "the season has become a real test emotionally and physically. It will be interesting to see how he plays from here on. The Soviet system is geared to prepare them for the Olympic Games, the world championships and the Canada Cup. The team has two months to prepare. They can practice so they peak emotionally and physically for those events. In the NHL, you play well one night and the next night you have to come back and play well again. You get to March and it's a grind."

While many of the observations about Fetisov were ominous, to say the least, Slava himself often took them with humor. Like Makarov, Fetisov was eligible for the Calder Trophy for rookie of the year although he knew that he had scant chance to win the prize. Slava just laughed it off. "I'm not a rookie," he giggled, flashing his toothy grin, "I'm a pensioner. I'm an old-timer in the Soviet Union. Here I'm a rookie. Actually, I would have liked to have won the Calder Trophy ten years ago, if I played here. It doesn't matter; individual prizes were never a priority for me."

Fetisov won back a large contingent of fans, if not rookie votes, on March 3, in a critical game with the Penguins at Byrne Arena. With Mario Lemieux sidelined with a back ailment, the Devils had an opportunity to create space between themselves and Pittsburgh. After trailing 1–0 in the first period, New Jersey rallied for a pair of goals, first by Kasatonov and then Fetisov, enroute to a 6–5 victory. "The team had come to the edge, you might say," said Fetisov while towelling himself in the jubilant Jersey dressing room. "You can't lose when you're at the edge. This win was very important for our team. We were losing our confidence."

The win also was important to restore off-ice confidence. Just when a thaw appeared to be developing in the frosty Fetisov-Kasatonov relationship, yet another revelation was made public that threatened to destroy whatever gain had been made. This time a story broke by way of Vladimir MacMillan, a sports reporter for Tass, the official Soviet news agency.

According to the Russian newspaperman, the genuine — as opposed to various other published explanations — reason why Fetisov had been giving Kasatonov the cold shoulder had absolutely nothing to do with Aleksei's friendship with coach Tikhonov and everything to do with a bit of spying Kasatonov had done while he and Slava were teammates on the Soviet national team.

Visiting Montreal on a North American vacation, MacMillan said Fetisov's gripe was that Kasatonov kept watch on him over a period of two years in the Soviet Union while they were roommates as well as a defensive tandem on the ice. MacMillan maintained that Kasatonov kept a personal log of Fetisov's violations of team drinking regulations as well as the times when Slava broke curfew.

In an interview with David Johnston of the Montreal *Gazette,* MacMillan added that the diary was given to Kasatonov's wife who, in turn, gave it to Tikhonov's wife, and eventually it landed in the coach's hands. According to MacMillan, Fetisov was shown the log by Tikhonov in 1989 when Slava told his coach that he wanted to leave the Soviet Union to play in the NHL. "Tikhonov told Fetisov he could make life difficult for him if he persisted in his desire to leave," said MacMillan.

The Kasatonov spy story, as MacMillan explained it, was originally revealed by Tass senior hockey writer Vladimir Dvortsov, who had not actually written the story. However, MacMillan added, "It's already a well-known story in Moscow."

The son of James MacMillan, a onetime television engineer at the American embassy in Moscow, Vladimir grew up in the Soviet Union as a result of an unusual romance. His father, a native of Washington, DC, married a Soviet citizen whom he met when she worked for the US embassy. James MacMillan and his wife remained in Moscow, where Vladimir MacMillan grew up and turned journalist.

In Montreal, conversing with Johnston, MacMillan delivered a free-swinging analysis of the NHL's Russians, criticizing some and lauding others. As for Kasatonov, MacMillan suggested that he was not as tough a character as Fetisov. "Aleksei is the kind of guy who, if you tell him, 'C'mon, guy, do this!', he'll say, 'Okay, I'll do it.' He doesn't have a tough character. Of all the Soviet players, Fetisov and Larionov have the toughest characters. Krutov and Mylnikov aren't very intelligent or very tough."

Having observed the hockey stars in Russia, MacMillan allowed that he wasn't the least bit surprised that Fetisov and others were having difficulties in making the adjustment to the NHL system. "It's an absolutely different way of life in North America," he pointed out. "In three days in Canada or the United States, you see more than you ever see in your whole previous life in the Soviet Union. For some guys it is really a shock. You think over where you used to live and how you simply served as a slave, seeing nothing, absolutely nothing, except hockey. Even when Slava and the rest of them toured North America when they played for the Soviet team, they only saw cities out of the windows of buses."

One of the Soviets continued to see North American cities exclusively out of the windows of buses and that was Sergei Starikov, forgotten by everyone except the Devils organization. Starikov's demotion to Utica of the American League meant long bus trips to such little-known places — at least to a citizen of Moscow — as Hershey, Pennyslvania, Newmarket, Ontario and Springfield, Massachussets.

Starikov adjusted well, in part due to the understanding of Tom McVie, the gravel-voiced coach of the Utica Devils and onetime NHL coach. McVie knew almost immediately that Sergei was not going to pout over his failure to make the NHL varsity and would contribute to his organization.

"He didn't speak much English when he arrived," said McVie, "but that didn't bother me a bit because the game of hockey overcomes a lot of barriers including language. I've been around hockey long enough to be able to recognize a skilled player on sight and this guy impressed me after a couple of workouts. The key to me was the effect Sergei had on my younger players and, do you know what, every player who skated with Starikov lifted his game a notch. That tells me that Sergei had a very positive reaction on everybody he skated with, especially the kids."

One knock against Starikov in New Jersey was his weight. McVie solved that problem by playing the Russian overtime. He took a regular turn, worked the power play and killed penalties. By playoff time, Starikov was not slim but he was in his best condition of the season and his movements reflected those of an international star.

"There were a couple of givens about Sergei," McVie explained. "For one thing, he never made a bad pass and for another he never got his team in trouble by overhandling the puck. The rough stuff didn't bother him and he took his man out cleanly. After all, the guy is built like a Zamboni machine. When he'd take a guy out along the wall, you'd hear a THUD! throughout the building."

Like many foreign players, Starikov at first fooled McVie into thinking he knew less English than he really did know. One afternoon the coach delivered one of his vintage vitriolic speeches, well-laced with expletives. A telltale smile broke over Sergei's face and finally McVie, himself, broke up, pointing at his defenseman: "You sonofabitch, Sergei, you understood every god-damned word I said!"

Starikov kept grinning, and finally replied, "Hey coach, no problem." With that, the room broke up with laughter.

McVie had steered Starikov to Whitesboro, a nearby community with a large Russian settlement. The natives welcomed him like a national hero and Sergei soaked up the sentiment, returning as one of the family whenever the schedule permitted.

"He could speak Russian there to his heart's content," said McVie, "and we even supplied him with a part-time interpreter in case he ever needed any more help. But after a while, I told the interpreter to stay home; I wanted Sergei to learn English on his own at the rink and darned if he didn't do well at it. As a coach, I found it a pleasure to work with this guy and, in retrospect, I don't know what I would have done without him."

Utica, located in central New York State, is a moderate drive to Buffalo, which meant that if he had any time off, McVie could catch some NHL hockey at The Aud. The lure was not merely the games but a chance to view the Russian who was supposed to be the brightest prospect of all, Alexander Mogilny.

In its report on the Russians, *Sports Illustrated* had given the 20-year-old a B-minus rating. "Some of the Soviets may master the NHL game in two years," said the magazine, "just in time for their marvelous skills to desert them. But by defecting at 20, Mogilny has time and perhaps the best set of legs in hockey on his side. After spending most of the first half of the season trying to beat people one-on-one, he is learning to use his teammates and showing signs of becoming a prolific scorer. The moral of the Mogilny story is that the team that shopped at the black market by hiring a defector seems to have gotten the best deal."

Perhaps it looked that way from the viewpoint of a magazine writer, but those within the Sabres organization knew otherwise. In plain English, Mogilny was an unhappy camper at a time when observers like the *Sports Illustrated* reporter were saying the sky was the limit in terms of his talent.

Then it happened. Mogilny became the centrepiece for a melodrama that wouldn't pass for bad fiction if it had come out of Hollywood.

CHAPTER 19

THE MOGILNY MELODRAMA

"Alex was a mystery to those in the motherland and he remains so to those in a strange land. Mogilny, himself, provides few clues. He will speak, but is reluctant to reveal too much of himself."

— *Steve Dryden,* Inside Hockey

There was something strange about Alexander Mogilny even when he was playing his best hockey in early January and totalled nine goals and 16 assists for 25 points. Elusive might be the best way to put it — both on and off the ice. As a Sabres forward, Mogilny had some of the classic dipsy-doodle moves displayed by Hall of Famer Max Bentley, one of the most difficult players to nail in open ice.

In the Buffalo locker room, Mogilny was just as difficult to corner. Between the Sabres PR people, who effectively shielded him, and his agent Don Meehan, it was virtually impossible to arrange a lengthy one-on-one with the Russian, as it was easy to do with the likes of Slava Fetisov. In late winter, this pattern was taken for granted by members of the press corps.

"Alex was a mystery to those in the motherland," commented columnist Steve Dryden of *Hockey News,* "and he remains so to those in a strange land. Mogilny, himself, provides few clues. He will speak, but is reluctant to reveal too much of himself."

During the first week of February 1990, he said even less to his general manager, coach and teammates.

To some of those who shared the dressing room, Alexander suggested that he had had it with the Sabres and would quit the team. While some may have taken him seriously, most of the players were shocked when the team emplaned for a match against the Blues in St. Louis without Mogilny. On Saturday, February 10, the Mogilny dream went up in smoke and nobody, least of all coach Rick Dudley, could discern precisely why, although there were theories galore.

The most obvious was Mogilny's fear of flying, a condition that became exacerbated as the season went on and more trips to distant Vancouver and Los Angeles became necessary. Another dealt with the culture shock of a youngster settling into new surroundings without the restraints of a totalitarian government to disturb him.

Not long before he had walked out on the team, Mogilny had completed the purchase of a townhouse in Amherst, New York, a middle-class suburb of Buffalo. His agent's associate, Pat Morris, was astonished how emotional Alexander was at the real estate closing. "On the day we completed it, Alexander cried, 'This is something that never could have happened in the Soviet Union.' It was like an advancement of freedom."

Yet for all the joy, there obviously was a powerful negative reaction to his new celebrity status. Dryden, one of the few journalists with whom he would confide, persuaded him to reveal his anti-media feelings. "I don't like when people read about me in the paper some BS," he said. "I know if I will say something the reporters are gonna write down different story. I know about that."

It was not an unusual response for Mogilny but now that he had engineered his walkout, reporters descended on the story like hyenas to a zebra's carcass. Since Alexander was nowhere to be found in St. Louis, journalists covering the club turned to teammates for clues to his unexpected exit. "I knew he had trouble with the flying," said Christian Ruuttu, "but no one knew how serious it was."

No one knew what to make of Mogilny; that was the dilemma. Just after the All-Star break he missed a two-game road trip to Philadelphia and Chicago. The first report indicated that he was suffering from the flu. That was cancelled by a later disclosure that his fear of flying aggravated an already weak stomach.

"Many were suspicious of the fear of flying excuse as Mogilny had been a world traveler in recent years with the Soviet national team," noted Jim Kelley of the *Buffalo News*. "While he appears to have a definite dislike for flying, there never were any reports Mogilny missed a trip with the Soviet Junior or National Teams."

The dark side of Mogilny began to surface in more and more of the analyses. Some players described his playing style as selfish, in that he would hesitate or refuse to pass the puck in obvious situations when a pass was in order. Others defended him. General manager Gerry Meehan, a master at public relations, asserted that the adjustment to North American ways was more difficult than people imagined. "We expected we would have problems with him adjusting," said Meehan. "He always has been extremely nervous and jumpy. It's not just the fact of flying, it's the frequency. With all the changes in his life, the fears and uncertainty, it builds up. Put that with the fact we have to get on planes three and four times a week and I think it all just overwhelmed him."

Armchair psychologists jumped into the fray offering "insights" faster than Mogilny could shoot pucks. Agent Don Meehan pointed out that his client may have been traumatized by seeing film or video of airplane crashes, something that he never had seen in Russia. There were skeptics within the Sabres organization. One suggested that Mogilny had a completely distorted view of what NHL life would be like: playing a game and then partying. "He had no concept of the training regimen, practices and other demands of the 80-game schedule," said the Sabres official.

Another questioned the sincerity of the fear of flying rationale. "He had been all over the world before he got here," said a source close to the Sabres. "Lots of guys don't like to fly, but they do it. He has done it, too."

Gerry Meehan was disturbed by the walkout but sympathetic to his forward. "He had big problems," said the general manager. "He had to adjust to the intensity of the schedule. I don't think he was ready for that. The cultural adjustment was slower than we had hoped."

Having missed the game in St. Louis, Mogilny now was faced with the question of when he would rejoin the club. He decided to take a train to Chicago two days later, but Dudley chose not to use him. Instead of returning with the team by plane to Buffalo, Mogilny took a bus. By this time it was impossible to discern the Sabres' plans for Alexander, or his own frame of mind.

On February 18, Mogilny celebrated his 21st birthday. He would practice with the team, be scratched from the lineup, practice again with the team and then be left waiting for further developments. As the controversy swirled about him, Alexander rebuffed the press. He seemed to have one notable confidante in the media, Steve Dryden of *Hockey News,* and on Saturday, February 24, he talked to the columnist.

Only a night earlier he had returned to the Sabres' lineup after missing six games. Buffalo beat Hartford 7–3 at The Aud. Mogilny scored a goal and registered an assist and was lustily cheered by the home crowd. Following the game he joined his teammates at a party but the festive spirit was gone by the next morning.

"I've got big problem," he told Dryden. "I watched on TV some plane crashes. I don't know. Everything up here in my head."

Dryden pressed him on certain issues such as his failure to live up to expectations. Mogilny allowed that he had not played as well as he was capable of performing but added that there had been extenuating circumstances. "You know this is my first season. There are a lot of problems, a lot of changes in my life. I don't think I can do my best right now."

Mogilny was circumspect about his Russian girlfriend, Alexandra, a model who was staying with him, and he discussed his confidante, Sergei Fomitjov, who engineered his defection from the Soviet Union. Some of Mogilny's critics accused Fomitjov of being a latter-day Rasputin, casting a negative influence over the man. On the other hand, there were those who insisted that

Fomitjov had been a major source of encouragement to Alexander.

"He help me always with my problems, with my relationships," Mogilny said in Fomitjov's defense. "I can't imagine if Sergei will be gone how I'm going to live here. He is my right hand."

Dryden came away from the interview as baffled by Mogilny as anyone. "There are no easy answers to him," he concluded and the speculation continued. It didn't help Mogilny's cause when a report surfaced in a New York paper that Alexander was using the fear of flying as a cover to be traded to another team, preferably the high-paying, high-profile Rangers.

Jim Kelley of the *Buffalo News* speculated that Mogilny might be seeking a life in the New York City area. Why New York? For one thing, a huge Russian community was growing in the Brighton Beach section of Brooklyn near Coney Island. The area is loaded with Russian restaurants, night clubs and stores of every kind. To Brooklynites it is known as Little Odessa, and the feeling was that Mogilny would feel more at home there than in Amherst. "He thought he'd feel a little more comfortable there," said teammate Benoit Hogue.

Despite talk that a deal with the Rangers was imminent, no trade was made and Meehan reiterated that Mogilny's potential was too enormous to allow him to forsake the player so early in his NHL career. "You don't just give up on someone like him," Meehan insisted. "Not as a person or as a player."

Another possibility was that Alexander was suffering the pangs of national schizophrenia, not knowing whether he was a Soviet or an American citizen. "I don't know who I am," he confessed. "Probably I'm still Russian. What can I do? But I don't want to be Russian. It's taking time."

The Sabres high command seemed willing to take its time in bringing Mogilny back into the fold. At first the club gave him an "indefinite medical leave of absence" in February so that he could receive therapy and counselling, and then he was welcomed back. To compensate for his fear of flying, the team arranged for him to travel by limousine to games. It was impossible to predict just how he would perform from game to game.

"There are some nights," noted Jim Kelley, "when he does not appear to be a factor on the ice or in harmony with what the rest of the players are attempting to do. There are other nights when Mogilny is the difference in the game."

Some of his teammates distrusted him, while others were more willing to be patient in order to make a determination later in the campaign. "At one point," said Hogue, "he thought the guys were talking behind his back about his fear of flying. We talked to him and told him we were on his side. We just want him to come every night and play."

The trade deadline came and went in March and Mogilny remained a Sabre. That is, he still wore the Buffalo uniform when Dudley decided to dress him and he was still admired by many fans. But his contribution to the team diminished in the final month.

Whether Alexander Mogilny would ever recapture the glory of opening night remained a moot point. If the answer was positive, the Sabres might be able to do something that had not been possible for too many years: get out of their division in the playoffs and take a run at the Stanley Cup. If not, Buffalo would suffer through yet another dismal hockey spring.

In the meantime the Sabres attempted to find solutions to the flying phobia. On the encouraging side was the knowledge that Wayne Gretzky had battled his flying fears for years and only in the late eighties and early in 1990 was he able to reach a level of security, if not comfort. Before reaching this state, Gretzky had tried hypnotism, sitting with the pilot, sleep, sitting in the back of the plane and sitting in the front of the plane.

Vancouver *Province* columnist Jim Taylor offered a possible solution. "Maybe," suggested Taylor, "the Sabres should keep punching him in the stomach and shouting 'TIKHONOV.'"

Buffalo hockey broadcaster Ted Darling wasn't so sure it would work. He remembered watching Mogilny on one flight and swore that Alexander lurched to the bathroom 15 times.

Don Meehan said his client was in a "panic" about his problem. Players asserted that Mogilny had a negative impact on the team. "It's affecting us," said defenseman Grant Ledyard.

Another source of potential irritation was the conflicting feelings of coach and manager about when and when not to play Mogilny. General manager Gerry Meehan said he backed Dudley's decision not to play Alexander when he was scratched from the lineup. "Rick was under no obligation to play him or not to play him," said Meehan. "Rick is the coach of the team and it was his decision whether to use him or not. I made it clear from the start that the decision lies with Rick."

Dr. Marilyn Ruman of Encino, California, a clinical psychologist who has helped entertainers overcome a fear of flying, chimed in, saying it has become an increasingly common phobia in the wake of much-publicized plane crashes in recent years.

"A phobia has a life of its own," she said. "It truly paralyzes an individual. It's as if the catastrophe is happening to them, and they can watch it. The problem is most people don't seek treatment. They spend their life avoiding flying, which, of course, makes it more frightening."

To which Dudley replied, "I don't think an English-speaking psychiatrist can help a basically Russian-speaking Soviet with a problem like this."

The coach appeared sympathetic although disturbed by the turmoil and distractions caused by the Mogilny mess. "I've watched the kid on planes," Dudley explained. "From the time we take off to the time we land he is in a state of terror. I can relate to that because I was a bad flyer myself. I'm still not a good flyer but I'm a lot better than I was. I really had to work on it, to concentrate on not being so paranoid and trying to relax, I had to learn some relaxation techniques. To deal with somebody's subconscious, you have to talk with the person — it's a pretty profound conversation and if you don't understand exactly what is being said, you can't work with the person. Unfortunately for Alex, he had nobody to talk to."

As Mogilny's woes circulated around the league, more players, coaches and managers reacted with sympathy. Former Detroit coach turned broadcaster Harry Neale claimed that every NHL player has at least two horror stories about air travel, and Mogilny's troubles brought them out.

"When I was coaching the Red Wings, we lost an engine on takeoff and we only had two to start with," Neale recalled. "The plane was vibrating and it was pretty scary. I remember John Ogrodnick had just signed a big contract after his 50-goal season [1984–85] and he looked over and asked me, 'Harry, am I going to get a chance to spend some of that money?'"

Ogrodnick remembered it well. "Sirens and buzzers were going off and we could see the firetrucks on the runway below. You might think after something like that you'd be more wary of airplanes but I actually think you get more confidence in them because, after all, you made it."

Neale disagreed. "We lost the game that night, 10–2. I think we were happy just to be there."

Other Sabres began to reveal their own personal distaste for air travel. The club's star scorer Rick Vaive would sit with the pilot when possible and found that it was comforting. "It helps," said Vaive. "You get more of a sense of what they're doing when you see how the plane responds you have a better understanding. It's a calming experience."

Mike Robitaille, a former Buffalo defenseman who became one of the team broadcasters, was another with flying problems. "Everybody's different and has different feelings about it," said Robitaille. "I know people who aren't bothered by it tend to laugh and say, 'just do it,' but it's not that easy. It's a very real problem, and if it's your problem, nothing anyone says or does can make it just go away.

"There were times when someone could have offered me $10,000 to get on a plane and it wouldn't have mattered. No amount of money or anything else can change the way you feel about getting on that plane."

Robitaille had counselling and employed mind control techniques to ease the anguish. "It's a serious problem," he concluded, "and it has to be dealt with in a serious way."

But those who probed into the Mogilny problem kept getting the impression that there was more to it than the flying. When the Sabres visited Winnipeg, *Winnipeg Free Press* columnist Hal Sigurdson cornered Buffalo's assistant coach Don Lever and asked him if there was more to the mess. "Maybe," Lever conceded in a telltale admission, "but we've been told to say the only problem is the flying thing. He really does hate it, by the way."

Lever added that Mogilny had, at times, been a discipline problem. "He's very good at negotiating," Lever added. "Just like North American kids, he likes to test authority to see how much he can get away with. And he's got a big ego."

Mogilny accepted the Sabres' offer of a chauffeur. For a game in St. Louis, the club went by jet. Mogilny arrived after a 13-hour car ride from Buffalo, chauffeured by Mike Winters, a friend of Sabres trainer Jim Pizzutelli. Also aboard was Fomitjov. The three stayed overnight and drove back to Buffalo the morning after the game.

The media reaction was mixed. Buffalo is a one-newspaper city with a main hockey writer, a back-up and a couple of columnists. One of them, Jerry Sullivan, spoke for thousands of fans when he concluded that the Sabres "should do everything possible to protect their investment. But they also have a large investment in this season. It's becoming more and more apparent that they'd be better off finishing it without him."

With the home stretch looming and first place slipping farther from the Sabres' grasp, that seemed like a good idea. But the ultimate decision would be made by Gerry Meehan, who had one thing going for him: at least his club was assured of a playoff berth. That was not the case in New Jersey where Lou Lamoriello was hoping that somehow his Devils could fit all the pieces into place and make a run for the top. To do so, they had to have Fetisov playing world class hockey and, considering the minefield he was skating through, that would not be easy, especially since Wendel Clark of the Maple Leafs still was after his scalp.

PART 3

CHAPTER 20

FETISOV - CLARK, ROUND TWO

"It's not entirely clear how these matters are handled in Russia, but around here Soviet defenseman Viacheslav Fetisov is, how you say, a dead duck."

— *Dave Fuller, Toronto* Sun

As any hockey fan knows, the most important segment of the regular 80-game NHL season is the period following the annual All-Star game. Then teams get truly serious about the run to schedule's end in early April, when the final determination of playoff berths is made.

But for most of the teams that had hired Russian players, a determination of a playoff berth had already been made. With one of the worst teams in league history, the Quebec Nordiques were so firmly ensconced in the Adams Division cellar that no manner of miracle could extricate them for the late season run. Goalie Sergei Mylnikov had virtually become a non-person in the eyes of coach Michel Bergeron. Sergei had played only five games through mid-January, had won nothing and was no longer a factor at the Colisée.

The Vancouver Canucks continued spinning their wheels and no manner of lineup juggling by coach Bob McCammon could save them from skating in mud. By the All-Star break it was apparent that Igor Larionov and Vladimir Krutov were consigned to a team that would have an early spring recess.

At the other end of the spectrum were the Sergeis — Makarov, the full-timer, and Priakin, the part-timer — in Calgary. The Stanley Cup champion Flames may not have been burning as bright as they had hoped but at least they were battling for the top of the Smythe Division, and there was no doubt that they would cruise into the playoffs, as would the Buffalo Sabres, with or without Alexander Mogilny on the roster.

That left only one team armed with full-time Soviets with a playoff berth uncertain — the New Jersey Devils. Rookie coach John Cunniff was continually striving for consistency and it was constantly eluding him. Unlike clubs in the five-team Adams, Smythe and Norris divisions, a Patrick Division outfit knew at the outset that not one but two clubs would be eliminated from the playoffs, because of the six that were in that sector.

"With the NHL enjoying the greatest parity it has ever known," said Devils vice president Max McNab, "it was a toss-up who would make it and who would not in the Patrick."

So complicated was the Patrick race that the New York Islanders, for example, got off to a dreadful start — they were counted out of playoff contention by Thanksgiving Day — then amazingly recovered in December and January, before faltering again in late winter. The Rangers zoomed into first place early in the season only to tailspin to the cellar in January before climbing back to the top.

The Penguins, who had not only made the playoffs a season earlier but reached the seventh game of the Patrick Division finals, confounded their critics. They fired coach Gene Ubriaco early in the campaign, and replaced him with Craig Patrick, who was both coach and manager. Patrick refused to hire a new full-time coach and found himself further burdened when superstar Mario Lemieux developed an agonizing back problem that wouldn't go away. The Penguins' fate hinged on Lemieux's health, and nobody could tell when he would be healthy and when he would be sidelined.

No less confusing were the Philadelphia Flyers, for

most of the same reasons. The balance-wheel of the Flyers' defense, Mark Howe, also developed a back ailment and he, like Lemieux, could not be counted on from game to game. Similarly, Ron Hextall, Philadelphia's crack goalie, aggravated a groin problem that had sidelined him early in the year and he, too, became a patient, not a player. Add to that front office bickering and the eventual trade of Flyers standbys Dave Poulin and Brian Propp and the Flyers were left in a state of disarray.

All of this should have helped the Devils and, to a certain extent, it did. "A year earlier we were trying to play catch-up from the start of 1989 until the end of the season," recalled forward John MacLean. "At least when 1990 rolled around we knew we had a good chance to finish in the money. We also knew that a lot of work had to be done if we were going to beat out Pittsburgh and Philadelphia."

Much of that work would have to be done by Viacheslav Fetisov and Aleksei Kasatonov. The latter seemed at ease throughout his transition period, even though Fetisov was not making it easier for him because of Slava's perceived feud. But Fetisov remained an enigma who often grated his coach with erratic play.

Cunniff, for his part, worked hard at remaining calm about it and succeeded. "It's going to take time for Slava to get used to playing in the NHL," the coach often repeated. "He has habits that he picked up over ten years playing in Europe. He's got to recognize it. He has to break some of those habits. Other teams are hitting him all the time, playing his body. Defensemen over here don't have the time to make the plays like they do in Europe; the game is so much faster here."

And tougher. Fetisov made that discovery after Wendel Clark of the Toronto Maple Leafs rained blows on him without fear of counterattack; he learned it again when Mario Lemieux levelled him with a thundercheck during a game at Pittsburgh. When it came to physical play, Fetisov seemed willing to engage the enemy but often he appeared hesitant.

One sports psychologist who observed the Devils believed that Slava's problem had much to do with his puzzlement over fighting in the NHL and the fact that it was something he had never done — no matter how courageous he was — in the European game. "He seems worried about being lured into a fight," the psychologist explained, "because of some anxiety about losing it and embarrassing himself. To avoid that perceived embarrassment, he simply does not choose to fight, even if the situation might invite such a reaction."

It wasn't that Slava didn't think about fighting. Shortly after the pummeling he received from Clark early in the season, Fetisov asked the Devils' enforcer Jim Korn to work with him on hockey fighting technique. "The next time I will be ready," Slava assured the media. "The next time will be different."

The "next time" arrived shortly after the All-Star break in late January. Clark and Fetisov would oppose each other for the first time since their one-sided bout in October, but the match had other significance. The game was being played exactly two years to the day that Doug Carpenter had been fired by the Devils, and the Maple Leafs coach was making the most of the occasion.

Early that Friday his club held its morning pregame skate at the Meadowlands rink — following the Devils' workout — and Carpenter held court like some visiting deity in the ramp between the two benches. His club was hot, having won four straight games and eight out of their last ten. They had become known as the Toronto Macho Leafs at home because of their penchant for punching out the opposition, while scoring at least four times for 12 out of their last 13 contests. Carpenter could hardly restrain his gloating although he made a modest attempt at it when a SportsChannel TV camera flashed on for an interview.

"We all have pride," said Carpenter, "and when I come to Jersey, because of what happened to me here, there's a little bit of revenge involved."

The magnitude of the meeting did not elude

Fetisov nor the sellout audience of 19,040 at Byrne Arena. "I'm ready tonight," Slava asserted.

However, the Devils were not ready. Early in the game defenseman Ken Daneyko handed the puck to Toronto's Gary Leeman for the 1–0 goal at 10:49 of the first period. New Jersey had one upbeat moment when Doug Brown forced a turnover by Tom Fergus of the Maple Leafs. Kasatonov got the puck and drilled a 15-foot shot between goalie Jeff Reese's legs for his first NHL goal. The score remained 1–1 until late in the second period when Leeman deflected a shot past Sean Burke while the Devils were on a power play. In the third period Toronto put the game out of reach and all that mattered to the fans was the Clark-Fetisov business. Would there or wouldn't there be a Round Two?

Slava would see that there would. After taking hard runs at several Leafs, Fetisov perceived an opportunity to nail Clark as the teams battled for puck possession at centre ice. A rather lumbering skater, Clark moved along the right boards past the visitors' bench toward the red line. Fetisov, who had been positioned a good distance away on right defense, detected Clark's advance early in the Leaf counterattack.

In a trice, Fetisov went into high gear and there was absolutely no doubt what he had in mind: a crushing bodycheck near the Devils' bench. Normally, in a situation such as that, the attacker is gambling. Because of the distance involved — in this case, about 30 feet of ice — the prospective victim has ample time to pick up the enemy on his radar and defend accordingly. That is, if he is not distracted by other matters, such as controlling the puck.

Fetisov was well into orbit before Clark even had a faint notion that he had been lined up for the assault. The Toronto forward was concentrating on the right side of the rink where the Devils were trying to stop him. About one second before Fetisov actually made contact, Clark detected the attacker. Since his dexterity is not up there with the Gretzkys and Lemieuxs of the NHL, Clark was unable to completely elude Fetisov. Wendel pulled up but the charging Devil managed to get a piece of the Leaf — and what a piece it was. Slava made contact with Clark's right knee, causing Wendel to wince in momentary pain.

Fetisov completed his orbit and returned to the play in his defensive end. Although some Toronto players screamed at the referee to call a penalty there was no whistle, and the puck skimmed toward the left boards not far from the New Jersey goal. Noticing Clark moving toward the gridlock, Fetisov made a beeline for the Leaf once again and hit him solidly.

There are some who would say that Fetisov should have been better prepared for the retaliatory moves that followed. Certainly, if the experience at Maple Leaf Gardens was an example, Slava should have expected the worst from Clark.

At best, he was semi-prepared. As Clark dropped his gloves for the traditional launching of a hockey fight, Fetisov did likewise, but that was as far as he would go under the circumstances. Clark tossed a mighty right cross that caught Slava over the left eye and sent the Russian down to the ice.

Superficially at least, the vignette was humiliating to the Jerseyites. In two out of two bouts, Fetisov had been overwhelmed by Clark's fists without returning a single blow. "Fetisov was an immediate loser when he was knocked to the ice with one punch that left him with an ugly cut outside his blackened and swollen left eye," commented Rich Chere in the *Star-Ledger*. "Or *was* he a loser?"

There was at least one other side to the story, and that was Fetisov's gumption in going after Clark — and several other Leafs, it should be noted — although he was acutely aware of the possible consequences. Fetisov showed guts, and many players sensed that at the time of the episode and in the dressing room an hour later.

"Clark made his point," said Jim Korn, "and Slava made his point with the bodycheck. He could have avoided Clark all night and he didn't. That showed a lot. Clark is one of the toughest guys in the league. They fought and Clark hit him with a punch. Big deal. Slava got up."

Fetisov's "point" was well-taken. Slava may have suffered another ego blow as the swelling grew into a grayish puff around his left eye, but Clark was betraying agony down the corridor in the visitors' dressing room. The original charge that Fetisov had put on Clark had damaged Wendel's knee sufficiently for doctors to wonder when he would be able to play again.

"I don't think Fetisov redeemed himself," Clark proclaimed as Toronto reporters crowded around him. "If you want to carry a big stick in this league you have to stick up for it sometimes. It's up to him if he wants to play that way."

Until the gravity of Clark's injury had been made known, Carpenter could hardly contain his gloating. During the latter part of the game, when the result was no longer in doubt, he vehemently cursed several of the Devils from his position behind the bench and singled out Fetisov for particular abuse. In the dressing room he was asked if he held bitter sentiments toward Lou Lamoriello, the man who had fired him in Jersey. Carpenter got right to the point. "Still do!" he shot back.

When Carpenter was advised that Clark's knee injury could be serious, the coach launched into a tirade against Fetisov. "He tried to cut the legs out from Wendel. It was a dirty, rotten trick."

That was debatable and Fetisov was in a debating mood, as were his supporters. The pro-Fetisov camp was quick to note that even though Slava had been cut at 8:57 of the third period and required stitches, he did not take the rest of the night off and returned to the ice. "He made sure to be back for the end of the game," noted Frank Brown of the *Daily News*. "If there were any questions about his toughness, Fetisov certainly answered them."

Perhaps, but there were as many questions raised about Fetisov-Clark Round Two as there were answers. For one thing there was the question of Slava's reaction to the fooferaw. "Clark was trying to show that I'm afraid of something," he said. "But I'm not afraid of anything at all on the ice. Maybe there are some things I don't know how to do, like fighting, but I'm trying to acquaint myself with all these activities."

That was a good idea because New Jersey and Toronto had a rematch coming up on February 17 at Maple Leaf Gardens, and already the warning signals were out both in New York and Toronto that this would indeed be a bloodbath. Both cities have tabloids struggling for circulation, and the Fetisov-Clark war was a natural for the sensation-mongers.

On the Devils' side the battle for readership featured the *Daily News, Post* and *Newsday,* all tabloids. Only the *News* (Frank Brown) and *Post* (Hugh Delano) covered the team on a regular basis and Delano, with more space at his disposal, was the more likely to grab the story and run with it.

In Toronto there are three English newspapers, the *Globe and Mail,* the *Star* and the *Sun.* Over the past decade the *Globe and Mail* has de-emphasized its sports section, whereas the *Sun*'s coverage of hockey has continued to grow. Over the years the *Star's* sports side has remained consistently strong. It was the *Sun,* Toronto's only tabloid, that exploited the Clark-Fetisov story more than the others.

The detonator for the exploding articles was a revelation from the Maple Leafs that Clark's collision with Fetisov had resulted in the Toronto forward suffering a partially torn medial ligament in his right knee that would likely sideline him for the remainder of the regular schedule. "Fetisov tried to cut the legs out from under him," said Carpenter. "You don't do that in the NHL."

Carpenter's carping was questionable, to say the least. To begin with there was ample proof that Slava had attempted to deliver a clean check and only Clark's last-second reversal caused the injury. And even if one assumes that Fetisov's motive was entirely vengeful and he was deliberately attempting to injure the Leaf, surely Slava had good reason to be angry, based on the unprovoked pummeling he had received in Toronto. Furthermore, Carpenter was being naive. As anyone who has watched and chronicled hockey over the decades knows, the knee check is not uncommon. In the 1990 playoffs for example, Rangers forward Kris King disposed of both Washington Capitals stars Dino Ciccarelli and Kevin Hatcher with questionable knee checks.

Fair or foul, the Fetisov maneuver and the Leafs attempts at retribution would continue to be exploited as much as the sports editors would allow. Certainly, the Toronto *Sun*'s Wayne Parrish would permit the brand of newspapering that would have made William Randolph Hearst's yellow journalism look pink by comparison.

For starters, in its January 29 edition, the *Sun* ran a photo of Fetisov with WANTED in bold letters above his head. Underneath, the *Sun* ran a checklist: Team: New Jersey; Position: Defenseman; Crime: Cheap Shots; Last Seen: Brendan Byrne Arena.

Although Fetisov didn't even receive a two-minute penalty on the play in question the *Sun* had unequivocally ruled him guilty and was depicting him as a convict on the loose. The inflammatory poster was accompanied by a story by Dave Fuller, who left no doubt that the *Sun* had stopped just short of branding Fetisov a criminal.

Fuller led off his article as follows: "It's not entirely clear how these matters are handled in Russia, but around here Soviet defenseman Viacheslav Fetisov is, how you say, a dead duck."

Here we have a clear presumption on Fuller's part that the Maple Leafs will be headhunting for Slava when the teams meet on February 17. Lest there be any doubt, Fuller continued: "The Leafs may well publish a batch of Most Wanted posters with comrade Fetisov's mug on them." Fuller reiterated Carpenter's accusation that Fetisov deliberately targetted Clark's knees.

Not to be outdone, Delano signalled a warning for the beleaguered Devil in the *Post:* "Viacheslav Fetisov may need a bodyguard when the Devils play in Toronto on February 17," Delano asserted. "Without saying so directly, the message from Toronto is that the Maple Leafs will be out to get Fetisov. Toronto management and players are furious at what they consider dirty tactics used by Fetisov to seriously injure Wendel Clark. Fetisov had better keep his head up when John Kordic, Lou

Franceschetti, Luke Richardson or Brian Curran are on the ice."

Interestingly, when questioned by Toronto journalist Tim Haffey, the Maple Leafs sounded considerably less hostile toward Fetisov than the tabloid journalists made them appear.

"I don't think it was a deliberate attempt to injure," said Richardson. "There've been hard feelings between the two and when that happens guys play hard against each other. When Fetisov went across to hit Wendel, Wendel tried to jump out of the way and they got their legs hooked. Maybe it looked dirty on tape but you have to realize that Fetisov was just trying to stand him up at the blueline. Those things happen a lot. So maybe it looked deliberate but I don't think it was."

Other Maple Leaf players reiterated Richardson's point. Yes, they were disturbed that their ace was injured and, yes, they would no doubt attempt some sort of retribution but, no, they didn't feel — as the tabloids insisted — that Fetisov had gone out of his way to hurt Clark.

"I don't think that when Fetisov hit Clark, Fetisov was thinking that he was going to tear his knee up," said Toronto defenseman Al Iafrate. "But I can tell you one thing; when Wendel hit him, he was trying to hurt him."

Fetisov's motives were irrelevant in terms of the retaliation possibilities when next they met. "I'm sure a lot of guys are going to want revenge for Wendel," assured Vincent Damphousse. "We'll try to hit Fetisov more than we usually do and I'm sure he'll be ready for it."

By now the confrontation began snowballing simply by virtue of one newspaper not wanting to be outdone by earlier reports. At first the "war" stories were limited to the tabloids, but soon the normally conservative journalists were joining in the fray. FETISOV BETTER WATCH OUT, HE'S BLAMED FOR CLARK INJURY, warned a headline in the *Newark Star-Ledger.*

Carpenter appeared determined to make the most of the propaganda in order to spur on his troops. "It didn't look bad at the time," snapped Carpenter of the Clark-Fetisov collision, "but Fetisov got him good. If they want to maim players and hurt players that way, it's okay. They'll learn."

Conveniently, Carpenter overlooked the fact that the Devils — as opposed to his goon squad — were one of the NHL's cleaner teams and that Fetisov's record as a clean defenseman was obvious to most opponents. It also was plain to Slava that he was fast becoming a marked man.

"I'm not a punching bag for anybody to take a shot at," Fetisov retorted. "Anybody who takes on me is going to have to answer back to me. I'll do what I can with my checks or my hands. I play hockey and because of one moment on the ice, they make big story. The NHL has its own rules and I still don't understand why things happen. One type of player practices hockey all the time and you have another type who practices on the speed [boxing] bag."

The Maple Leafs roster was sprinkled with players who worked out on the boxing bag, with John Kordic the most notorious of the bunch. Kordic had been in and out of trouble with both the league and his teams ever since he had broken into the NHL with the Montreal Canadiens. When he wasn't driving coach Carpenter to distraction with his off-ice shenanigans, Kordic was a somewhat effective fourth-liner whose primary focus was on hitting and, as they say in hockey's major league, enforcing. If there was a quintessential NHL goon it was John Kordic, and it would be Kordic that Fetisov would have to fear the most.

Acutely aware of thc buildup on the other side of the trenches, the Devils' Lou Lamoriello had to devise a strategy of his own. And since the Maple Leafs — abetted by the Toronto media — seemed bent on turning the next meeting into a blood war, Lamoriello had to decide whether he would sacrifice any of his regulars in the battle or bring in reinforcements.

New Jersey's top hitters included Ken Daneyko, David Maley, Jim Korn and Brendan Shanahan. Each of them was necessary to perform a playing role in the club — as opposed to fighting — and hardly could be wasted in a mere police action. With that in mind, Lamoriello sent an SOS for Troy Crowder.

A towering presence, the 21-year-old Crowder measured 6–4, and 215 pounds, which he had demonstrated could be put to good boxing use. Despite these assets, Crowder had some qualms about being pigeonholed as an enforcer and left the Devils during the 1989 training camp. He gave his hockey pants to his brother and gloves to his dad and lost track of his skates altogether. Instead of hockey, he pursued a career with his landscaping-construction company in Sudbury, Ontario.

Fortunately for the Devils, Crowder stayed in touch with Lamoriello and, by mid-season, had an itch to return to the NHL. In January he began working out and declared that he was ready to return. Appropriate, in view of the storm clouds emanating from Toronto.

Just two days before the scheduled Devils-Maple Leafs rematch, the Devils revealed that Crowder would be ready to suit up in Toronto. "I can play a few shifts a period and play tough," Crowder said. "I've heard a lot of yipping from the Maple Leafs about Clark. Personally, I don't think Toronto has the team to do anything about it. It might just be idle threats, but somebody might do something stupid."

So intense was the interest by this time that even the staid *New York Times* got into the act. Alex Yannis, who regularly covered the Devils for the newspaper, noted "the Maple Leafs have implied that they will seek retribution against Fetisov."

The primary topic of conversation at the corner of Carlton and Church streets outside Maple Leaf Gardens an hour before game time was the anticipated bloodshed. Questions were being asked and nobody had the answers: Would the Leafs go after Fetisov? Who would be the primary attackers? How effective a deterrent would Crowder be and if he needed help, who would assist him on Jersey's side?

The fans didn't have long to wait. Less than seven minutes into the game Crowder and Korn took the ice for the visitors while Kordic and Curran were dispatched by

Carpenter. Crowder wasted little time attempting to waste Kordic and the two heavyweights slugged it out in a fight that proved to be a standoff. Just as the officials were ready to restart the game after the fight, Curran threatened Kasatonov and that moved Korn into action. Clearly the aggressor — he later was assessed a fighting penalty and a game misconduct — Korn belabored Curran with blows until the linesmen restored peace. As Korn left the ice an irate Maple Leafs fan reached over and tried to attack the Devils forward. The unruly spectator was taken away by security police.

Once the fights were dispensed with, the teams settled down to hockey and, again, the Devils fell short of their mark although they outplayed the Maple Leafs territorially. Sean Burke was guilty of blunders on Toronto's first and third goals, enabling the Leafs to skate off with a 5–4 win. New Jersey outshot them 45–25 and Fetisov, unfazed by the furor, played commendably enough to win kudos even from his most severe critics.

"Give Slava credit," said Delano. "He showed poise and composure and played a good game in a difficult atmosphere."

What remained to be seen was whether Fetisov — and his friendly enemy Kasatonov — would show poise and composure in the most critical segment of the season, the home stretch, as the Devils strained to make the playoffs.

CHAPTER 21

HOME STRETCH HEROICS

"I know in the NHL, players dream of the Stanley Cup. I play now in the NHL and I have the same dream. The team is playing well and I think the team will go far."
— *Slava Fetisov, New Jersey Devils*

There are two overall goals for every National Hockey League team. The ultimate, of course, is to win the Stanley Cup, emblematic of the professional championship of the world. But in order to qualify for the Cup competition, the other goal must be attained, and that is to be among the 16 teams that reach a playoff berth from among the 21 starters.

This has never been a simple feat for the New Jersey Devils. The franchise was a disaster in its original form — the Kansas City Scouts — and was no bargain after moving to Denver, where it became the Colorado Rockies. When John McMullen purchased the club and moved it to the New Jersey Meadowlands, he understood that a long rebuilding process would be necessary.

Sure, enough, it was long and agonizingly painful. Once, after the powerful Edmonton Oilers had defeated New Jersey, superstar Wayne Gretzky referred to the Devils as a "Mickey Mouse outfit." This was an unfortunate commentary for several reasons: Gretzky had been quoted out of context and he never had meant any harm to either McMullen or the team. (Actually, Gretzky was upset because his personal friend, Ron Low, had been suffering in goal for the Devils, and Wayne was empathizing with

Low more than anything.) But, as so often happens with a chance remark, it was not only blown out of proportion by an eager media looking for a story, it had lengthy ramifications. (To this day, the Mickey Mouse label still shows up in stories.) McMullen, naturally, was furious and Gretzky apologetic. Meanwhile, the Devils had been stigmatized above and beyond the call of their play and just about everybody was unhappy about it except the reporters on the beat.

Compounding the felony was the Devils' chronic inability to gain the one measure of respectability that separates the Mickey Mouse teams from the others: the elusive playoff berth. Try as they might under an assortment of coaches, the Jerseyites just couldn't put enough wins together to pass two other Patrick Division teams and qualify.

The 1987–88 season didn't appear to be any different. As always there was some promise early in the season but the inevitable slump followed, and then the sacking of coach Doug Carpenter. His replacement, Jim Schoenfeld, showed promise at first, then slumped, and by early March appeared incapable of producing any significantly different result.

Poof — something unusual happened. Trailing the Capitals in Washington, the Devils rallied with a pair of shorthanded goals and came away with a victory in an arena where they almost never won. Then they caught fire. Win followed win in late March until New Jersey actually moved to within sight of a playoff berth.

Unfortunately, it was late in the season and the fourth-place Rangers seemed to be too far ahead to catch — barring an unforeseen collapse. Incredibly, the pieces began falling into place. It started a week before season's end when the Devils clobbered the Rangers at Byrne Arena, in a game that featured a decisive penalty shot goal by Pat Verbeek, who beat John Vanbiesbrouck in the New York goal. The Devils were still alive. It came down to the final night of the season. New Jersey at Chicago. To make the playoffs the Devils had to beat the Blackhawks in Chicago Stadium, and they did it on a sudden-death overtime goal by John MacLean. After that the Devils whipped the Islanders and Capitals, before succumbing to Boston in the Wales Conference finals.

A year later the franchise fell on its face again, to the abject disappointment of McMullen. The hope, now, was that 1989–90 would be different. The playoff berth that had seemed so promising after the opening night win at Philadelphia had become an uncertainty. On February 18, the Devils occupied fourth place in the Patrick Division but their position was precarious. They were two games under the .500 mark (25–27–7), had an unimpressive 57 points and were ranked 14th overall in the league.

"In a sense," said Ken Daneyko, "we were fortunate that nobody was running away with the division and we still had time to straighten ourselves out."

Inconsistency drove coach Cunniff to distraction, yet despite all manner of line changes and defensive combinations New Jersey could not extricate itself from the morass. At the week ending February 25, the Devils had dropped to four games under .500 (26–29–8) with 60 points, hanging in fourth place as if by a gossamer string.

As luck would have it — Devils' luck, that is — the Islanders had developed an even worse slump, if that were possible, and were plummeting to the subterranean depths of the division. Philadelphia had lost aces Ron Hextall and Mark Howe for the rest of the season due to injuries and Pittsburgh learned that Mario Lemieux would not be available until the final weekend of the campaign, if at all.

And still the Devils floundered. By the week ending March 4, they were four games under .500 (27–31–8) for 62 points. Throughout the February-March doldrums members of the press corps alternately wondered about and clamored for a trade. Some players felt the same way. Randy Velischek, outspoken before training camp opened — he was openly critical of Fetisov's signing — turned vocal once more.

"I pray that I get out of here," he asserted. "I've had enough. It's time to move on."

If nothing else, Velischek's timing was exquisite.

The trade deadline — March 6 — was just around the corner and there were several clubs anxious to land an experienced stay-at-home defenseman like Velischek. The Quebec Nordiques was one such club, and a likely one, as Lamoriello had a history of dealing with them.

But there were other uneasy Devils as well. Craig Wolanin, the young defenseman with all-star potential, continued to believe that he was being showcased for a deal, and then there was Reijo Ruotsalainen, who had become more recognizable in civilian clothes than in uniform. Rexy seemed destined for Edmonton since Oilers general manager Glen Sather had gone public stating his desire for a mobile defenseman who could play the point on the power play. Ruotsalainen had played for Sather once before and was considered a good possibility to do it again.

One thing was certain; if Lamoriello did not make a deal, the prospects for the Devils hanging in for a playoff berth did not appear bright. "A deal would not be enough," one newsman said at the Byrne Arena press room on March 6. "It will have to be a BIG deal."

The official trade deadline was 3 p.m. but, historically, deals often have been announced much later because of any number of bureaucratic obstacles that could hamper the negotiating process.

At 2:45 p.m., some members of the SportsChannel television crew entered the press room. One of them headed for the Devils front office to get late news.

Yes, a deal had been made. New Jersey had traded Jim Korn to Calgary for a fifth-round draft choice. Someone asked a front office secretary, "Is that all?" The woman smiled. "That's all — for now."

It was 3 p.m. and, ostensibly, all dealings should have been complete. As the press room began filling up, the journalists couldn't help but discuss the critical situation. The moving of Jim Korn, who played only occasionally, hardly was the stuff on which playoff hopes are built. Surely Lamoriello would not stop there.

By 5 p.m. the tension in the press room could be sliced with a hockey stick and the same situation held 20 yards down the hallway, where players filtered into the Devils' locker room. It was common knowledge that Craig Wolanin was one of the Jersey players being bartered and it also was known that Quebec Nordiques captain Peter Stastny was being offered around the league.

Only days earlier reports from Buffalo indicated that the Sabres had a lock on Stastny and would trade Benoit Hogue for him, but the exchange never was consummated. Some players were unsure whether Wolanin should — or would — dress for the pre-game warmup.

Meanwhile, Lamoriello was busily tying the pieces of his package together. Ruotsalainen was moved to Edmonton after his puzzling five-month stay in East Rutherford. In exchange, the Devils obtained young defenseman Jeff Sharples.

"In New Jersey I didn't feel anything," said Ruotsalainen, who said more upon leaving than he had all season. "For me it was all hot dogs in the press room. I didn't play any and I never felt a part of the Devils. After what we were talking about when they signed me, I was a little surprised the way they used me. They didn't feel I could help the team. I could feel it right away when the season started. I wasn't the right guy there. They signed me to help the power play but when you don't play, how will you ever get going?"

It was the typical plaintive alibi of the failed player. In truth, Ruotsalainen was a disaster for the Devils. He was given an opportunity at the start of the season and constantly was guilty of the giveaway, the missed pass or the errant shot. Unlike his dressing room mates, he never seemed to be a part of the team. One reporter suggested that Rexy held the NHL record for getting dressed and leaving the rink faster than anyone in history. In effect, when they obtained Sharples the Devils were getting something for nothing — no matter what Ruotsalainen would do for the Oilers.

Game time at Byrne Arena is 7:45 p.m. As time marched on word was passed around the press room that Lamoriello would meet the media before the national anthem was sung. Now the rumor was spreading that the

Devils' leader had, in fact, completed a truly major deal. Peter Stastny had become a Devil and not a Sabre, as most had thought. To obtain the Slovak centre, Lamoriello had to give up 22-year-old defenseman Wolanin and future considerations. Some reporters speculated that the future consideration was defenseman Randy Velischek.

The passing of the trade deadline — and the movement of three teammates — had a positive effect on the Devils. "We had a lot of bodies here," said captain Kirk Muller, "and some of them couldn't get ice time. Now we're down in numbers and those of us who are left know what we have to do."

Two of those were Viacheslav Fetisov and Aleksei Kasatonov. Hockey's odd couple still were at odds with each other, two months after they had been reunited on the Devils' blueline. Making matters even more ironic was Cunniff's etched-in-stone decision to pair Slava and Alex together on defense through the end of the 1989–90 campaign, no matter what transpired between the trade deadline and the final game of the season.

"They may not talk to each other," said Cunniff, "but one thing they do is read each other. They're terrific defensively. Of course, sometimes I have my heart in my mouth the way they go up offensively but I can play them together and know I'll get a solid game."

Frigid as their social relationship may have been, both Fetisov and Kasatonov agreed that their professional relationship was positive for each other as well as the team. "It's normal for us to be together on the ice," said Aleksei. "We've practiced and played together for ten years. We've played in the same pair and felt comfortable with each other for a long time. It took a while to get it together but our skills eventually fell into place.

"As for our personal differences, we've put them aside for now. The first order of business is to win. The team is going to be first for both of us. The way we're playing together Slava wants to win and play well with me."

Reporters who followed the team were constantly searching for signs — even little hints — that there was some warming of their relationship. And there was, tiny though it may have been. After a goal, they were seen giving each other the traditional players' high-five signal and there was a beginning, at least, of on-ice dialogue. Somebody asked Fetisov if personal relations were better with Kasatonov. "If we didn't score," said Fetisov, "would it be worse? It's our work."

Thus, it was no secret that their off-ice cold war would continue indefinitely. Meanwhile, the Devils players, placed in a weird situation, did their best to ignore the hostilities, or the truce, as the case may have been. They also understood that Fetisov remained the heavy, so to speak, the one who would determine whether a genuine peace pact would be struck.

For his part, Kasatonov was just tickled to be in Jersey and to be recognized as a prime factor in the home stretch run for a playoff berth. "I'm delighted to be in the NHL," he continued, "and for me it's easier playing here on the same defense line with Fetisov. I know where I can go to get open. I can predict what he's going to do. The more we play together, the better things work out. We give up the puck less often, and make more passes.

"You will see that we haven't really shown the type of game we are capable of playing. We're going to be consistent on defense but also try to help on offense."

The night of the Stastny trade the Devils edged the St. Louis Blues 2–1. It was not a pretty win but it was meaningful, because the visitors had come to New Jersey as one of the NHL's hottest teams (14–4–2) since the All-Star break. But Fetisov and Kasatonov helped hold the NHL's leading goal scorer, Brett Hull, in check most the night, and goalie Chris Terreri once again produced a clutch performance.

Two nights later Terreri was in the nets again as the Devils whipped the still slumping Islanders 4–2. Peter Stastny made his New Jersey debut and while he didn't dominate the game, he played commendably enough to win raves. More than that, he helped both Fetisov and Kasatonov. Although born in Slovakia, Stastny was a master of the Russian language and could communicate easily with the two Soviet aces both on and off the rink.

Cunniff's decision to unite Fetisov and Kasatonov paid dividends almost immediately, and continued to strengthen the Devils' defense while providing a boost to the attack. On March 10, the Devils played host to Quebec. Stastny starred against his former teammates but it was Fetisov who made the game-breaking play. Slava sidestepped a Curtis Leschyshyn check, allowing the Nordiques defenseman to crunch face-first into the right wing glass. Fetisov regained the puck and slid it to Kasatonov who used David Maley as a screen for a 25-foot wrist shot and a 2–1 Devils lead at 8:09 of the first period. New Jersey went on to a 9–3 win.

But the Fetisov-Kasatonov on-ice marriage was hardly without its flaws. On March 15 the Devils skated on to the Saddledome rink for a match with the Stanley Cup-champion Flames. The champions scored five goals for a 5–4 victory — and the Fetisov-Kasatonov combine was on the ice for four of them.

Moving on to Edmonton, the Devils celebrated St. Patrick's Day with a 4–1 win over the Oilers and all was well again with the Soviets. They played a solid game, and the club climbed to the .500 mark (32–32–8), only six points behind the first-place Rangers. "We're having the same excitement we had two years ago," said Brendan Shanahan. "It's a confident, exciting feeling."

With eight games remaining in the schedule, the Devils' record was their best since the 1988 playoff season, the only other time New Jersey had recorded 30 or more wins. New Jersey still had time for a final run at first place, which was the good news. The bad news was that the team still was an enigma, to the fans, to the critics and to the players themselves.

"We've been a team without an identity," explained defenseman Bruce Driver. "We didn't know whether we were a defensive team or an offensive team. I'd say we're a defensive team — we've got to play that way to win because we don't usually blow teams out of the water."

Coach Cunniff couldn't determine whether it was wiser to look ahead to the still-catchable Rangers or to the four teams behind him; the most distant, the last-place Flyers, were to visit the Meadowlands on March 20.

Judging by the media horde that descended on Byrne Arena for the New Jersey-Philadelphia contest, it was difficult to determine which had the greater attraction, the ascent of the Devils or the descent of the Flyers.

Edward Casey, a Philadelphia priest who also was a professional hockey writer and expert on goaltending, had accompanied the Flyers to Byrne Arena with other journalists who would not normally travel with the team for a regular season game. "The difference," said Father Casey, "is that nobody in Philadelphia viewed this as just another regular season game. In the view of several editors, this game was to be the final burial of the Flyers for 1989–90. Their slump had been interminable; they were riddled with injuries and they were playing a team that not only was hot but was at home and in a position to hammer the final nail in the Flyers' coffin. That's why Philadelphia sports columnists and others considered this an historic event. As everyone knew, it was a long, long time since they Flyers had missed the playoffs."

The burial appeared to be in order as the Devils took a 1–0 lead after 9:05 of the first period when Sylvain Turgeon scored his first goal in eight games. But the Jerseyites alternated between careless and lackadaisical and seemed not to possess an ounce of the killer instinct so important to a playoff-bound team. Philadelphia rebounded to tie the game at 1–1, and then Brendan Shanahan set up Kasatonov at the left point for a power play shot that went through a crowd of players and beat goalie Ken Wregget.

Kasatonov looked to be at the very top of his game but his teammates couldn't exploit the lead and the Flyers pecked and pecked away in the second period, scoring twice and then hanging on. The Devils never scored again and exited with a terribly depressing 3–2 defeat.

"We didn't play well," said goalie Sean Burke, "that's all there is to it. We have to play better than that."

Burke was understating the case. With one defeat, the Devils had suddenly placed themselves in a precarious situation for the playoffs. Not only did they lose a game they should have won but they gave the seemingly-dead Flyers a new life. Even worse was the prospect of having to play at Philadelphia's Spectrum the upcoming Saturday afternoon, and then flying to Buffalo to play the Sabres on the next afternoon. Further complicating matters was the injury factor. Turgeon, who was counted upon for late season goals, left the game with a serious groin injury that would deactivate him for the rest of the season, and Randy Velischek left the game with a concussion.

It was on to Chicago for the Devils before the weekend matches in Philadelphia and Buffalo. If ever a game demonstrated the powerful effect — for better and worse — the two Soviets had on their team, the Blackhawks affair on March 22, 1990, was it.

Kasatonov scored a strategically important goal early in the third period to spur a New Jersey comeback from a 4–1 deficit, ultimately bringing the score to 4–3 for Chicago with 12 minutes remaining. But just when the comeback appeared ready for completion, Steve Thomas of the Blackhawks skated up the middle and put an outside move on Kasatonov. Thomas fired a 35-footer past goalie Chris Terreri. Fetisov also had his problems, especially with the physical game, and once was checked so heavily he went flying backward, "like a turtle," according to the *Daily News*.

The final score was 6–3 for Chicago; the Devils had burrowed from the trouble level to a position of deep trouble. Waiting for them at the Spectrum were the Flyers, now in a position to thoroughly demoralize the Devils and send them reeling out of playoff position. If ever a big game was needed from Slava and Aleksei, this was it. And if ever the Russians came through for their adopted team, the afternoon of March 20 had to be circled on their calendar.

"Before the game," said Cunniff, "we talked about this being playoff hockey. We didn't want any highs or lows. We wanted to keep our composure."

A victory for New Jersey would give them a five-point cushion on Philadelphia. A defeat would mean a precarious one-point lead. "We just wanted to come in and stop the bleeding after losing two straight," said forward Pat Conacher.

The bleeding continued as Ken Linseman scored the game's first goal five minutes after the opening face-off. Peter Stastny tied the score a few minutes later and then the Devils went ahead to stay, thanks to the brilliance of Kasatonov. Aleksei combined with Stastny to feed John MacLean a radar-like pass. MacLean teased the Flyers for several seconds before shooting and scoring.

Philadelphia came close, scoring late in the second period to close to within a goal of tying, but the Devils scoring burst in the third put the game out of reach. It ended 5–2 and Frank Brown's *Daily News* report stated unequivocally, "Kasatonov and Fetisov were basically magnificent on defense." On to Buffalo.

It was amazing what one win could do for a hockey club. Overnight the world was right again for Cunniff's sextet, and it would be even better if they could complete the road trip with a win over the Sabres. How much better? Well, a triumph could mean clinching a playoff berth for the second time in franchise history.

For a change, the Devils showed a zest for going to the jugular. They scored two quick goals in the first period, exited with a 2–1 lead, went up 4–1 after the second period and held fast as the Sabres closed the gap to 4–3 with five minutes and ten seconds remaining in the third period.

Buffalo pressed the attack in the final minute, getting two faceoffs in New Jersey's end with goaltender Clint Malachuk pulled for an extra attacker. With 12 seconds remaining, hard-shooting Sabres defenseman Grant Ledyard wound up for a powerful slapshot from the left point. Fetisov anticipated the play and hurled himself in front of the drive, blunting the shot and assuring the Devils' victory and his own first Stanley Cup playoff in his rookie NHL season.

If there was any doubt that playing on a playoff club had added significance for Fetisov, one only had to peek into the Devils' dressing room following the game.

Slava was spotted turning each of his hands into a little cup. He then held the hands about six inches from his face, forming a frame of fingers. With a smile more in his eyes than on his lips, he announced to all who would listen, "I want a BIG beard!"

Fetisov knew that the longer his team marched in the playoffs, the longer his traditional playoff beard would grow. "I know in the NHL players dream of the Stanley Cup," Slava explained. "I play now in the NHL and I have the same dream. The team is playing well and I think we will go far."

Somebody asked Fetisov if he had felt added pressure to help the Devils get to the playoffs. He wasted no time replying. "No, because hockey is a team sport. Everybody does what he can for the team and in this case the team did well. For me it was difficult in the beginning of the season because of so many different kinds of players."

Having achieved a playoff berth, the Devils now aimed higher. Their next game was at home to the third-place Washington Capitals. A victory would clinch second place for New Jersey. What's more, the contest also loomed as a playoff preview, with one of the two clubs likely to finish second and the other third, meaning they would collide in the first round of the Patrick Division tourney.

The 4–1 win over Washington was almost too easy for words, and Capitals coach Terry Murray had the best words for the evening. "The Devils worked harder than us. They came out with a lot more intensity."

To which Cunniff added, "We're turning into a solid team. I can feel the confidence that I've been looking for all year."

The confidence built two nights later on the finest night of Fetisov's NHL career, March 29. More than 19,000 fans had filled Byrne Arena in anticipation of a match between the Rangers and Devils that was seen as a portent of a more distant meeting in the Patrick Division finals.

Slava set up the first of two Dave Maley goals. He sprinted into the attack, powered to goalie John

Vanbiesbrouck's left and rammed in a diagonal Kirk Muller pass from the left wing circle for the 2–0 goal at 10:24 of the first period. Next, Fetisov arranged Patrik Sundstrom's backhand from Vanbiesbrouck's right at 17:26. In the second period Fetisov set up Brendan Shanahan's goalmouth tip-in to give the Devils a 4–1 advantage. When the Rangers showed signs of making a comeback, Slava repulsed them, driving into the slot for a snap shot that was deflected, but then buried for the winner by rookie Jon Morris.

The sum total was a five-point performance for Fetisov that set some Devils' rookie records and matched others. "Slava is in the Paul Coffey-Ray Bourque class when he's on his game," said teammate Ken Daneyko. "I saw him in 1986 in the world championships when I was playing for Canada. He's shown flashes of this for the past 20 or 30 games."

Towelling after the 6–4 win in front of his dressing room space, Fetisov was advised that he had become the first Devils rookie to collect five points in a game. He shook his head. "I don't classify myself as a rookie. I was playing against professionals when some of our Devils players were still kids."

Slava's performance just barely overshadowed an equally impressive effort from Kasatonov, who now was regarded as one of the league's better defensemen. "The game established overwhelmingly the superiority of Fetisov and Kasatonov," commented Alex Yannis in *The New York Times*. "They were the dominant players in the game."

David Maley: "The way Slava and Alex are playing is really rubbing off — on all the defensemen and the whole team."

Since Fetisov and Kasatonov had emerged as a dominating defense pair, it was only natural that journalists ponder the possibility of not merely a truce but a gesture of true friendship between the Russians. Before leaving the dressing room, Fetisov was asked about the possibilities. "I don't know," he said, obviously uncomfortable about discussing the matter. "A lot of things can happen in life."

A lot of things would happen to the Devils' odd couple before the season would officially close. One episode involved a new shipment of sticks Slava had obtained. As it happened, Kasatonov had been complaining about the quality of the sticks that had been sent to him almost from the time he had arrived in New Jersey. The combination of language difficulty and the fact that stick manufacturers these days seem to have trouble satisfying the meticulous demands of NHL players combined to leave Aleksei with a stick that did not suit his standard.

Kasatonov did, however, notice that Fetisov's shipment was to his liking and he asked one of the Devils' equipment men if he could use a few. "Take some," the equipment man suggested and Kasatonov did just that.

When Fetisov realized what had happened, he asked the equipment man, "Why did you give them to him?" Slava was told that Aleksei needed them but Fetisov was unimpressed. "Anybody else but him!" he barked.

Later Fetisov gathered his best sticks and drew the international circular sign with the diagonal line signifying "off-limits" on a piece of paper and hung it on the stack of lumber. The extras — ones with which he was not delighted — he set aside for Kasatonov.

The reject sticks certainly did not limit Kasatonov's game. In the Devils' last regular season home game he collected three assists as New Jersey defeated Detroit 5–1. Fetisov must have been happy with his sticks as well, judging by his dynamic shooting. "On one occasion," said John Dellapina of the *Bergen Record,* "a Fetisov slapshot nearly put a hole in Red Wings goalie Glen Hanlon's belly."

As the Devils emplaned for Boston and their final game of the 80-game schedule against the Bruins, the club was wearing a distinctly happy face. Not only did they have a firm grip on second place but a win or tie at Boston Garden would break the franchise record for points in a season. In 1987–88 the Devils went 38–36–6 for 82 points. They now were 37–34–8. They were a far different club than the one Kasatonov encountered when he arrived in New Jersey at the end of December. "Tactically, things are good," Aleksei observed. "Technically they are good. And physically, no problem."

There was a slight problem in Boston; for a change the Devils did not win. They did, however, come from behind a 3–2 deficit to tie the game with 26 seconds remaining in the third period. And this without Fetisov, who was given a rest for all his good work in the home stretch.

"Slava is playing as well now as in his best years in Europe," said Kasatonov. The same could be said for Aleksei and because of them, the enthusiasm not only within the dressing room but the press room as well was overflowing with giddy predictions.

Even Hugh Delano, the *Post* hockey writer who had been so critical of Fetisov early in the season, now conceded that Slava had significantly improved his game and, as a result, the Devils had emerged as a major playoff threat.

"Bring on Washington! Bring on the Rangers or Islanders!" Delano wrote after Cunniff had shepherded his team home from Boston. "The Devils are confident they can beat any of them, win the Patrick Division playoff championships, and go on to make a serious challenge to bring the Stanley Cup to New Jersey."

Not only had they completed the most successful regular season in their eight-year history, but the Devils finished the campaign with a 5–0–1 flourish — and closing streaks of 10–3–1 and 13–5–1 — after a near-fatal 1–8–3 slump. In the final 14 games, as Fetisov and Kasatonov established themselves as a premier defense unit, the club surrendered an average of only 2.57 goals against a game.

"I see no reason why we can't go all the way," said defenseman Bruce Driver.

David Maley agreed. "Our defense has really learned a lot from the Russians. It took Slava and Aleksei a while to get going, but the whole team picked up when they started going."

The presumption was that Fetisov and Kasatonov would maintain their world class play in the playoffs. Slava indicated he was ready for his biggest test with a concise comment: "Every soldier wants to be a general."

They seemed truly excited about the opportunity to pursue the trophy Lord Stanley of Preston had donated to hockey in the 19th century.

"The way Fetisov and Kasatonov have been playing recently is evidence of their desire to have their names engraved on the Stanley Cup in their first year in North America." And this from the conservative *New York Times.*

One thing was certain, the Devils would live or die in the playoffs on the performances of their Soviet defensemen.

CHAPTER 22

THE 1990 PLAYOFFS — LIVING AND DYING WITH THE SOVIETS

"What is past is past; this is the playoffs. We'll see how they do now."
— *Terry Murray, coach, Washington Capitals*

Viacheslav Fetisov had come a long way since opening day of training camp at South Mountain Arena in September 1989. He knew from the start that professional hockey at its highest level would be different in North America than it was in the Soviet Union, but he could not imagine how much of a change it would be until he finally experienced the contrast first-hand.

Now that he had his first full regular season under his belt, he could sit back at the South Mountain training facility and reflect on his fascinating but often bumpy odyssey. "Every game is important here and nobody knows before the game who will be the winner," Fetisov said. "In the Soviet Union, we know the winner most of the time in advance because some teams are stronger. We learn that some games are more important than others."

Fetisov explained to some media friends that in Russia, the Soviet hockey leaders train its players to be most competitive in tournaments such as the world championships and the Olympic Games. That is when they raise their level to its highest pitch. Slava experienced that feeling as captain of the Soviet national team for almost a decade. He had never felt anything like the day to day pressure of the NHL nor the intense competition of the Patrick Division, where the last two teams — Philadelphia and Pittsburgh — were not eliminated until the final weekend of the campaign.

It was Alexander Mogilny who played a part in the Penguins' eventual demise. Pittsburgh had appeared to be a cinch to clinch fourth place during the latter weeks of March as the Islanders and Flyers were locked in a dreadful tailspin. But without Mario Lemieux's help, the Penguins slipped as well.

On the final Saturday of the season, the Islanders played Philadelphia at Nassau Coliseum while the Penguins were host to the Sabres. An Islanders loss would eliminate them, whereas a Pittsburgh win would guarantee the Penguins a playoff berth.

The Islanders game began earlier than the Penguins game and ended well before Pittsburgh and Buffalo had completed their match. With the home crowd cheering them on, the Islanders defeated the Flyers and now awaited the final score from the Civic Arena in Pittsburgh.

The Penguins were favored for two reasons; Lemieux had finally returned after his lengthy sabbatical and was expected to be both an emotional and physical catalyst to his teammates. Second, the Penguins were considerably more motivated than their opponents. Buffalo had long before clinched a playoff berth and, at this point in the season, the Sabres were more concerned about avoiding injuries before the Stanley Cup round than anything else.

If the Sabres were intent on taking it easy, you couldn't tell by their performance. Rather than take the night off, they stayed with the Penguins and managed to keep the enormous Lemieux in check for a good part of the game.

Neither team scored in the first period, but Pittsburgh broke the ice in the second and appeared ready to break the game open until Mogilny converted passes from Pierre Turgeon and Dave Andreychuk to tie the score at 9:50 of the second. It was one of the few meaningful goals the Russian had scored in some time for Buffalo but, from the Islanders' viewpoint, it couldn't have been bigger simply because it had stemmed the Penguins' offensive and turned the game in the Sabres' favor. Less than six minutes later Rick Vaive put Buffalo ahead 2–1, and underlined the point that Pittsburgh would have to work hard if it was going to win.

Lemieux finally tied the count at 2–2 in the third period but the game went into overtime, setting the stage for a long shot by defenseman Uwe Krupp that eluded goalie Tom Barrasso. With a little help from Mogilny, the Sabres edged Pittsburgh 3–2, enabling the Islanders to clinch a playoff berth.

Sabres fans were a lot less enthusiastic about Mogilny at the time than grateful followers of the Islanders. Like several of his comrades, Mogilny was an enormous disappointment to those who had worked so hard to secure his NHL citizenship. He had not come close to solving his flying problem and except for the occasional goal, he no longer was considered a major scoring threat; the Buffalo general staff was hoping that would change now that the Sabres were preparing to meet Montreal in the opening round.

There would be no playoffs for Vancouver's Vladimir Krutov or Igor Larionov. At season's end, Krutov was rated an unmitigated flop, whereas Larionov obtained positive notices but, overall, did not live up to his billing. Considering the $315,000 a year they were receiving — the highest-paid Canucks — Krutov and Larionov made president Pat Quinn and coach Bob McCammon wonder whether they had erred in signing them in the first place. The conclusion, of course, was that they had no alternative and there was little second-guessing.

"Granted, they haven't lived up to expectations," said McCammon, "and certainly the adjustment has hurt our hockey team, but we had to take those players because their skill level is so high. Our problem was that they couldn't be the supporting cast. They were supposed to be our two best offensive players.

"They just can't believe how hard the games are over here, every night. They play 45 league games and maybe five are hard. By the end of the first period with the Red Army team, they're up 5–0 and having fun throwing the puck around.

"Coming over, they had a lot of confidence. They had played all the best in the NHL: Wayne Gretzky, Paul Coffey and Mario Lemieux. They figured they're not that tough. And they're right. They're all offense. But after a while, my guys are looking at the back of jerseys and saying, 'Who's this Troy Murray slashing, hacking, riding on my back all night?' They see Lemieux and Gretzky from a distance from our bench. But when they go out, the grinders are all over them.

"Then they wake up at six in the morning, take a three-hour plane ride and do it all over again. They're wondering, 'What happened to the 6–5, run-and-gun games we played in the Canada Cup?' "

Sergei Mylnikov was another Russian whose team missed the playoffs. But the Quebec Nordiques were so egregiously abysmal, it was unfair to place any blame on a foreign goaltender whose coach, Michel Bergeron, had given up on him before the season had even started.

Sergei Makarov was another story, and a good one, the Calgary Flames hoped. A year earlier Hakan Loob had scored eight goals and nine assists for 17 playoff points enroute to the Flames' first Stanley Cup championship. With Loob returned to his native Sweden, Makarov was designated to pick up where the Swede left off. In 1988–89, Loob's final NHL season, he totalled 27 goals, 58 assists and 85 points in 79 games. Makarov, in his first NHL campaign, played in all 80 games, scored 24 goals, 62 assists and finished with 86 points.

Makarov's coach, Terry Crisp, hoped that the Russian would pick up his game a notch for the playoffs. "Their whole system of hockey is getting ready for tournaments," said Crisp. On the whole he was pleased with Sergei's efforts. "For a while there, I was telling him this was a big game and the next game was a big game and there was a big game after that.

"One day he comes back at me with, 'Hey, is every game a big game?' I guess if you're a coach, every game is a big game. But like most players, there are games when you like to turn it up a bit. And with all the games, I think the Soviets were a little confused. It's not like Europe.

"What we've seen is that Makarov, and any other Soviet in the playoffs, will really turn it on. It will be like a big tournament for them."

It would not likely be a big tourney for Sergei Priakin, Makarov's teammate. Limited to only 20 regular season games, the fourth-stringer scored only two goals and two assists. If nothing else, he provided Makarov with a Russian-speaking comrade to keep him company when he got homesick. "Priakin," quipped Canucks executive Brian Burke, "is the most expensive baby-sitter in history!"

Many critics pointed to the Stanley Cup round as the litmus test for the Russians. Al Morganti, hockey editor of *The National,* an American-based sports daily, needled the Soviets for their regular season effort but added, "There is a feeling that the world-class players from the land of glasnost will finally show their true talents in the playoffs."

The intangibles were pressure and officiating. Nobody could be certain how the Russians would adapt to the high-intensity atmosphere of a playoff series, nor whether they would get a fair shake from the referees. "Because I'm Russian," said Makarov, "the refs let them slash me, hit me, anything."

"He's like a human space invaders game," added Flames defenseman Brad McCrimmon.

The same could be said, to a lesser extent, of the Devils Fetisov and Kasatonov. Each absorbed a substantial amount of physical abuse, essentially turned the other cheek, and hoped that the referee would punish the offender. In time they came to realize that NHL officials see approximately 60 percent of the infractions committed on the ice and call only about 40 percent. Through the end of the regular schedule, Slava and Aleksei seemed to adjust to the realities of that system without undue harm being done to them or their team.

If anything, the Devils' home stretch run — beginning with the pivotal win at the Spectrum — indicated that Fetisov and Kasatonov would flourish in the upcoming playoffs. "It's reasonable to assume that the Soviets will be geared up for the playoffs," predicted Lamoriello. "Every indication that we've seen is that they play better in the more important games. There has been some unevenness in their play, but when the playoffs come around, we hope that gets better.

"The one thing we have to worry about is the short time between the end of the regular season and the start of the playoffs. I don't think they're used to a quick turnaround like that."

Just as the onus was on Jim Schoenfeld to help the Russians adapt to the NHL at the start of the 1989–90 season, so now the challenge before Cunniff was to extract the best from Fetisov and Kasatonov in their first playoff experience. Cunniff let them do their thing and remained neutral and distant on their endless cold war.

But nobody had to tell Cunniff about Stanley Cup pressure. He had worked as Boston Bruins' assistant coach under Terry O'Reilly when the Devils were eliminated in seven games by Boston in 1988, and had seen his share of world championships. "The intensity for the Stanley Cup playoffs is just unbelievable," said Cunniff, "and I think Slava and Alex will feel it. The fact is that the world championships they've been used to might be prestigious but it's dull hockey.

"Sure, there is a high skill level and great skating and speed, but the world championships are nowhere near the intensity of the Stanley Cup playoffs."

The teammate best able to provide a clear understanding to the Soviets — in their own language — was Peter Stastny. Not only was Stastny a veteran of the world championships as captain of the Czech national team, but he'd also captained the Quebec Nordiques in several stirring Stanley Cup rounds.

"You cannot compare the Stanley Cup playoffs with the world championships," said Stastny. "This is especially true for the Soviets because whenever they went into the world championships and the Olympic Games, they went into just about every game knowing they were going to win.

"Here in the NHL it will be much different. I know how they must be feeling for their first playoffs. Everybody tells you, 'Wait till the playoffs, wait till you see what it's like.' And it is very different, very intense. But what will be the same is that players like Alex and Slava have learned to keep their cool and play their best when it really matters. I think that will happen."

Having finished in second place, the Devils would meet Washington in the best-of-seven opening playoff round. It would open at Byrne Arena, supposedly giving New Jersey home-ice advantage. The Capitals, despite — or because of — their Russian training camp in September, had not played up to potential and finished the season under the .500 mark.

Most writers, such as Rich Chere of the *Star-Ledger,* favored the Devils to win the series in six games. One reason for such New Jersey-based optimism was the play of the Russians. "Fetisov (plus-8) and Kasatonov (plus-15) are at their best," noted Chere in his pre-series analysis. "Fetisov had 1–6–7 in his final two games, while Kasatonov could be the Devils' best defenseman."

Cunniff knew that his team would live or die on the performance of his Russians. If he harbored any doubts about their ability to deliver in the clutch, he never betrayed them to anyone. Like most observers who watched Fetisov and Kasatonov assure New Jersey of a playoff berth, Cunniff hoped they would ride their late-season momentum right into the Cup round.

"Both guys have so much maturity and experience," he said, as if to reinforce his thoughts. "In these big games they don't really get hyper. They've found that maturity level. Younger Russian players work with sport psychologists about that."

Playoff fever had engulfed the New York-New Jersey area by the start of April. For the first time in

NHL history, not one, not two, but all three teams — the Islanders, Rangers and Devils — would be involved in the Cup challenge. Across the Hudson, the Rangers were gearing up for their playoff with the Islanders and newspapers were giving hockey the top play for one of the few occasions in the season.

For the Devils, the euphoria of playoff-clinching had worn off and now the attention was focussed on the series ahead. Players like Stastny, Muller and Burke understood that, as much as the fans delighted in having them in the playoffs, once the first puck was dropped in Game One, any regular season accomplishments are forgotten and winning in the playoffs is all that counts. The buzzword at Byrne Arena was "pressure" yet the Soviets seemed above the anxiety.

"Honestly," said Kasatonov, "I think the Olympic Games were much more pressure-filled. I was a lot more worried. There, one game can decide four years of training. Here, you have a lot more chances to correct your errors. I'd say I'm in the stage of my career when I don't worry about nerves or pressure. All my nerves are burned up already."

Fetisov: "I feel I'm ready. I feel something different. This is going to be different than the world championships. It's a bad athlete who doesn't get nervous. I don't believe anyone who says he doesn't get nervous. It's a normal state of mind. You just can't get too nervous. I think I still have some more to offer. I can play better."

The "experts" were almost unanimous in picking New Jersey to breeze past Washington. The *Post*'s Hugh Delano picked the Devils in five games, as did both Frank Brown and Barry Meisel in the *Daily News*. Nobody seemed concerned that the Capitals had won the season series from the Devils 4–3, or that Washington boasted one of the biggest, most experienced defense corps in the league. In his preview, Brown actually gave the Jersey defense an edge, pointing out, "Fetisov and Kasatonov are playing at their absolute best."

Capitals coach Terry Murray digested the reports that had his club rated as distinct underdogs, examined the Russians' inexperience in Stanley Cup competition and said, very simply, "What is past is past; this is the playoffs! We'll see how they do now."

After exactly 83 seconds of the first playoff game, Murray's point was well taken — and so was his strategy. Murray and his assistant Rob Laird had mapped out a simple plan: the Russians were to be rushed, forechecked, bodychecked and generally harassed at every turn. The thinking was simple; a combination of physical, mental and general playoff pressure would throw them off their game. If the Devils' best two defensemen could be proven vulnerable, the entire team would go down with them.

Precisely as planned, the Capitals' strategy immediately paid dividends. Murray sent Dino Ciccarelli, a pesky, talkative and highly-skilled scorer, onto the ice. A veteran of the 1981 Stanley Cup finals when he skated for the Minnesota North Stars, Ciccarelli knew that a quick Washington goal would completely defuse the capacity crowd of more than 19,000 fans and possibly unnerve the favored Devils.

Seeing the puck skim behind the New Jersey net, Ciccarelli pursued Fetisov, who was attempting to tame the loose puck. Weighing 45 pounds less than the Russian, Ciccarelli was not one who normally would win a duel against a more powerful man along the boards. But, somehow, Ciccarelli not only wiggled free, he had the puck as well and skated directly in front of the goal where he stuffed the puck behind Sean Burke. The time was 1:23 of the first period and the crowd was stunned to the core.

Before the announcer could finish giving the details about Ciccarelli's goal, Dino found another opening and scored again, 24 seconds after his first red light. In time the Devils would recover and tie the score 4–4 in the third period, but that was the extent of their production. Ciccarelli got the winner at five minutes and 34 seconds of overtime to stake the Capitals to victory.

It would be folly to suggest that after one loss, the Devils suddenly had become the underdogs but there was enough evidence to warrant more than passing concern. Certainly, Fetisov's failure to contain Ciccarelli along the wall was symbolic of the general inability of the Soviets to employ their bodies as blocking devices as often as necessary. Unquestionably, it was necessary on the opening play.

Neither Kasatonov nor Fetisov were the kind of formidable defending-attacking defensemen that they had been during the last two weeks of the season, and the Devils as a group appeared to falter, at least in part because their imports were not up to par. Still, it was only one game and there was plenty of time for redemption. “Fear,” said coach Cunniff, “is a big motivator.”

Fear surely occupied a large part of the Devils’ psyche in Game Two in New Jersey. If it was a motivator, as the coach insisted, the Devils cashed in on the motivation early in the game. First, Brendan Shanahan opened the scoring and then Fetisov orchestrated the second goal on a power play, starting the play with a pass to Stastny who threw a cross-slot feed to John MacLean. MacLean’s one-timer beat goalie Mike Liut inside the left post.

The 2–0 lead was deceptive. Washington found soft spots in the Devils’ defense and eventually tied the score 4–4 in the third period. New Jersey went ahead 6–4 but Kasatonov lost the puck to Ciccarelli on the end boards and the smaller man skated out the left side of the net to beat Chris Terreri.

With a minute remaining, Murray pulled his goalie and sent an extra attacker into the Devils’ end for what amounted to a full-court press. Time and again the Capitals came agonizingly close to putting the puck past Terreri as the Jersey skaters piled up in front of their goaltender. A final Washington shot had goal marked all over it as the rubber sailed toward an opening, but Fetisov’s hand shot up and knocked the puck to safety, enabling the Devils to skate off with a 6–5 victory.

“My record for the game,” chuckled Fetisov in the crowded dressing room, “is one assist and one save. I learned that in volleyball!”

That Fetisov and Kasatonov were left on the ice at that critical juncture of the game said volumes about Cunniff’s determination to play them in major moments.

Whether they could continue to hold up under the increasingly heavy fire was still an uncertainty, particularly now that the next two games were to be played at the hostile Capital Center in Landover, Maryland.

After two games a pattern had been set that would go a long way in determining how the series would finish. A bigger, more aggressive team, the Capitals had established a policy of both legal and illegal punishment for their smaller foe. In addition to heavy hitting from the likes of Scott Stevens and Kevin Hatcher, the Devils had to endure incessant verbal needling from the master, Neil Sheehy, as well as the inevitable cheap shots delivered by pesky Dale Hunter, who was notorious, league-wide, for his use of high sticks, checks after the whistle and general disturbing in front of the enemy net.

Cunniff had warned his players before the series that they had to maintain discipline, turn the other cheek when necessary and get even by scoring more goals. On their home rink, the Capitals would be even more ornery, and yet the Devils prevailed although the statistics hardly would support that claim.

Over three periods Cunniff's skaters took only a grand total of ten shots on goal. Somehow they managed to score on two of those shots while Terreri limited Washington to only one goal. As for the physical battering absorbed by the Devils, it could be summed up in one word — brutal.

Fetisov was a marked man, mostly by Hunter. Early in the second period, the Capitals disturber went into the corner after the defenseman, crunching him with an elbow. Slava was shaken up on the play but was able to continue, although Hunter showed no mercy and battered him later in the game.

"The [rough-housing] tactics being used against us are going against them," said Cunniff. "Our discipline was terrific. We don't want to have our top players off the ice."

With a two games to one lead, Cunniff could afford to be optimistic, especially since he had won with an absolute minimum of shots. "After losing game one," said Sean Burke, "this is the best scenario we could hope for. We're in a position where we can really put them behind the eight ball."

Cunniff's hope was that the Capitals' hyper-aggressiveness would result in additional penalties that would be exploited by the Devils' power play. His concern was that the game-by-game pounding would weaken his aces — especially the Russians — and they would wilt as the series continued.

Indubitably, Washington was on the spot. Another loss at home would drop them to a one-three deficit in the series with little chance for recovery. When a team limits the opposition to ten shots and still loses, it is in big trouble. But Cunniff, to a certain degree, played into the Capitals' hands. Instead of sticking with his winning goaltender, Terreri, he announced that Burke would be back in the nets for Game Four.

"We were happy they made the goaltending change," said Murray. "I really believe that's page one of the coach's manual. You don't change a winning goalie."

Burke did not play badly for New Jersey. He had limited Washington to one goal well into the second period and Kirk Muller had tied the score for the Devils at 13:02 of the second period. The scenario was ideal for the visitors to pull away but their concentration, or whatever the intangible was that limited them, was not there. Just 15 seconds after the Jersey score, Fetisov allowed Washington forward John Druce to skate into the slot behind him and whip the puck past Burke. That was all the Capitals needed. The Devils couldn't muster another goal, while Washington added an insurance goal in the third period enroute to a 3–1 triumph.

The series not only was tied at two games apiece but an uneasy feeling had overcome the Jerseyites. Four matches into the series they were not receiving the world class performances they had expected from their imports. Fetisov and Kasatonov may not have been panicking but they certainly were not playing anything like the grade A defense they had exhibited late in the season.

To some that was negligible compared with the Devils' offense, which had become almost non-existent since Game Two. They had won the third game 2–1 on only ten shots on goal and scored just once on 24 shots in Game Four.

"We're playing well defensively," said captain Kirk Muller, "we have to stay patient offensively. If we can break their line at the blueline and get more shots, things will go our way."

Against the formidable Washington defense, getting the first goal meant a lot to the Devils, and preventing Washington from scoring was just as important. When the Devils had won — in games two and three — they had scored first. But again Fetisov was victimized early in the game. He misplayed a clearing attempt behind his net before getting checked hard by Kevin Hatcher. John Tucker controlled the weak clearing try in the right corner, centring a pass to Hunter, who deflected it past Terreri at 9:03 of the first period.

Still, there was time for a Russian to emerge as a hero in this encounter. New Jersey tied the score early in the second period and went ahead 2–1 on a play engineered by Kasatonov. The Devils took the one-goal lead into the dressing room at the end of the second and hoped to preserve it with a combination of tight defensive play and energetic forechecking.

It was a good idea that died 27 seconds into the third period when Mike Ridley backhanded a rebound past Terreri to tie the score. At 4:30 of the final session Ciccarelli picked a pass out of the air and tipped it in to snap the 2–2 tie. Washington won the game 4–3, putting the Devils right on the brink of the playoff abyss.

"We have to regroup," said Cunniff. "We haven't done anything easy all year so this is nothing new to us."

"We can't afford to be down right now," added Muller, "We seem to play better on the road anyway."

What had appeared to be a sensible Devils' blueprint early in the series now was terribly obsolete. The idea of turning the other cheek and luring Washington into penalties only was providing the Jerseyites with an unlimited collection of bruises and black-and-blue marks. Intimidation was working for the Capitals.

"The referees allowed the Capitals to play a physical, often cheap-shot style of hockey in the early games," commented Rich Chere. "The Devils' strategy of walking away from such tactics wound up serving as an open invitation to players such as Dale Hunter and others to simply take out several of New Jersey's key players."

Cunniff was not unaware of Murray's plan and attempted to counter it by using his enforcers, particularly Jamie Huscroft and Troy Crowder. Unfortunately, the officials suddenly began enforcing the rules against unsportsmanlike conduct and the Devils lost Crowder and Brendan Shanahan in Game Five with ten-minute misconduct penalties.

"We'd send a guy like Huscroft out there, who would do anything to win," said Burke, "but guys like Kevin Hatcher and Scott Stevens would not fight Jamie. It may have been beneficial for us to go up to a Hatcher and smack him around a little. He has been in total control of the series. Hatcher and Stevens know that no one was going to come after them."

But by Game Six at Capital Center, Fetisov and Kasatonov knew full well that somebody — sometimes it appeared that it was everybody — would come after them and lay a heavy bodycheck or apply the lumber, especially if the opponent happened to be Dale Hunter.

"The Caps hit Slava and Alex until they were gun-shy and ineffective," added Chere. "The Soviets wilted under the intensity and physical pounding of the playoffs."

With at least one more game remaining, the Russians had an opportunity to redeem themselves and help salvage the series. "In games four and five we didn't match Washington's intensity," analyzed Burke. "That urgency didn't seem to be there."

It was there when they skated onto the Capital Center ice on April 15. Cunniff's team was as ready as it would ever be for an important test. Even injured players such as Pat Conacher, John MacLean and Sylvain Turgeon suited up and made it clear they would expend every bit of energy to keep the club alive. And the Devils were very much alive in the opening period, when they matched the home team check for check, shot for shot and save for save.

When Kasatonov took a two-minute crosschecking penalty at 1:48 of the first period the Devils checked fiercely and eliminated all Capitals' power play chances. Just as Aleksei stepped out of the penalty box the puck skittered into the Washington zone where goalie Don Beaupre moved out to steer it out of danger. Somehow, the goaltender misread the play and was caught helplessly out of his crease.

Kasatonov, with the puck on his stick and the net wide open, moved in from the left side — not the best of angles under the circumstances, but not the worst either — and positioned himself for what appeared to be the first goal of the game. The Russian must have suspected that an opponent was right behind him because he didn't take the extra strides that would have enabled him to move right in on the goal. Instead, he released his shot — and watched it hit the left post and carom harmlessly away.

"I was getting to the end of the ice," Kasatonov explained, "and I saw one of our guys coming in on the right. I wanted my shot to get in close to the pipe."

Still, the Devils persisted. Muller caught Beaupre out of his crease but Capitals defenseman Bob Rouse covered up in time. Finally, it was Fetisov's chance. A half-minute before the ten-minute mark in the first period, Slava bisected the Washington defense and cruised in, one-on-one, against Beaupre. An artist to the end, Fetisov attempted the difficult play — a stickhandling maneuver to slip the puck between the goalie's legs — and brought the puck to his backhand.

Beaupre read the play well and got just enough of the puck to brake its speed. The rubber slid through his pads and was about to cross the goal line for New Jersey's first score when defenseman Rod Langway interceded and brushed the puck out of danger. After ten minutes of play, the Soviets had the game's two best scoring chances but had nothing to show for it on the scoreboard.

"Maybe we were too confident in ourselves," said

Kasatonov in post-game reflection. "Perhaps we were thinking, 'if we don't score now, we'll score later.'"

But the Devils did not score in a superbly-played first period that looked to end in a 0–0 tie. That would have suited Cunniff just fine. Holding Washington scoreless in the first period on their home ice was not the worst thing in the world. Additionally, his club was carrying the play and, sooner or later, Beaupre could be expected to crack.

Those thoughts were dancing through the heads of Devils players in the final minute of the first period with Fetisov and Kasatonov working the defense. Washington dumped the puck into the enemy end as the seconds ticked away. At 19:40 puck control went to New Jersey. The Devils must have been concerned that Slava would make that odd play that had gotten the team into so much trouble during the regular season.

Fetisov took possession off the wall in the left corner after taking a short pass from Kasatonov. His options included a retreat that would leave him in possession or a shot off the boards to send the puck out of danger. Inexplicably, Slava opted for the difficult play, a pass into the neutral zone. The idea may have worked if he had clear vision to his receiver or if he had not been hounded by Washington forechecking. The Capitals' forward Steve Leach was too close; he intercepted in the left circle, skated out while teammate Michal Pivonka set a pick on Fetisov and beat Terreri on the stick side at 19:49 for a 1–0 Washington lead.

"When things aren't going well, you make one mistake and a goal is scored," Fetisov said later.

To minimize the effect of the goal, one could say it was devastating. Having played so well for so long, the Devils expected to skate off the ice at least tied 0–0. Now they were behind again, facing a hot goalie and a rugged defense. Still, the cheerleaders among the New Jersey players kept up a live patter between periods and left their dressing room feeling they had at least 40 minutes of life left in their season.

A breakaway goal by the Capitals sobered them at 9:27 but MacLean, suffering from what the training staff called a "major league hip pointer," reduced the margin to 2–1 at 13:21 of the middle period. Once again the Devils were coming on strong. Once again, the Soviets deserted them.

As the final minute of play began, Hatcher carried the puck into the Devils' end, circled behind the net and centred a pass to John Druce, who was being covered by Fetisov. Obviously, he was not being sufficiently covered because Druce easily circumvented the Soviet and banged the puck past Terreri's stick side on his second poke at 19:06 to give Washington a 3–1 lead.

Terreri was furious as he left the ice. Galumphing past the television studio enroute to the clubhouse at the end of the period, he shouted, "Why the fuck didn't he [Fetisov] knock him [Druce] on his ass?"

Well, for one thing, Slava may just have been too tired to knock Raggedy Ann on her derriere. "I tried the best I could," Fetisov said in retrospect.

Perhaps, but that third Washington goal was a killer. Two down, the Devils pulled out all the stops in period three and moved to within a goal when Stastny converted a Bruce Driver pass and beat Beaupre at the right post at exactly five minutes. With 15 minutes remaining, the Devils stepped up the pressure and came close to scoring the tying goal innumerable times. In the final minute Stastny appeared to have the Devils' third score on his stick but the puck eluded him and the Capitals ran out the clock.

When the losers completed the ritual mid-ice handshake they returned to their room almost too fatigued to even curse. Not surprisingly, the media singled out the Soviets for criticism. In the *Star-Ledger,* Chere opened his obituary with these words: "The Devils season ended much the same way it began — with their two Soviet defensemen intimidated into making costly mistakes while absorbing bone-rattling hits."

Chere charged that the imports "wilted under the Stanley Cup intensity," and an almost identical verdict was delivered by Delano in the *Post.* Slava and Alex made easy targets, particularly in view of the pair of opening period scoring chances that they missed and the two easy-to-see errors by Fetisov late in the first and second periods.

Neither of the Russians ducked the media after the game. They patiently answered questions that ranged from the intimidation factor to fatigue. "I'm stunned and upset," said Fetisov. "I don't think the Capitals are a better team. Luck was with them."

The analysts insisted that it was anything but luck, and some of the Devils seemed to side with the intimidation element. "We did get physically handled in some of the games," said Burke. "I don't know if that was the turning point. That's the way the Caps saw it. But if your guys are able to hit the opposing defensemen and go into the corners and rough guys up without anything being done about it, that gives you a lot of confidence."

Too much blame was being heaped on the Russians and too little on other Devils who had failed in the clutch. Team captain Muller was virtually a non-factor when it counted, and other defensemen were just as culpable overall as Fetisov and Kasatonov.

Lamoriello was pressed continually about the abuse absorbed by Slava and Aleksei and repeatedly blunted the questions. "After the fact," he replied, "when you have results, you can go back and say that [intimidation] was Washington's plan. If those were their plans, fine. They got Alex and Slava in a couple of situations, but we have to look at the positive things Alex and Slava did, too."

Positively, the Russians were responsible for getting the Devils into the playoffs. At times they were among the best players in the league. For the most part, they tried their best although they had never experienced anything so physically and mentally draining as an 80-game season. Never, ever, had they been a part of so intensely-fought a tournament as a Stanley Cup playoff. The ledger, in the end, indicated that the Devils lived with the Soviets during the season and died with them in the playoffs.

However, that should not have been taken personally. After all, a lot of teams — including Doug Carpenter's Toronto Maple Leafs — were making their playoff exit in the first round. What made 1990 unique was the pattern involving New Jersey, Buffalo, Calgary and Minnesota.

CHAPTER 23

WHAT HAPPENED TO MAKAROV WHEN THE FLAMES BURNED OUT?

> "I don't think anybody wants a good season like ours to end so early in April."
>
> — *Joe Nieuwendyk, Calgary Flames*

From the very start of the Russian invasion, the media as a whole was overwhelmingly unfair to the Soviet hockey players, and none was more representative of this attitude than hockey writer Al Morganti. New England-bred, Morganti had been raised on Bobby Orr and The Big, Bad Bruins, a swashbuckling team that had raised intimidation to such a high level that the Philadelphia Flyers — alias The Broad Street Bullies — eventually patterned their style after the Bruins.

Morganti became a sportswriter for the Philadelphia *Inquirer* and he revelled in the bashing-crashing of the Flyers, who sustained their aggressive play through the 1980s. Morganti left the *Inquirer* during the 1989–90 season to work for the newly-minted sports daily, *The National,* and wrote frequently about the Soviets, usually with a disparaging view. At one point he noted that if Providence-born Lou Lamoriello had his choice of player it would be a Soviet who played for Providence College.

Morganti, along with many other hockey reporters, established an unrealistically high standard for the Soviets and then unabashedly tarred and feathered them at season's end when they failed to reach that level. "The performance of the Soviet players in the NHL has not been overwhelming," Morganti asserted, "which is surprising. Some observers figured the Soviets would take a hammer and sickle to the NHL record books."

This was a misstatement at the expense of the Soviets. Perhaps the Russians did not overwhelm the NHL, but who were the "observers" who figured that Fetisov and Company would rewrite the record books? In fact, no media personalities ever came out in print or on radio or television to unequivocally state that the Russians would be in the Wayne Gretzky-Mario Lemieux mold.

What was stated, many times, was that the adjustment would be difficult. And it was. The playoff problems encountered by Fetisov and Kasatonov were no different from those that confounded their comrades in Calgary, where Sergei Makarov and Sergei Priakin were enjoying the fruits of the Flames' first-place finish.

The regular season could not have finished on a higher note for coach Terry Crisp's defending champions. They played their 80th game at home while 20,107 fans watched what would be a preview — they hoped — of the upcoming playoffs. It was now guaranteed that Los Angeles, locked into fourth place, would oppose Calgary in the first round, and the Kings would be the ideal sacrificial lamb.

With a surgeon's precision, the Flames calmly dissected the visitors, led by none other than Makarov. Calgary jumped into a first period 3–1 lead and Sergei supplied goal number two and formulated goal three with a neat pass. After Los Angeles rallied in the second period, Makarov responded with the game-winning goal early in the third period. He later added an assist as the Flames walloped the Kings 8–4.

Calgary finished the season with a record of 42 wins, 23 losses and 15 ties. The Kings were an unimpressive 34–39–7 and entered the playoffs shaken by a report that their ace, Wayne Gretzky, would be unable to play for the first two games because of an ailing back.

There were no doubts at all that the Flames would steamroller the Kings. The question was whether Calgary was strong enough to win a second straight Stanley Cup. The *Hockey News* experts believed they would, as did *Sports Illustrated.* "The Flames will roll," *Sports Illustrated* predicted, noting the club's "bottomless depth" and that Makarov had replaced Hakan Loob. "Makarov," the magazine added, "might be the world's best right wing."

Makarov was in good company. Players like Doug Gilmour, Joey Mullen and Joe Nieuwendyk enabled the Flames to lead the NHL in offense. They also boasted the league's best power play and ranked fifth overall in defense. "You win the Cup one year and people wonder if it was a fluke," said Crisp. "Now the guys should want to prove that we are legitimate. Our first concern is healthy goaltending and we have that. Our second concern is goals against and we're cutting down on that. Our third concern is the guys up front. We lost two grinder-type wings but depth wins for you."

Makarov was a key to that depth. It was a factor that was conspicuously missing in the Kings. Not only was Gretzky injured, but also key players like goalie Kelly Hrudey, defenseman Tom Laidlaw and penalty-killing ace Steve Kasper. LITTLE HOPE FOR TORN AND TATTERED KINGS, pronounced a headline in the *Windsor Star.*

Crisp's final message: "When you get a team by the jugular, you should slice them from ear to ear. Never let them off the mat. If we can get them on the run, we should keep them running."

The message was clear enough, except nobody was listening. Leading Los Angeles 3–1 at the four-minute mark of the third period, the Flames must have thought the jugular was located somewhere around the big toe. Instead of wiping out the visitors, the Flames suddenly disintegrated, allowing four consecutive Kings goals, as the champions were stung with a 5–3 defeat.

"I can't figure what the heck happened," said Al MacInnis. "When we went up 3–1, I figured the game was in the bag."

Makarov did nothing. Absolutely nothing. Gary Roberts and Joe Nieuwendyk had also been silenced. But the Calgary media would not be quiet. *Calgary Herald* columnist Alan Maki urged Crisp to replace goalie Mike Vernon with Rick Wamsley. Others wondered whether the team would panic. The players emphasized the need to retain their composure. "It's never too early to start worrying a little bit," said defenseman Dana Murzyn, "but I don't think there's any reason for us to panic. If we come out and play the full game like we played the first two periods of the opener, we'll be fine."

They would be if they got a big game out of Makarov and, this time, they did. After the Kings had rallied from a 2–0 deficit to make it 2–1, it was Sergei who arranged Calgary's third and fourth goals. He also received an assist on their final score, the eighth goal in an 8–5 rout.

The series was tied; good news for Calgarians. The bad news was that it now moved to Inglewood, California, for games three and four. What's more Wayne Gretzky, who had missed the first two contests, was expected back in the Los Angeles lineup. The final decision would be made by Kings physician Steve Lombardo. After the morning workout, The Great One convinced Lombardo that he was fit enough to play. "The important thing was, I asked him to be honest with me because I knew he wanted to play," said Lombardo. "Wayne said he felt great."

The jammed Great Western Forum was the site of a magnificent hockey game. With Gretzky captaining the team once more, the Kings played a disciplined, defense-oriented game. They took a 1–0 lead on Tomas Sandstrom's second period goal and appeared capable of nurturing Kelly Hrudey's shutout until Joey Mullen tied the score at 14:08 of the third period. It remained 1–1 through regulation time.

At 3:34 of the sudden-death period, Jim Korn of the Flames received a two-minute penalty for roughing, but Calgary's penalty-killers did their job efficiently. At 6:52 Mike Krushelnyski took a two-minute holding penalty for Los Angeles.

Calgary was due for a goal. Their power play

during the regular season worked to 27.7 percent efficiency whereas the Kings' inability to stop disadvantages was fifth worst in the league (76 percent). For more than a minute and a half the Flames' power play was ineffective once more. Regrouping at mid-ice, Gary Suter attempted a pass. Penalty-killer Tony Granato read the plan, intercepted the puck and raced in on goalie Mike Vernon. The shot went right over Vernon's glove and into the net at 8:37 of the first overtime period. Los Angeles now had a 2–1 lead in the series.

As stunning as anything was the abject failure of Calgary's power play, on which Makarov had played so well during the regular season. "We've been dissecting, analyzing, looking and probing," said Crisp. "Maybe we should just start reacting. It boils down to work. We've X'ed and O'ed these guys for three years now. Our five guys have got to outwork their four.

"We've been spoiled. We've depended on our rush for a long time and usually it's come through for us. Now it's time to get our fingernails dirty, our knuckles skinned. We can't just try to dipsy-do our way into the zone, be stopped and think, 'Oh, well, we'll make another rush.' We've got to put all that BS aside."

The "dipsy-do" was Makarov's forte. Take it away from him and there's not much left to his game. And if there was not much left to his game, there would be not much left to the Flames.

Makarov did collect a pair of assists in Game Four but his first one — on Calgary's first goal at 9:16 of the second period — was delivered after the Flames had been buried by seven straight Los Angeles goals. It was 4–0 Kings after the first period and 7–0 at 7:58 of the second. The final count was 12–4, which rendered Sergei's contribution null and void. Makarov was not alone. Calgary's key line of Doug Gilmour, Brian MacLelland and Joe Mullen was a combined minus-18 with only seven points. The power play was 1 for 21, the lone goal coming on a penalty shot, of all things!

Nobody had to tell Crisp about the depth of the hole his club had dug for itself — and him. A Calgary defeat in the series would almost surely cost him his job and some journalists, Alan Maki for one, already were demanding Crisp's dismissal. "We'll suck it up," Crisp vowed. "In Game Four absolutely nothing went right. If we can't pick ourselves up now, if that wasn't embarrassing enough, we never will be embarrassed."

If anyone was embarrassed, it was Makarov. In a desperate effort to generate more offensive punch, Crisp removed the Russian from his regular spot on the Nieuwendyk-Roberts line and put Theoren Fleury in Makarov's place. The move worked. Minus Makarov, the line came along, and so did the Flames, who blasted the Kings 5–1. Los Angeles still led the series but now the margin was only 3–2. A victory in Inglewood would tie the series for Calgary.

"I don't think anybody wants a good season like ours to end so early in April," said Nieuwendyk.

The pressure was not off the Flames by any means. Certainly, the media, which had become relentless in its criticism of the team, was not about to let up. "Send this shell of a team to Moscow and make it stay," wrote Maki. "Send it in a rowboat with a slow leak. Put it in an airplane — third-class or baggage — with only one movie to watch, the disgraceful loss at Los Angeles."

On the tenth day of their title defense, the Flames showed up at Great Western Forum determined to turn the series back in their favor. They battled the Kings even (1–1) in the first period and took a 2–1 lead in the second, when Makarov and defenseman Brad McCrimmon combined to set up Doug Gilmour's goal. The Kings regained a tie early in the third but Mullen staked Calgary to a 3–2 lead with less than five minutes remaining. Then Steve Duchesne beat Vernon at 18:17 to send the game into yet another traumatic sudden-death period.

Somehow the Flames managed to kill off a two-man-short situation and the teams slogged through the first overtime; the Flames appeared to win the game when Gilmour made a centring pass that seemed to have eluded Hrudey. The puck rolled off the goaltender's leg and fell between his pads, which appeared to be behind the goal line. The red goal light flashed and the Flames celebrated, but referee Denis Morel disallowed the goal. At different times, Morel offered different explanations. At first he claimed that the puck never went into the net although TV replays indicated that it had crossed the line. "It was in by six inches," claimed Brian Burke of the Vancouver Canucks high command. Later, Morel argued that he had whistled the play down, presumably because he had lost sight of the puck.

"Morel compounded a lie with a lie," barked Crisp after hearing the two versions.

What mattered was that the goal officially was disallowed and the game would continue, tied 3–3. The first overtime was completed without a score and the second opened with an early Kings threat. Duchesne took a shot at 3:10 of the second overtime with the puck rebounding to Krushelnyski, who was apparently well-covered. As he was being tackled to the ice, Krushelnyski somehow flicked a high shot over the groping glove of Vernon. It hit the net at 3:14 and the Flames' one-year reign was kaput!

The post-mortems were long and bitter. Many fingers were pointed at Crisp for his coaching. "The Flames went backward under Crisp," sniped Larry Tucker of the Calgary *Sun*. "One look at the standings and the sorry way they disappeared from the playoffs tells you that."

Others singled out individual players, including Makarov, who was accused of merely floating and not adapting to NHL playoff hockey, among other things. Sergei did not stay around Calgary very long to absorb much criticism. He took the first available jet to Bern, Switzerland, where he joined the Soviet national team, which was competing in the World Championships. So did several of his teammates, including Doug Gilmour and Theoren Fleury, who would sign up with Team Canada.

Ironically, Makarov would go head-to-head with Fleury on at least two occasions in the World Championships, and in each case the unpleasantries were hard to accept to those who recalled that only a few weeks earlier they had been roommates.

When the Russians routed Team Canada 7–1, Fleury attempted to intimidate Makarov, alternately pushing, shoving and sticking him. Fleury also verbally assaulted Makarov and even head-butted the Soviet ace.

"That bleeping Fleury," Makarov later explained. "You know what he said? He said, 'Why don't you play like that in the playoffs?' I said, 'Why didn't you?'"

Makarov and Fleury challenged each other in two matches but when the tournament had ended, and the Soviets had won an unprecedented twenty-second gold medal, the two Flames forwards had an amicable reunion and a good laugh over their battles.

And just to show that their friendship was genuine, Makarov pulled Fleury aside and presented him with a gift — his gold medal. Crisp got his "gift" a few months later. He was fired.

CHAPTER 24

ANOTHER MOGILNY MESS

"The unknown factor is Mogilny."
— Buffalo News *writer*

Alexander Mogilny had become a poster boy in the New York Islanders publicity department. But then again, so had Uwe Krupp. Both had been instrumental in torpedoing the Pittsburgh Penguins on the final weekend of the season, enabling the Isles to clinch a playoff berth at the eleventh hour, while the Penguins went down the tubes.

However, Mogilny was not held in such high esteem in Buffalo. The Sabres had clinched a playoff berth, to be sure, and would face the Montreal Canadiens in Round One. But there was absolutely no certainty that Alexander would be more than a modest contributor to the Buffalo organization.

Topping the list of problems of which general manager Gerry Meehan had a surplus was the business of flying; or, to put it another way, Mogilny's abject refusal to get into an airplane. It had been hoped that a month or two of therapy would have "cured" Mogilny of his phobia, but results were nil. Fortunately for the Sabres, the first playoff round would open at The Aud in Buffalo, guaranteeing two games without any need to take to the air. Games three and four would be at the Forum in Montreal, followed by a fifth game at The Aud, a sixth at the Forum and seventh, if necessary, back in Buffalo.

Much of the lustre that had accompanied the Sabres' early-season renaissance had long since been dulled by slumps and the eventual ascendancy of the Bruins to first place in the Adams Division. Buffalo's second place finish was hardly something to mourn but the expectations for a Stanley Cup victory were muted by the time coach Rick Dudley put his club through the final pre-playoff practices.

The Sabres had one factor on their side as they awaited the Canadiens arrival for Game One. With a better record than Montreal — and with Norris Trophy-winner Chris Chelios out of the Canadiens' lineup due to injury — Buffalo was favored to win Round One and meet the survivor of the Boston-Hartford series.

It is worth noting here that each of the three play-off teams fortified with a Soviet skater was favored to advance past the first round. The Flames with Sergei Makarov were listed by Las Vegas bookmakers as the overwhelming choice to beat Los Angeles; and the Devils, employing Viacheslav Fetisov and Aleksei Kasatonov, were believed a good bet to top Washington.

The difference in the Sabres' case was that Mogilny was not regarded as a chief protagonist anymore; certainly not in the class of a Makarov or Kasatonov. During his pre-playoff practice, coach Dudley had buried Mogilny on a line with enforcer Mike Hartman and fourth-stringers Mitch Molloy and Bob Corkum. It was a fourth line, which was as low as one could get.

In its pre-series preview, the *Buffalo News* predicted a Sabres victory in six games. As for Mogilny's anticipated contribution, it commented, "Buffalo's younger players have shown a penchant for kicking in a timely goal of late. The unknown factor is Mogilny. If he arrives in this series, it's a boost for Buffalo."

Mogilny was an unknown factor but, then again, so was the entire Sabres team, from coach Dudley on out. A day before the opener they appeared more jittery than their opposition. The general staff, no doubt under orders from Meehan, discouraged television cameramen from filming their scrimmage and in the evening, as the Montreal *Gazette*'s Bob Morrissey observed, "players are as hard to get hold of as Wayne Gretzky."

Meehan had sequestered his players in an unidentified hotel, adding to the mystery. "We want to make sure our players stay focused," was his rationale.

They certainly appeared consumed with the game and only the game for the next 24 hours. And when the Sabres took the ice on April 5, Meehan's strategy was impeccable. Buffalo contained Montreal in the first period and then went ahead briefly in the second before the Canadiens tied the count. After that it was all Sabres — a power play goal by Rick Vaive and a dazzling play by Dave Andreychuk put the Sabres up 3–1.

Dudley had been spotting Mogilny in a variety of offensive roles and on several different lines. In the third period Alexander proved useful, contributing to the insurance fourth goal. Defenseman Dean Kennedy started the play with a hand pass that Mogilny gathered. The Russian then broke free for a two-on-one break with Bob Corkum, who beat Patrick Roy in the Montreal goal. It was the final score in the 4–1 victory.

For Game Two coach Dudley promoted Mogilny to a more prominent line, this time with Christian Ruuttu and Rick Vaive. It was a game that could have pushed the Sabres over the hump in their attempt to conquer the Canadiens, but Patrick Roy was giving away nothing in the Montreal goal, while the Habs' forwards collected three goals and left Buffalo with just what they wanted, a 3–0 victory and a split in the series. "We got some respect back tonight," observed veteran Canadiens forward Mats Naslund.

With the series moving to the Forum, attention turned to Mogilny. Now that the regular season schedule had been completed, it was a matter of concern how Alexander would handle the playoff pressure and, as well, how he would deal with the airplane travel. Would he accompany his teammates on the jet from Buffalo to Montreal or would he take other transportation?

The question was important enough for the *Buffalo News* to feature it as the lead sports story on Monday, April 9. "It was hoped," wrote Jim Kelley, "that the Sabres' celebrated Soviet winger would fly to Montreal with the team for Game Three of their Adams Division semi-final series.

"He didn't make it through the air. Instead, Mogilny took to the highways again. In terms of coming to grips with his apparent fear of flying, this is not a catastrophic event."

The Sabres had not considered his independent motor trip to Montreal an act of rebellion because Mogilny had never received an ultimatum from the team, neither from Meehan nor anyone who had been treating his flying phobia. Management, coaches and players all remained at least superficially supportive. "It is the approach everyone involved with the young forward is hoping will be successful," Kelley observed.

Mogilny continued to reject interviews, with the exception of a March telephone conversation with Steve Dryden of *Hockey News*. "He's been good for the last month and a half," teammate Benoit Hogue said.

He was good enough to produce a team-high four shots on goal in Game Two but was a non-factor in Game Three, which the Canadiens won 2–1, on Brian Skrudland's sudden-death goal at the Forum. Adding to the confusion was Mogilny's absence from the Sabres' practice the following day. He was seen limping about the Forum — rumors spread that he had suffered a hip pointer injury — but nobody would confirm that the Russian had been hurt. Speculation was rampant that Mogilny would miss the fourth game, which also would be played at the Forum.

Mogilny was scratched from the lineup and whether it was coincidence or not, the Sabres went out and played a superior game, defeating the Canadiens 4–2 to tie the series. Pierre Turgeon's two goals made the difference, while Dave Andreychuk contributed four assists.

Having tied the series, the Sabres now held the upper hand since games five and seven (if necessary) would be played at The Aud. For a time the Sabres were making the most of the home crowd's noisy support. They had a 2–1 lead when Rick Vaive scored his third goal of the series at 10:58 of the second period, but the Canadiens counterattacked with two goals in 72 seconds late in the period, and went on to win 4–2. Nobody could blame Mogilny for the setback since he watched the game from the press box for the second straight time. However, he was pronounced fit for Game Six back at the Forum.

Dudley, who had inserted centres Ken Priestlay and Donald Audette into the lineup in Mogilny's absence, benched them for the critical game in Montreal. It didn't help. The teams battled through most of the second period tied at one, but Brent Gilchrist gave the Habs a 2–1 lead, sending the Sabres into a disorderly retreat. By the time they straightened themselves out, it was too late. Pat Burns' skaters had poured through the Buffalo defense with impunity and emerged with a 5–2 victory. Apart from taking an elbow from Skrudland that produced a Buffalo power play, Mogilny was a non-factor in the final game; a non-factor, that is, until coach Dudley met the press for the series post-mortem.

Meeting the press after the traditional handshakes and other pleasantries and unpleasantries, Dudley delivered a not-so-veiled criticism of his boss, general manager Gerry Meehan. "I feel I made some mistakes," said Dudley. "I definitely should have stuck to my guns and gone with the lineup I wanted. I will not elaborate on that, but I should have."

The statement oozed with controversy and conjecture. Exactly who would have been in the lineup Dudley had preferred? Who was he compelled to play against his better judgement? How much of a role did Meehan play in the lineup scenario? These questions provoked the media to pursue Dudley. The coach shrugged them off with a powerful "No comment!"

That only served to fuel the controversy. Almost immediately a source tipped off some reporters that Dudley and Meehan had strongly disagreed as to who should play in the final game. And just as swiftly Alexander Mogilny's name became an issue. Was he the player Dudley felt obliged to play, despite the coach's wish to employ Ken Priestlay? Jim Kelley believed that was the case.

"The use of Mogilny over Priestlay appeared to be the crux of the issue," wrote the *Buffalo News* reporter.

Priestlay, himself, had thought he was going to dress for Game Six and added that he was surprised that he had been scratched from the lineup without being given any reason by management.

Meehan, who usually manages to conceal a fiery temper behind his normal attorney-like decorum, attempted to subdue any anger he harbored over Dudley's outburst. "Until I talk to Rick," said Meehan, "I'm not going to say this or that is untrue or true. The decision as to who goes in and who comes out is a coach's decision. A manager certainly expresses his views, but I didn't hand him a lineup card. He has the responsibility for who goes in the lineup."

The Mogilny affair had begun to take on epic proportions. Dudley, who had been accused by Buffalo writers of poor coaching throughout the series, now had some critics suggesting that he might lose his job after only one year behind the bench. His boss obviously was unhappy, to say the least, and more likely furious. Dudley's next move would be critical, and what he did was attempt some damage control.

For starters, the coach charged that his remarks had been "misconstrued badly" and insisted that there was no feud with Meehan. Dudley accepted blame for playing certain players and benching others and added that the trouble occurred in Game Five, not Game Six.

"I had a gut feeling I should have made a roster change and I didn't," said Dudley. "I didn't follow my instincts. I took a safe out. Instead of making what would have amounted to maybe an unpopular decision with some people, I took the easy way out and that angered me."

Dudley continued to remain mum over the specific players involved, although insiders continued to point to Mogilny as the coach's bête noire. But the coach sidestepped any indictment of individuals and pointed the finger at himself.

"It's hard to describe what goes through your mind after you lose a playoff series," he added, "but all I could think of was that I didn't have the guts to make a decision. It was interpreted that I was directing that at Gerry, and that simply was not the case. It was directed at myself, all at myself."

Pressed on Mogilny, Dudley finally denied that the Russian was the player involved. The absolution of Mogilny from the furor did not gain acceptance among all members of the media, but it served the coach's purposes at the time.

If Dudley believed that it would get him off the media hook, he was sadly mistaken. *Buffalo News* columnist Jerry Sullivan tarred and feathered the coach a day after Rick had delivered his explanations. "The best thing about Buffalo's abrupt demise," said Sullivan, "is that it gave Dudley an early vacation. Heaven knows, he needs one. You could analyze the series until Alexander Mogilny became fluent in English and it would come back to one essential fact: the Sabres didn't have enough offense."

And one good reason why they didn't was that Alexander Mogilny was not the offensive force the Sabres had hoped he would be.

The Sabres' unexpectedly quick playoff exit consumed six games. Coincidentally, both the Flames and Devils also departed from their first playoff rounds in six games. By mid-April every regular Soviet player had been eliminated from Stanley Cup competition. This was not what Lou Lamoriello, Cliff Fletcher or Gerry Meehan had in mind when they imported the likes of Makarov, Fetisov and Mogilny, but those were the facts of NHL life and now the general managers went back to their drawing boards to determine what to do next with their Russians.

Meehan's primary concern was Mogilny's future. During the summer of 1990, Alexander was occasionally spotted in Brooklyn's Russian-speaking Brighton Beach community confiding to friends that, if he had his way, he would leave the Sabres and play in New York for the Rangers. Meehan, however, was determined to retain his ruble-in-the-rough.

CHAPTER 25

LOSING AND WINNING WORLD PRESTIGE

"I don't know whether to weep or cheer. Fetisov looked dead to me when he left and, all of a sudden, he becomes a star."

— *New Jersey fan*

The rapid elimination of Soviet players from the Stanley Cup playoffs did not go unnoticed in the North American media. Russophobes such as Don Cherry lambasted the likes of Sergei Makarov and Viacheslav Fetisov for their inability to perform at a higher level and enable their teams to advance farther in the playoff hunt.

However, this was not a unanimous opinion. In each case — the Flames, Devils and Sabres — there were extenuating circumstances. Calgary had been extended to seven games the previous season without Makarov and barely escaped being eliminated in the opening round by a weaker Vancouver team than the Los Angeles club that deposed the Flames in 1990.

Buffalo had a history of playoff failure that extended back more than a decade. "The Sabres had done what they have learned to do automatically," observed *Buffalo News* sports editor Larry Felser, "congratulate the victors and unlace their skates for the final time in a season without winning a playoff series." They did it for years without Mogilny, so why should an only-occasionally-used forward take the brunt of the blame?

As for the Devils, this was only their second trip to the playoffs. Granted that Fetisov and Kasatonov both erred in the sixth and final game against Washington, both played admirably on other occasions. "The six playoff games were a microcosm of the season," said Devils radio analyst Larry Brooks. "It had been said that Fetisov had been intimidated in the third game by Dale Hunter. I don't buy that. He was battered, yes, but not intimidated. Nobody intimidates Slava Fetisov.

"It is very difficult for a defenseman to break into the NHL. This was their first year in the league but they were not perceived by the fans or the media as rookies. They were regarded as Soviet defensemen and that was the mistake. They should have been viewed as NHL rookies; then their mistakes would have been more acceptable."

For Fetisov and Makarov there still was time to redeem the 1989–90 season, although not for their North American teams. Each had accepted an offer to temporarily return to the Soviet national team and perform in the 1990 World Championships being played at Bern, Switzerland.

Although Fetisov had reservations about playing again for Soviet coach Viktor Tikhonov, he was persuaded by teammates to put his nationalism above any personal disputes. The headstrong Fetisov was as adamant about Tikhonov as he had been about Devils teammate Kasatonov.

No sooner had Slava arrived in Bern than he let the media know exactly how he felt about his old boss. "With Tikhonov," Fetisov asserted, "every fault on the ice is a catastrophe. A game lasts 60 minutes and for Tikhonov, it is 60 minutes of catastrophe after catastrophe.

"The reason I came is that Viacheslav Bykov and Valeri Khomutov called me and asked me to come and help the team, so I'm here. I did not come for Tikhonov."

Makarov echoed Fetisov's views. "I'm not playing for Tikhonov. I'm playing for my country. I play for the team to win. I don't care who the coach is. Tikhonov, Terry Crisp — it makes no difference."

Fetisov appeared infinitely more relaxed and cheerful now that he was reunited with his Russian comrades and once again was able to perform on the larger European ice surface. "It's a different style of hockey," Slava explained. "In Europe it's a more tactical game. In the NHL, the high-sticking, the checking from behind, is not a good thing."

There was considerable conjecture about the Russians' chances of winning another world championship. Tikhonov and the Soviet Hockey Federation had embarked on a youth movement. After examining the lineup, Fetisov conceded that the 1990 Russian sextet was not in a qualitative class with others he had captained.

"There are many younger players who need another two or three years to develop," Fetisov said. "But it's a good team and there would be no surprise if we won the tournament."

At first the Canadians looked like they might win a gold medal. With time-proven aces such as Paul Coffey, Steve Yzerman and Jamie Macoun, Team Canada wasted Norway 8–0 early in the tourney and gave indications that coach Dave King could very well have the best team of the bunch. When the Canadians defeated powerful Czechoslovakia 5–3 in the preliminary round, and Sweden edged the Russians 3–1, more evidence was piling up in Canada's favor. A 3–1 win over Sweden boosted Canada to sole possession of first place with a 6–0 record. It marked the first time since the present world championship format was adopted in 1982 that Canada had been in first place at this stage of the tournament.

Team Canada went unbeaten (6–0–1) in the seven-game preliminary round-robin, enabling them to finish first, and caused considerable speculation that the Canadians — and not the Soviets— could take the gold medal.

When the medal round began, Canada opened against the Czechs, a team they had beaten 5–3 in the earlier competition. But on this night Czechoslovakia received outstanding goaltending from veteran Dominik Hasek and edged the Canadians 3–2. "We stunk the place out," concluded Al Eagleson, Canada's spokesman.

That was an understatement compared with Team Canada's abject failure two days later when the Soviet Union humiliated the Canadians 7–1. "We fell behind by a couple of goals and some guys took undisciplined penalties," said Canadian centre Ron Sutter of the Philadelphia Flyers. "Against the Soviets, with all the power they have, you have to play disciplined hockey and battle your way back into the game. We took ourselves out of the game."

There were excuses galore for Team Canada but they could not erase the losses, which included still another defeat administered by Sweden. By contrast the Russians got better as the tourney progressed. They outscored their opponents 15–1 in the medal-round games, culminating with a final test against the pesky Czechs.

Tikhonov, who rarely inspired so much as a smirk, had his players smiling in the steamy Allemand Arena, mostly because of his overcoat. The Russian leader stubbornly refused to remove his outer garment although he was red-faced and perspiring profusely from the heat.

"I am superstitious," Tikhonov revealed after the final buzzer had sounded. "This is my lucky coat. Sure, I was hot and with ten minutes remaining, I tried to take the coat off but my players started laughing. They wouldn't let me. Eventually, they pulled it off with ten seconds left."

By that time it didn't matter. The Russians had a 5–0 lead and preserved the advantage to win their record-setting twenty-second world championship. "This is something special for the Soviet team," said Tikhonov. "This is the first time I ever summoned players from the NHL. This was different. Every day of the tournament we were forming this team. This is unique and was difficult."

Perhaps it was for Tikhonov but the series was a breeze for Fetisov, who had seemed so bewitched, bothered and bewildered at the conclusion of the Devils-Capitals playoff. Veteran NHL reporters who watched Slava dazzle with his leadership, defense and playmaking ability during the medal round could not believe it was the same player they had seen just weeks earlier across the Atlantic.

"The Fetisov who played at the World Championships in no way resembled the defenseman who played his home games this season at the Meadowlands," said Steve Simmons of the Toronto *Sun.* "He was the best defenseman in the tournament and likely the best player."

Slava collected two goals and eight assists in the ten games he played. "This European style is still my game," Fetisov said when it was over, and there was no one who could deny that statement. Nor could anyone deny that the Soviets still were the best, overall, when it came to winning the world championship.

"The Russians," added Simmons, "were at their dominating best. They were so dominant that any pre-event forecasts of their demise were rendered ludicrous."

Back in New Jersey the Devils fans were confused about the reports emanating from Bern. "I don't know whether to weep or cheer," said one season-ticketholder. "Fetisov looked dead to me when he left and, all of a sudden, he becomes a star again. I can't figure what it means for next season."

Vancouver Canucks executive Brian Burke witnessed the tournament and agreed that Fetisov was *the* dominant player. "The fact that Slava was the best," said Burke, "will be good for him and the Devils next season. He needed a year to adjust to the NHL and this experience in the Worlds just proves that he has all the skills. He'll be a much better NHL player in 1990–91. And so will the other Soviets playing in North America.

"If anything, the world championships proved that the Soviets still have prestigious hockey players. How many more they'll deliver to us is a moot question."

The Russian experience in the NHL proved a lot of things but, more than anything, it demonstrated that John McMullen was absolutely right when he originally drafted Fetisov and Kasatonov and said, "The inclusion of Soviet players in the NHL will be good for hockey."

CHAPTER 26

THE SOVIETS KEEP COMING

"What's happening is that every NHL team is looking for the best players available; and if they happen to be Russian, why not take a chance?"

—*Neil Smith,*
General Manager, New York Rangers

To gauge the impact of Soviet hockey on the NHL, one had only to open to page five of the *Hockey News'* Draft Preview '90, a slick, multi-colored annual that listed the best professional prospects available to the major league. His picture dominating the lead story, Viacheslav Kozlov, a five-ten, 172 pound centre, was rated "among the most talented prospects in the world."

Also noted among the "Top Prospects" were Alexander Godiniuk, a defenseman for Sokol in Kiev, and Sergei Zubov, a defenseman with CSKA.

"I'm not surprised," said New York Rangers general manager Neil Smith. "What's happening is that every NHL team is looking for the best players available; and if they happen to be Russian, why not take a chance?"

The Washington Capitals nearly took a chance during the 1990 playoffs. After eliminating both the New Jersey Devils and then Smith's Rangers in the Patrick Division finals, Washington went up against Boston for the Prince of Wales Conference championship. Until then, nobody at Capital Center in Landover, Maryland, had heard much about Mikhail Tatarinov. But with the Capitals' top defenseman Kevin Hatcher sidelined for the duration with a serious knee injury, general manager

David Poile scrambled for an adequate replacement.

On May 3, the *Washington Post* declared that defenseman Tatarinov might jet from the World Championships in Bern to Boston in time for the Stanley Cup semi-final series between the Bruins and Capitals. Tatarinov, whose home team was Moscow Dynamo, had been paired with Viacheslav Fetisov during the Soviet annexation of their twenty-second world championship.

But much as the Capitals might have wanted Tatarinov to suit up as soon as possible, there still was the issue of getting approval from both the Soviet Hockey Federation as well as Tatarinov's team. Then there was the matter of age. Tatarinov would be 24 when the 1990–91 season got underway. The Soviet Hockey Federation had not yet allowed players under age 28 to join the NHL. Finally, there was the arrangement of financial compensation in the event that the Federation did approve.

Tatarinov never made it to the 1990 playoffs, nor did Soviet centre Dimitri Hristich, whom the Capitals drafted in 1988 and consider a sure-fire NHL prospect. Hristich would be 21 in time for the 1990–91 season and was not likely to be released. Still, with the dramatic changes taking place in the Soviet Union, NHL teams had become more optimistic than ever about signing players who had been regarded as untouchable only two or three years ago.

"Now the players are free to talk to anybody," said Jack Button, the Capitals' director of player personnel and recruitment.

Certainly, the Soviets sounded a more liberal tone. Igor Dmitriev, assistant coach and chief spokesman for the Soviet national team, indicated that the Russian hockey authorities were more anxious than ever to see their players do well in North America. Dmitriev conceded that the Soviet Ice Hockey Federation had been embarrassed by the less-than-spectacular performances of Fetisov, Krutov, et al.

To avoid another such sub-par season, Dmitriev proposed that the Federation would hold a special camp in Moscow during the month of August 1990 to prepare the Soviets for their second NHL experience. "There were a lot of problems," Dmitriev said. "It wasn't just a new team and new country. The biggest thing was training. They were not so prepared for the NHL. You have to understand, they were in training their whole lives. They didn't have to do anything on their own before."

Dmitriev was acutely aware that the five Soviets who had taken part in the playoffs combined for no goals, 12 assists and a minus-six rating in 24 playoff games. He also had been stung by criticism from the likes of Don Cherry who had described the Russians as "money-grubbing Reds" who wanted to lose so they could join their national team for the world championships.

Perhaps they were "money-grubbing Reds" but the Edmonton Oilers didn't seem to mind. Nor was club owner Peter Pocklington averse to emptying his bank account even more to accommodate a couple of additional stars — even though his club was in the midst of its annual playoff struggle.

His Oilers had just disposed of the Los Angeles Kings in the opening game of the 1990 Smythe Division finals when Pocklington introduced Anatoli Semenov and Sergei Yashin to the media. That Pocklington and general manager Glen Sather would consider intruding the Soviets onto the scene during the pressure cooker playoff atmosphere was surprising enough. Even more arresting was the Russians' absence from the World Championships in Bern. Their representative, Soviet television executive Sergei Levin, explained that they opted for Edmonton rather than Bern "because they wanted to go to the the NHL more."

No less intriguing was the manner in which the original announcement was made. Normally, a team tries to capitalize on a breaking story by revealing it on an off-day. Instead, the Oilers' public relations department made the disclosure during the first period of Game One.

Yashin and Semenov inspired mixed reactions. Los Angeles Kings owner Bruce McNall, who had earned a reputation as a wheeler-dealer but had not signed any

Russians, dismissed the move as a bummer. "I hope the Oilers sign those two Russians," barked McNall. "Maybe they can screw things up in Edmonton."

Others took a wait-and-see attitude although there was little time to wait or see; a day after the announcement the two Soviets skated with the Oilers' farmhands and then walked over to an empty dressing room where they met the press. Their aide, Levin, accompanied them as an interpreter. Without further ado, the journalists jumped over them with questions. "Have you ever heard of Don Cherry?" one asked. After Levin delivered his translation in Russian the two shook their heads. Someone immediately piped up, "You will!"

Another asked about their adjustment problems in view of the difficulties faced by Fetisov and friends. "Everybody has to adjust to a new style of hockey and a new style of life and obviously that was a problem for the players who came over in 1989–90," said Semenov. "But it will be much easier for us because the guys who came first had to experience more troubles and more special circumstances. We will learn from what they've experienced."

Yashin admitted that he had followed the trials and tribulations of Krutov and Mylnikov as closely as anyone in the Soviet Union. He allowed that their failure had caused some concern, but added that it would prove to be a motivational factor for himself and Semenov. "I know people were disappointed," Yashin conceded. "I also knew I would come here with a more serious attitude and planning more professional play. I want to play here and I want to play well.

"I know what happened to Krutov in Vancouver but, in a way, I'm happier to be in Edmonton than Vancouver. The weather here in Edmonton is the same as Moscow — cold. I like that."

Cold was the best way to describe the reception Don Cherry had for Semenov and Yashin. "You'd think Glen Sather would have learned with Vladimir Ruzicka. Maybe the two Russians should play on the same line as Ruzicka. They're the same talent. But I guess they'd have to bench Mark Lamb and Craig MacTavish. They finally see the light and put Ruzicka in the press box and then they bring in two Russians. Unbelievable."

Semenov and Yashin couldn't have cared less. They were given the grand tour, including a visit to the awesome and seemingly endless West Edmonton Mall and other testaments to affluent capitalism. "My wife will have to adjust to things like being able to go to a store and buy anything," chuckled Semenov. "As for me, I'll have to try first for a place on the team and then wait for the coach to let me play."

His wait was a lot shorter than anyone had imagined. Oilers coach John Muckler dressed Semenov for the critical fourth game of the Campbell Conference finals — Edmonton trailed two games to one — and while he made only a cameo appearance it was significant that the general staff had enough confidence in the Russian to thrust him into a cauldron of sound like Chicago Stadium.

Cherry's bleats had no influence whatever on the continuing on-ice thaw between the NHL and the Soviet Union. Wherever one turned during the spring of 1990 another new development took place, but one of the more surprising was the disclosure that an NHL prospect would be playing in Russia for the 1990–91 season.

Winnipeg Jets general manager Mike Smith designated 22-year-old Tod Hartje as his hockey guinea pig, doing the reverse of such Soviet-turned-NHL players as Larionov and Makarov. Smith told the Harvard senior that he wanted him to play all of the 1990–91 season for the Kiev club in the Soviet Elite League. Thus the Anoka, Minnesota, native would become the first American to play in Russia's top league.

"I think it was the first agreement worked out between any professional team in North America and a sports club in the Soviet Union," said Smith. "We've sent first-year pro players to Finland for the past several years. Mike O'Neal, an All-America goalie at Yale, played in Finland.

"In the case of Hartje, we knew it would take an extraordinarily strong individual to do it. He's bright and will look upon it as an exceptional opportunity that won't happen to anybody else."

When Hartje originally conferred with Smith, the collegian had no idea what the Jets general manager had in store for him. "Never in my wildest dreams had I anticipated anything like this," said Hartje. "My first reaction was that it's one of those opportunities in life that comes along and you can't pass it by. The only thing I know about the Soviet Union is what everybody hears. I've never been there and I have no idea what to expect."

Smith expected Hartje to succeed. "Hockey-wise," Smith explained, "he has good skills. He's a strong skater, sees the ice and is extremely adaptable. This will help him gain that half-step needed to play in the NHL."

Sokol Kiev coach Anatoli Bogdanvov sounded as enthusiastic about the exchange as Smith and Hartje. "If Mike Smith tells me he's a good player," said Bogdanov, "then he must be a good player. He won't have any trouble adapting because most North American teams play the way we do."

One of Hartje's first lessons upon arrival in the Soviet Union was that Russia's premier hockey league was in just as turbulent a period of flux as its North American counterpart. If "parity" was the byword of the NHL, the same could be said of Russia's Elite League.

For 13 years Central Red Army dominated the division until Fetisov, Makarov, Larionov, Krutov, Mogilny, Starikov and Kasatonov left for the NHL. But on March 15, 1990, Moscow Dynamo nosed out Viktor Tikhonov's army club by three points for the gold medal. The last time a team other than Central Army won the Soviet championship was in 1976 when the Spartak team led by Alexander Yakushev turned the trick.

While always a contender, Dynamo had won only two previous gold medals. The club had won the first ever Soviet championship, played outdoors on a soccer field in 1947, and won again in 1954. Tikhonov was a defenseman with the 1954 team.

The Hartje experiment was just another of a growing number of Soviet-North American exchanges. Some of them had been planned years in advance, while others developed almost spontaneously. One of the most surprising was a visit of the 16-member Moscow Select teenaged team, which embarked on a week-long exhibition schedule in the spring of 1990 throughout the New York City area.

"They showed up on the spur of the moment," said a surprised Warren Ernst, international director of youth hockey in New York. "We had sent an all-star team of 15-year-olds from the Long Island Hockey League to Moscow, Helsinki and Vienna during the winter. We developed a relationship and invited them to New York."

Sergei Altunin, director of the Red Army organization, accepted the invitation but didn't notify anybody in New York. "Just before they arrived we got a fax from Altunin saying, 'We're on our way.' We had to get families to house them and iron out details."

That done the Russians played a series of games and won the hearts of oft-critical New York audiences. "Our people liked them so much," said Ernst, "we didn't want to see them go home. We just fell in love with them."

As with Slava Fetisov and the Devils, the young Russians demonstrated to their hosts that language was not a barrier. "We used sign language, pointing to light switches, how to run the water, how to turn on the television or VCR," said Andrew Loyal, whose son Darrin hosted Sergei Trahanab of Moscow. "Neither speaks the other's language but they communicate. Sergei is a typical youngster. Right away he went to the Atari set and at the arenas, right to the video machines. Typical kid."

CHAPTER 27

THE SOVIETS AND THE STANLEY CUP

"We consider Canada the mecca of hockey. As far as being with the Edmonton Oilers is considered, it is an honor to be with this great hockey club."

— *Yuri Moiseev, former Moscow Dynamos head coach*

When the New Jersey Devils, Buffalo Sabres and Calgary Flames departed from the 1990 Stanley Cup scene it was logically assumed that the NHL had seen the last of the imported Russian stickhandlers until, at the very earliest, training camp the following September.

The assumption was wrong. Quietly, the Edmonton Oilers had been considering the possibility of inserting a Soviet player, Anatoli Semenov, into their lineup at some point during the long playoff grind. The Oilers had barely squeezed out a seven-game opening round playoff win over the Winnipeg Jets and then walloped the Los Angeles Kings in four straight games to reach the Clarence Campbell Conference finals. Their opponents would be the Chicago Blackhawks.

Edmonton easily defeated Chicago in the opener at Northlands Coliseum but absorbed a surprising loss in Game Two at home. When the Blackhawks won Game Three at Chicago Stadium, an SOS was sounded by the Oilers general staff. It was then, to the astonishment of just about everyone but general manager Glen Sather and coach John Muckler, that Semenov suddenly emerged.

This in itself was amazing stuff, but even more astonishing was the manner in which the Edmonton club paved the way for Semenov's May 1990 playoff premiere all the way back in September 1989. It was then that Yuri Moiseev, a 49-year-old ex-Moscow Dynamos head coach, showed up in Edmonton and became a member of the Oilers' scouting brain trust. Sather had been tipped off about Moiseev's technical ability years earlier by Soviet goaltending immortal Vladislav Tretiak, whose acumen was widely respected.

"Tretiak told me that Yuri was the best technical coach they had," said Sather. "At the end of training camp we'll see how we get along, how the coaching team accepts him and how he accepts the change. Then, we'll work it out after that."

Moiseev, who spoke no English, arrived with an interpreter. "We have a great deal of respect for Canadian hockey," Moiseev said. "We consider Canada the mecca of hockey. As far as being with the Edmonton Oilers is concerned, it is an honor to be with this great hockey club. If my presence helps even a little bit, I will be a very happy man."

Some of the Oilers personnel were not as tickled about the intrusion of the Russian. "First, you can't get them to come over here," snapped Craig MacTavish, the veteran forward, "now you can't stop 'em coming. But I guess in five or six years, when there's ten Russians on each club, you'll need a guy who speaks Russian."

More important than any strategic contribution made by Moiseev was the talent connection he arranged between the Oilers and Soviet players. Before leaving Edmonton, Moiseev accepted a job as Edmonton's talent scout in Europe and, Sather hoped, he would also arrange for delivery of two Oilers draft picks, Semenov and Sergei Yashin.

Sure enough, Moiseev delivered — and Semenov eventually emerged as the mystery man accompanying the Oilers from city to city across North America as they made their 1990 trek toward the Stanley Cup.

The mystery ended on May 7, when the Edmonton *Sun* blew the lid on the Russian. RED TO THE RESCUE —

OILERS MAY USE SOVIET IN GAME 4, blared the headline on the sports page. Muckler's Oilers had been trashed 5–1 at Chicago Stadium in what was described as the club's "worst playoff performance this year." It was time for drastic action to shake up the tentative team.

Muckler already had indicated a preference for Semenov in Game Three of the series. He ordered the Russian to dress for the pre-game warmup and when the Oilers took the ice, Semenov was there along with extras Dave Brown and Jeff Beukeboom. At the last moment Muckler opted for Beukeboom and Semenov was scratched from the lineup.

"Muckler made a mistake," commented *Sun* columnist Terry Jones. "He admits that the 28-year-old Soviet has opened a lot of eyes."

So many, in fact, that the guessing before Game Four was that the coach had to insert Semenov into the lineup based on his performances in team scrimmages. "He's looked very impressive," said Muckler. "He's the most talented player we have who isn't playing."

Muckler would not admit that Semenov might be dressed for Game Four but there was so much conjecture about it on the day off between games that several of the Oilers players were asked about the possibility. Would they object to the Russian suddenly moving in at the most critical point in the season for the club? Speaking for his mates, captain Mark Messier insisted that there would be no beefs.

"Anatoli is a tremendous player," said Messier. "And the people on this team are big enough to let a player like him step in the same way Esa Tikkanen did against the Flyers a few years ago."

Sather had stunned onlookers during the 1985 Stanley Cup finals with Philadelphia by unexpectedly thrusting Finnish rookie Tikkanen into the series. Until then Tikkanen had not played a single NHL game. "This is too late in the year to worry about hurting anybody's feelings," added Messier. "If playing Semenov is what it takes, then that's what it takes."

Muckler had been unhappy with the play of

veteran Glenn Anderson, while some members of the media complained about the underachieving Czech Petr Klima. Meanwhile, Muckler played it close to the vest. "One quiet move to substitute a Soviet might help," said Terry Jones.

Semenov knew that he was moving toward centre stage but there was not much he could say about it since his English was more limited than his shooting ability. "Forecheck," said Muckler, "he understands that. Backcheck. He understands that, too. Some of the people who speak English don't understand backcheck."

Talk about playing the Russian became more intense a day later. This time the Edmonton *Sun* headline asserted GET THE RED OUT? "I want to play," said Semenov. "I want very bad to play." A natural centre, Semenov was advised that if he were to play it would be at left wing. "In Russian hockey," he replied, "you play centre and wing at one time."

Perhaps the scariest aspect of Semenov's expected debut was the locale. Chicago Stadium had long ago earned its reputation as the most difficult NHL rink in which to play. Crowd noise is deafening under normal conditions, a huge foghorn blares for Blackhawks goals and the oversized organ is played incessantly. Surely this could unnerve a Soviet rookie as much as it does NHL veterans. Semenov indicated that he couldn't have cared less about the Stadium trappings. "In Russian hockey," he explained, "people sleep. I like noise."

No less remarkable was the lack of communication between Muckler and Semenov and the dearth of knowledge about the new player except for the raw essentials. "I know he can skate," said Muckler. "I know he can shoot the puck and he has good hands. We played him in one practice on left wing with Messier and he looked good. I think he can score too."

He understood enough English for Klima to tell him he might be playing. "I don't know if he was sure what Petr was saying, but I guess he got through to him," said Muckler, "because all of a sudden he said, 'thank you.' "

The tip-off that Semenov would play finally was

uttered by Muckler as his club finished preparations for Game Four. "Maybe," said Muckler, "it's time for a risk."

Muckler followed through on his hunch and, for the first time in NHL history, a Soviet player appeared on the ice in a Campbell Conference final game. However, Semenov's debut hardly was worth writing home to Moscow about because of its brevity.

"If you went to the fridge or took the garbage out," quipped Jim Matheson of the Edmonton *Journal,* "you might have missed it."

Semenov was on the ice for a grand total of 40 seconds. Muckler dispatched him near the completion of a first period power play and twice Semenov was whistled offside.

"Going offside wasn't his fault," Muckler argued. "If he'd gotten the puck once, he'd have been right in."

The problem, for Semenov, was not his play but rather the Oilers' good fortune. His teammates as a whole performed splendidly with Messier doing an exceptional job as the Oilers won 4–2. "It was pretty hard to get him out there on a fourth line the way Messier was playing," Muckler explained. "We wanted Mess to get the maximum ice time."

Following the victory, which tied the series at two games apiece, Muckler was asked why he selected Semenov to replace Kelly Buchberger. "I thought we might need a goal," he replied.

It was mentioned to Semenov that he didn't play very much.

"Is that a joke?" he chuckled.

With the series deadlocked and Edmonton ready to move past Chicago, the jokes came easier in the Oilers' locker room. When someone mentioned that Semenov does, in fact, know what NHL checking is all about, another journalist piped up, "And he knows pay check, too!"

Nobody credited Semenov with turning the series around but it was undeniable that after his appearance, Edmonton dominated, and they eliminated the Blackhawks in six games. The Oilers then moved on to

Boston where they challenged the Bruins for the Stanley Cup.

For Muckler's sextet it was a remarkably easy series. They defeated Boston in five games and at the end Anatoli Semenov became the second Russian (Sergei Priakin being first, with the Flames in 1989) to drink champagne out of the Stanley Cup and earn an NHL championship ring.

"TOP ROOKIE MAKAROV PREDICTS BETTER YEAR"

So blared the headline of the Toronto *Sun* on June 7, 1990, the day after Sergei Makarov had gone to the NHL awards celebration at Toronto's Metro Convention Centre, wearing a tuxedo for the first time in his 32 years.

"I came here to win the Stanley Cup, not the Calder Trophy," was the remark Sergei had made several times during the regular season. In fact, at one point in the midst of the 1989–90 season Makarov had planned to withdraw officially from the Calder Trophy race for Rookie of the Year, in order to remove some of the pressure from himself and hopefully improve his play.

But he didn't withdraw and on June 6, he made history. Sergei and the Flames had sputtered, but Makarov the Rookie had beaten his closest freshman competition Mike Modano and Jeremy Roenick — by more than 80 votes.

"He's a first-year player, the same as Mike and I," said Roenick graciously after the award ceremony.

"He had just as hard a time adjusting to the NHL as we did," added the equally generous Modano.

"My number one plan was to play the best I can," Makarov told his audience, as he accepted the Calder, "and right now, this is the most important award [of his enormous collection of international trophies]."

Makarov's impact extended beyond his winning the Calder Trophy. Less than a month later, the NHL Board of Governors convened in Vancouver and passed what has come to be known as the Makarov Rule — an age restriction for rookie of the year eligibility. The Makarov Rule states that a player may not have attained the age of 26 by September 15 of the season in which he is eligible.

"We had to make sure the trophy justly goes to a person who's in his first year of competition at this level," concluded New York Rangers general manager Neil Smith

After the award celebration someone jokingly asked Sergei if he expected to receive a congratulatory telegram from his former Red Army coach Viktor Tikhonov. "I don't think so," responded Makarov, with a wry smile, adding that NHL-watchers could expect to see better performances in 1990–91 from the Soviets currently in the NHL, as well as more Soviets coming to North America to play.

Makarov's prophecies would be echoed 24 hours later at the Hotel Waldorf-Astoria as the prestigious Canadian Society of New York for the first time in its history honored not one but two players: former superstar goalies Ken Dryden of the Montreal Canadiens and Vladislav Tretiak of Soviet Red Army. Dryden and Tretiak had faced each other as opponents several times, beginning in 1972 and ending after Dryden's retirement in 1979.

"When I first skated on the ice in Montreal in 1972," recalled Tretiak, "before the game, I had no thought about Soviets ever playing in the NHL. After the game, when we had won, yes, the thought instantly occurred to me: we could do this, we could play in the NHL.

"Then, over the years, because I was asked this question so many times, it became a certainty in my mind. Yes, I would say, I think that we can play in the NHL. Sometimes I even said, I think we will play in the NHL."

Tretiak, accompanied by an interpreter, gave an eloquent speech of thanks, admitting that he envied his former teammates because they had played in the NHL and he had not, predicting that they would do better next year, and thanking Canada for giving "the most wonderful game of hockey" to the world.

It was Ken Dryden, paraphrasing from his book *The Game,* who put the whole Soviet-NHL rivalry in perspective, as he thanked the Canadian Society for the award.

"What the Soviets were," said Dryden, "was a good opponent, a rare and treasured thing for any team or player. For a good opponent defines a player or a team...stretches the boundaries of your emotional and playing experience, giving you...your best and worst and hardest moments.

"...It is why good teams and good players, good enough to stand alone, stand straighter and more vividly with a good opponent...so when a career ends, when the passion of the game subsides, towards a good opponent you feel only gratitude."

Dryden thanked Tretiak for being a good opponent and sat down, while the spotlight panned to Tretiak. As it did so, it paused on a figure in the row in front of Tretiak, while simultaneously highlighting another figure sitting next to the former Soviet netminder. The man in the front row was Aleksei Kasatonov; the man next to Tretiak was Kasatonov's former mentor and current New Jersey teammate, Slava Fetisov.

The ceremony ended and a swirling crowd of fans mounted the dais to garner autographs from the celebrities, who included Gordie Howe, Bobby Hull, Frank Mahovlich and Paul Henderson, who had scored the fateful final winning goal in Moscow in 1972. Slava stood in one corner, the only one of the Soviets present who understood and answered the fans' questions in English. Finally someone congratulated him on his performance in the world championships and asked him when he would go back home to Russia for the summer.

"I am not going 'home' to Russia," said Slava in his clear but heavily-accented English. "My wife and I will perhaps go to Europe for a few weeks, but there is no place for me to practice and work in Russia.

"This [North America and the NHL] is not my opponent now...I am happy here. I...we...we will be better this year. This is home now." It would be home for many more and they would come in different ways. In July 1990 Sergei Federov bolted from the Soviet national team at the Goodwill Games in Seattle — he left a team dinner in Portland — and signed a five-year contract with the Detroit Red Wings.

The "Year Of The Russians" was over. Soviet players had come, had played, had won and lost. The Russians weren't coming; they were here and would stay.

NOTES, QUOTES, AND ANECDOTES BY AND ABOUT THE SOVIETS

VARIOUS NHL PLAYERS COMMENTING ON THE PLAY OF THE SOVIETS

NEW YORK ISLANDERS

Goalie Glenn Healy: They didn't do as well as expected. Obviously, they're talented, world-class players but you have to remember that they're in the latter stages of their carbeers. A young Fetisov or a young Krutov would have had much more impact. Of the bunch, Makarov made the best impression, partly because he played on one of the best teams, Calgary, and with one of the best lines with Joe Nieuwendyk and Gary Roberts. But I wouldn't use the word "sensational" to describe any of them. The best way to put it is that they belong in the NHL because they have top-flight talent, but I wouldn't go farther than that.

Would I want to reverse the procedure and play in the Soviet Union? No way! I've already been over there, playing with the Canadian national team. Russia is the kind of place about which you say, "It's a nice place to visit once but I wouldn't want to stay there."

Centre Pat LaFontaine: The difficulty for the Russians who came to the NHL in 1989–90 was that they had been so accustomed to playing with each other for so many years that they couldn't easily make the transition to the new system. And, believe me, it was new for them. There were so many adjustments to make, from living style to rinks to the longer schedule.

I know some NHL players were upset about their coming over here and taking jobs but my feeling is that Europeans have been signing on with NHL teams for years, so why get upset now? It makes the NHL a truly international league and gives the fans different styles to watch. Now, thanks to the Soviets, we have more exciting players in the NHL than ever before. I appreciate the Russians because they are so good with the fundamentals — skating, shooting, stickhandling. They're great to watch.

Defenseman Jeff Norton: It's kind of ridiculous to be paying these guys all this money and sending it back to the Russian Hockey Federation for their youth programs instead of having some North American who is just as good or better play in their spots. I think the NHL made a bad move allowing the Soviets over here. There are enough quality hockey players around.

Defenseman Gary Nylund: From the advance notices, I expected them to dominate because of their skill and training. I didn't see that. What I saw was average players with the exception of one or two. Makarov is the best of the bunch. I saw him do things with the puck I've never seen anyone do. Krutov was the biggest disappointment. When I saw him in Russia, I figured him for the best player I had ever seen. He was unbelievable. When he came here he looked like he had put on 130 pounds and lost his drive. If I'm disappointed in him, imagine how the Vancouver Canucks must feel.

ST. LOUIS BLUES

Defenseman Mike Lalor: The travel and grinding style of NHL hockey got to them. After a strong start, they seemed to tire. Some of them got a second wind after they adjusted to the new surroundings. The only two who made an impression on me were Makarov and Fetisov. I have no quarrel with the Soviets being here. This is the best league in the world so we want the best players here. If they make a team better, it makes sense to welcome them.

Goalie Vincent Riendeau: The game belongs to the fans so if the Russians make the game better, then as many as possible should be able to come here. In the process, I might lose my job because of it. So, I'll just have to find another job.

BOSTON BRUINS

Centre Dave Christian: I was in Russia with the Washington Capitals when they had their pre-season camp there and being exposed to a different culture made me understand how tough it was for the Soviet players who came over here. I don't know if I could have handled it if I were in their shoes.

Goalie Andy Moog: Some people expected the Russians to dominate when they came to the NHL, but I never felt that way. Their schedule in the Soviet Union is set up for three key periods during the season: their own playoffs, any international competition, and the world championships. A lot of their time is spent preparing for those events and that's different than the regimen in the NHL We prepare for two weeks at the start for 80 games, during which you have to be at peak performance. Once you've done that, you have to take it a step higher and play a bit better. I knew they wouldn't be accustomed to our style of season. I felt they'd have either good halves of the year or a good playoff. I'm still skeptical about their ability to keep up the tempo for the whole year. They're all great players but it's the adjustment that's so difficult.

HARTFORD WHALERS

Right Wing Pat Verbeek: They have to learn to make plays faster. They're learning that they don't have the time they did in Europe. Makarov really impressed me but his downfall is that he doesn't want to shoot, always passing, passing. If he ever learned to be less unselfish, he'd be scary.

LOS ANGELES KINGS

Defenseman Marty McSorley: The Russians are not geared for dumping the puck in and getting it out of the corner. Give them the puck in the neutral zone and they'll do well with it. They remind me of a lot of the Europeans who came over here in the 1980s and were supposed to do well, but didn't. There was a part of their game that was missing, a part that is essential in the NHL.

MONTREAL CANADIENS

Left Wing Mike McPhee: Sergei Mylnikov, the Quebec goalie, was the biggest letdown of all in a group that, overall, was a disappointment. The Mogilny kid will be a good one. He's got some unbelievable moves and he can skate. He's more of an individualist now but once he learns to play with his linemates, he'll be dangerous.

Defenseman Craig Ludwig: Makarov has lived up to his notices better than any of the other Russians. The guy is a threat every time he touches the puck. I know I've learned a lot just watching him play.

Centre Ryan Walter: In time Mogilny will be one of the better players in the league. He's encountering the same maturing process that Canadian kids face when they move from the junior leagues to the NHL, or from college hockey to the top. The Russian who impressed me the most last year was Fetisov. He was the premier prospect and the steadiest of any who came over.

CHICAGO BLACKHAWKS

Defenseman Steve Konroyd: One reason why they struggled was because of age. Most of the guys they sent over were up in years and had lost a stride or two. That becomes evident over an 80-game schedule when they're not used to playing every second and third night. It took a toll on them.

PHILADELPHIA FLYERS

Defenseman Gord Murphy: Everything I heard about them is true. They're strong, fast and have all the tools. Their big problem is dealing with the change in lifestyles but, from what I've seen, they've adjusted well under the circumstances.

Left Wing Murray Craven: I can speak firsthand about their problems because I went to Europe for a month in 1989 to practice with a European team and it was quite a transition for me. Well, if I had problems with just a month, knowing that I would be going home soon, imagine what these guys have gone through. It's tough for them on the ice and off the ice.

WASHINGTON CAPITALS

Goalie Mike Liut: The advent of the European player in the NHL has made the game better. There's no doubt about that. They bring over a different type of game, based less on the physical aspect, that is, bodychecking and toughness. They emphasize more finesse, skating and passing. And that's good.

The Russian game has a little of the NHL flavor now and we've taken some of theirs. It's been an exchange of hockey ideas. Because of the bigger ice surfaces in the Soviet Union, they play more of a tactical game. In the smaller NHL rink you have more forechecking, dump-and-chase because it's so easy to clog the centre of the ice and hold the line at your blueline. That's almost impossible on a larger surface because there's so much room to go wide. There's not a strong side or a weak side; it's just a lot of side all over the place.

IGOR LARIONOV INTERVIEWED BY JOURNALIST DIANE GERACE

Cordial to a fault, Larionov did not hesitate in answering questions about his adjustment to life in North America.

"It's a new life," he said, "and a new system and, of course, a different team. In the first months everybody helped me and my family. People understood that I was a new player and that I had come from a place where it was a hard life and the change was great for me. I like the NHL atmosphere. Every day I learn something new."

Gerace asked Larionov about his most difficult adjustment. Again, he was comfortable with the response.

"There's a lot of travelling — much more than I was used to doing — and that has been the hardest part. The first two months especially were very difficult. In the Soviet Union we play a total of 44 games all season. I had played 48 by the middle of January."

Finally, he was questioned about his adaptation to the English language.

"I understand English," he concluded, "and I try to speak it, even in practice. My wife is better than me; she took English lessons."

DEVILS COACH JOHN CUNNIFF

ON THE FETISOV-KASATONOV FEUD

We've sat down with them to discuss it and they've gotten better. We said, "You have to show some emotion together when goals are scored. You know, come in and greet your teammates." They have been.

In terms of the feud, it's strictly Slava. The other guy is fine. It's Slava with the grudge and I don't know if it will ever be forgotten. We can only hope. You know it doesn't help anybody and it's not going to help him. It's something Slava is going to have to come to grips with sooner or later. But he's a pretty — I wouldn't say stubborn — determined guy. He thought he went through quite a lot as a leader of people. He stuck his neck out and took responsibility for basically all the athletes in the Soviet Union.

ON THE LACK OF PHYSICAL PLAY BY FETISOV AND KASATONOV

They don't use their bodies a heck of a lot. What they do is take the opposition out of the play without crunching them. That's smart sometimes but I'd also like to see them crunch once in a while. Every now and then one of them will get mad and Slava will occasionally crunch. They're smart about physical play in their own way. They play under control and take a man out but it won't be a crunching check. They get body position and take the man out hard. They do that very well.

ON OTHER ASPECTS OF THEIR GAME

They see everything. Sometimes I wish they wouldn't see as much as they do but they're unbelievable at seeing the whole ice. On penalty-killing, they see the different two-on-ones developing. What I'd like to see them do a little more is make that outlet pass quicker. What they do is weigh the two or three different options. Because they just started the North American game, they're not used to the aggressive forechecking so they don't have room in their end. What they see is a play here and a play there and still another play over there and what they do is run out of time thinking about their options.

VANCOUVER CANUCKS GENERAL MANAGER PAT QUINN ON THE FIRST YEAR OF HIS SOVIET PLAYERS, AS TOLD TO REPORTER DAVE STARMAN

We were optimistic about Larionov and Krutov because we knew they had shown success on the small rinks during the 1987 Canada Cup so we felt they would be able to handle NHL arenas. What concerned us was the increased number of games and the competitive style of the games. One other thing we learned was that they weren't accustomed to the intense competition every night. I had been told that in Europe they might have had to play three or four tough games a year. Because of their superior skills, they reacted to the rest of their games as if they were exhibitions rather than regular contests. Once we finally got into the season Larionov and Krutov mentioned that they were having trouble competing every night.

When it had become apparent that they would not be overwhelming it was not all that surprising to me because I really haven't seen a European player come here and dominate in his first year. There are a number of factors involved in that, such as the social part — learning the language, getting accustomed to a new way of life. In Krutov's case, he could not speak any English and since he was a guy with a very simple lifestyle, he seemed to struggle a lot more than Larionov. Igor's family was more worldly and sophisticated than Vladimir's. The Larionovs had ability in English and were eager to learn. They took to English right away and really worked on their studies. This was an adventure for them. With the Krutovs it was different. The parents and the younger boy really struggled with being here but their oldest son was all right. They were more reclusive and not as adventurous as the Larionovs.

In terms of their natural ability, there's no question that they are skilled players. They are stars and I don't think anyone will deny that.

FORMER NHL COACH AND TV HOCKEY ANALYST DON CHERRY ON THE FIRST SEASON OF THE SOVIETS IN THE NHL

It's the old story; we don't bring them over here to hit, we don't bring them here to check or fight, so we must bring them for their offensive power. Yet, if you check the final statistics for 1989-90 there are no Russians among the top ten scorers. Let's put it this way; if they don't check, hit or fight and they aren't among the top scorers, what the hell are they doing here? Nothing says it better about their failure than the Vancouver Canucks. This was a good bump-and-grind hockey club with guys like Richie Sutter and Trevor Linden who got them into the playoffs in 1989. Then, they bring Krutov and Larionov over and immediately put them on the power play with Linden. The power play didn't work and guess who went off the power play — Linden!

In New Jersey, the word was that Fetisov was a world class player, the Bobby Orr of the Soviet Union. That really got me! Orr used to get in one game what Fetisov got in a season. Look at Makarov, whom they raved about; he didn't get that many goals even though he worked on the number one power play in hockey. It makes me mad when I read that a guy like Harold Snepsts is making only $125,000 after 15 years and a guy like Makarov is getting $375,000.

The reality about the Russians is that they have propaganda spread about them. They're supposed to have great upper body strength yet they get pushed around — and they're too small. They can't take the travelling; they can't take the constant pressure of the NHL where they must win every game. Over there, they were number one and the games hardly meant anything. They'd get primed for a big tournament and then, after the ten games or so, that was it.

VIACHESLAV FETISOV SUMMING UP HIS FIRST NHL SEASON.

The NHL is very difficult and it was harder for me than usual because so much time was spent in the summer of 1989 trying to get things in order so that I could make my move from the Soviet Union to join the Devils. There were so many distractions that I was unable to prepare for the season the way I wanted to and it showed in my play.

For the first 25 games or so, my partners didn't understand my style and I didn't understand the style of the NHL. But we all learned a lot and I thought I had a very good second half. I had hoped to be in the playoffs longer with New Jersey but when we lost in the first round that was it. Then I got phone calls from Andrei Khomutov and Viacheslav Bykov, asking me to come and help the Soviet National Team in the World Championships at Bern, Switzerland.

I had just come through a long and tough NHL season but I always liked to play the more tactical game on the big ice so I decided to go. When people heard that I would be playing on the team coached by Viktor Tikhonov there was a bit of surprise because I once said, "The best thing about coming to the NHL was that I will never play for that man, Tikhonov, again." So, when the reporters asked me how I could line up with the national team with him behind the bench, I explained: "I am not here for Tikhonov; I am here to play for my country!"

SERGEI MAKAROV ON THE DIFFERENCES BETWEEN NHL AND SOVIET HOCKEY

The differences are everywhere. It is a totally different hockey in North America. Maybe from the stands it seems the same but the hockey player who experiences it can definitely feel the contrast.

One area of difference is in the understanding of collective play. In the Soviet Union it is not important who scores the most goals, who makes the greatest number of assists. In the NHL, however, it is listed in contracts — how many goals you score and how many assists you will get. For this we get bonuses. This is why it happens in the NHL that a linemate will not pass the puck but will rather try to score himself even though he is not in the best position to do so. That would not happen in Soviet hockey. I disagree with the theory that the NHL has too much freedom and therefore the Soviet players — not being used to freedom — find it harder to play. We are just used to another hockey. Most of us are thirty years of age and over. It is very difficult to retrain at that age.

The NHL has its critics but I found it a very good organization. Every little detail is thought of here but some things I did not expect. For example, there is no travel fatigue. Everything is properly scheduled. In the Soviet Union constant delays are normal. Sometimes we had to sleep in airports. There is no such thing here. I am able to rest spiritually. There's no such thing here as those ridiculous meetings before each game at which we'd get a spiritual push from the administration.

In Calgary I live with my family. Over there I communicated with my wife over the phone. Here we try to solve our problems together. From this I argue less with my wife.

As for the future, my plan is to help the Flames win the most prestigious prize in world hockey, the Stanley Cup. This is the only prize in hockey that I have not won yet.

ALEXANDER MOGILNY DISCUSSES HIS NHL ADAPTATION WITH MIKHAIL VAPNE, SPORTS CORRESPONDENT OF *NOVOYE RUSSKOYE SLOVO*

It is more difficult to play in the NHL but more pleasant. I have no problem whatsoever in communicating with the guys. During the summer (1989) I took an intensive course in English and now am able to converse somewhat. I wanted to show that I did not come here to play for no apparent reason. The game comes first. Only after that comes the financial and social side. In Soviet hockey I achieved everything possible by a Soviet player and I felt that my game level was going down. I always love to score although, to be honest, I do not get enough ice time. I feel as if the coaching staff do not completely trust me yet. I know that, as a player, I do not produce even fifty percent of what I am capable of. Much to my regret, my friends do not live in Buffalo but I find chances to meet them. We call each other on the phone. After one game a reporter from a Soviet television show, "Posie Polunochi" (After

Midnight) approached me and said, "Hello, Alexander Mogilny! We are from the Central Soviet Television. I calmly answered that I had nothing to talk with them about, that I am a "traitor." I turned around and headed toward the exit. They tried to catch me, screaming, "What are you going to do when you finish playing hockey?" I replied to them, without turning around, that I will move to Hawaii where it is always warm. I like it here. I bought myself a new house in a prestigious neighborhood. I drive a brand-new sporty Corvette. It is not just a car, it's an airplane! I love New York City. Those skyscrapers and gatherings of crowds bring me to a total state of joy. I would love to live there, but I am bound by contract with Buffalo. I get enormous pleasure from Brighton Beach (Brooklyn, near Coney Island). All those Russian stores, Russian restaurants, Russian signs and advertisements. I love it. In the United States I feel like I am at home.

WHAT OTHERS HAD TO SAY ABOUT THE RUSSIANS

Bobby Orr: I would like to see every player be given the same opportunity. We need skilled players. There's nothing wrong with Soviets and Europeans coming here to play. Just maybe these players might make our players work a little harder and give an honest effort.

Guy Lafleur: They're over thirty, but I'm thirty-eight so I can't talk. They're very good players, and they're going to help teams. They deserve to be here. I think it's good for hockey.

Darryl Sittler: They're great players, obviously. They're on the down side of their careers, but they can probably help some teams. Some teams have got to improve their clubs, and they will go to any extremes to do it. I don't know if I agree with them playing here one or two years then taking everything home with them. They do have some great players, and only time will tell if this was a good move.

Bobby Clarke: They don't belong here, they shouldn't be playing in our league. I'm totally against having them in our league. Why should Russians come over here, get paid a lot of money and take away jobs from Canadian and American players?

Ken Dryden: The danger in relating sports to a bigger subject is the exaggeration. But sports is the metaphor. It is the most vivid example we have. Sports, very simply, is part of life everywhere it happens to exist. And so when you get into things like the Soviets and their decision to allow these players to come and play in North America, you look at the story and it comes from somewhere. It comes out of conditions in both places, particularly those in the Soviet Union. It says something about the country and the relationship between those who are home and where all the power lies. And yes, absolutely, there is certainly something happening.

Mark Messier: My brother Paul went to play in Germany and couldn't speak a word. Now he speaks fluent German. I can really relate to how the Soviets feel. I know how Paul felt. It's given me a good appreciation for what Europeans go through. I think I'll run down to a bookstore to see if they've got any English-Russian dictionaries.

Jim Taylor: Send the Russians back to the Soviet Union? What — and rob the players and customers of a matched set of scapegoats? Igor Larionov and Vladimir Krutov are struggling, but they're by no means alone.

Paul Coffey: If they're the hockey players everybody says they are, they'll be able to adjust. Fetisov isn't used to dumping the puck around the boards or anything like that. He's used to always having a guy there to give it to.

Marty McSorley: Bump them extra hard. Not because they're Soviets and I say, "Well, I hate these guys." That has nothing to do with it. It's like a new kid comes into the league and he's a good hockey player, I'm going to bump him and see how he reacts, see if you can shy him off the puck.

NHL President John Ziegler: We don't ask where a player has played before, or where he was born. We only ask, "Can you play at a premier level?"